THE ARCHES

of

ARCHES NATIONAL PARK

A Comprehensive Study

By

Dale J. Stevens
Professor of Geography
Brigham Young University

and

J. Edward McCarrick
Moab, Utah

Mainstay Publishing
1988

Library of Congress Cataloging-in-Publication Data

Stevens, Dale J, 1936-
   The arches of Arches National Park: a comprehensive study

   Bibliography: p.
   1. Natural bridges-- Utah--Arches National Park.
   2. Arches National Park (Utah)
I. McCarrick, J. Edward, 1920-   II. Title.
GB565.U8S74 1988   557.92'58--dc19   88-9217
ISBN 0-9620168-0-2

© 1988 by Mainstay Publishing. This publication may not be reproduced in whole or in part by any means without prior written consent of the publisher.

Graphics & Printing: Geography Department of Brigham Young University

Binding: Brigham Young University Print Services

Scheduled Publications:

Fall 1988:   A 1:50,000 scale 4 color map, "The Arches of Arches National Park" showing the location of all arches described in this book.

Winter 1989:   A Supplement to this book documenting all arches in Arches National Park reported since field work ceased for this volume in 1986. See Appendix.

MAINSTAY PUBLISHING

471 West 650 South   1170 West Kayenta Drive
Orem, Utah 84058   Moab, Utah 84532

INTRODUCTION

Almost everyone knows what natural arches are, but few realize how varied and complex they are unless a methodical analysis is made of them. Several new insights are presented in this book which should help readers to become more fully informed on the arches and bridges in at least one small corner of the world, Arches National Park. Arches and bridges have long been noted as landscape features, but with little attention given to any distinctions in the detail of their characteristics. The terms "arches", "bridges" and "windows" have been used in a generalized way to describe several different types of natural rock openings in the past, but in recent times the word "arch" has become the designation most frequently used to identify all such openings.

Authorities in the fields of geology, geography and others interested in the study of arches are not generally in total agreement on a system that classifies and defines the different types of rock openings and spans that exist. This is probably due to the independence of each researcher and to the lack of any formal cooperative work to devise such a system.

When this project was undertaken there was no previous comprehensive study of natural rock openings within such a concentrated area. Previous studies on arches, however, have provided an excellent base from which an extensive classification and list could be compiled. The system of describing and measuring arches outlined in this book has undergone several modifications since its inception some years ago and now seems to work well for the 527 arches included in this study. We are fully aware that it is impossible to say with certainty that **all** arches have been located, mapped and measured, but we are confident that through our efforts, the great majority of them have been. Since completing the field work, other arches have been reported. A list of them is included in the Appendix. Documentation on each arch is rather extensive, including maps, tables, geographic coordinates, photographs, dimensions, etc., but no attempt has been made to describe specific routes to any of the arches. Such instructions might be confusing and difficult to follow because of the intricate topography of much of the Park. We concluded that it would be best to use maps and give straight-line distances to show location. In many cases certain arches can be seen from many vantage points and getting to them is fairly easy, while finding others requires climbing in and out, up and over, or through and around mazes of rocks. The authors know from first hand experience that it is almost impossible to explain in words how to reach many of the arches.

Much more information was collected on each arch than appears in the statements, summaries and conclusions of this book. As time permits more detailed analysis of this additional information will be made and published to help provide a more complete understanding and explanation of these landform features. In other parts of the world geologic and environmental conditions exist which are often quite different from those found in Arches National Park. Thus the origin and formation of arches elsewhere may be dissimilar to those found in southern Utah's sandstones. In spite of these differences, the criteria used in this book could provide a basis for more accurate and unified studies of these unique landforms. It is our hope that this comprehensive study will be useful for those interested in these landforms and that it can serve as a standard for greater understanding of natural arches and bridges everywhere.

ENVIRONMENTAL CONSIDERATIONS

Arches National Park is located in a desert environment and contains a number of plants and animals that are rather fragile and delicate in their natural setting. One of the most fragile is the cryptogamic soil, a very primitive form of plant life. They are black or dark brown crunchy looking material which form a crust over the sand in many places. They are important to the development of many plants and help prevent soil erosion. One footstep will destroy the cryptogams, requiring fifteen to twenty years for new ones to grow. In many cases the cryptogams may have difficulty in returning as surface erosion often prevents them from becoming established again. Anyone hiking off the established trails into the backcountry should avoid stepping on cryptogams.

During the spring time and at certain other times of the year, several animals and birds (particularly raptors) may be disturbed by constant human intrusion. It is advised that all wildlife be left alone and undisturbed as much as possible. Information on nesting seasons, cryptogamic soils and other aspects of the local ecosystems can be obtained at the Park Visitors Center.

ACKNOWLEDGEMENTS

The field work required to collect the information needed to complete this book would not have been possible without assistance from others. We would like to give special thanks to several people. Reuben Scolnik and Doug Travers were very helpful in sharing their knowledge and opinions on many arches they had personally documented. They also guided us to arches that they had found in many obscure places in the Park. Valuable help was provided by Seasonal Rangers Jim Stiles and Mike Salamacha who kept us informed on new discoveries and led us to many arches they had previously found. Special assistance was given by Geography Student Carl Horton, who as a rock climber helped us to reach many arches, then as a computer specialist put his skills to work to summarize, tabulate and chart much of the statistical information used in the book. The late Joan Swanson, Chief Park Ranger, encouraged and supported our work and was very cooperative in all aspects of the project.

Others whom we give special acknowledgment are cartographers Kelly Nielsen, Jeff Bird, Thomas Hinckley, Steve Brush and Warren Muensch of the BYU Geography Department who designed and produced the maps and prepared the photographs. The printing was supervised and carried out by Thomas Hinckley who freely gave of his time and expertise. We sincerely thank him. Appreciation is also extended to Rodney Horrocks, a BYU Geography student who prepared the illustrations depicting the ten arch types. Seasonal Park Rangers Alice Drogin and Damian Fagan were always on the lookout for new arches and consistently helped us by adding new arches to our list.

Park Technician Maxine Newell aided us in researching the archives of Arches National Park for historical information that proved to be very useful. Former Park Ranger Slim Mabery gave helpful information on some known arches. Other staff members of Arches National Park and Canyonlands Natural History Association gave encouragement and assistance throughout the study. Mitch Williams and Sam Taylor of Moab provided some valuable information on the early history. All those people whose names appear in the table **Alphabetical Listing of Arches** were very important behind-the-scenes contributors in reporting or naming arches.

Special thanks is to be given the College of Family, Home and Social Science and the Department of Geography at Brigham Young University for financial support and continual assistance. Without this help it would not have been possible to have completed so much work in such a relatively short time. Last but not least we wish to thank our wives Mary and Claire for their patience and endurance through the entire project.

Dale J. Stevens & J. Edward McCarrick

TABLE OF CONTENTS

                                                                                       page

HISTORY Chapter 1. 1

    Figure 1 Historical Map of the boundary changes of Arches National Monument and Park . . 3

GEOLOGY Chapter 2 7

    Figure 2 Geologic Timetable of the exposed rocks 9

    Figure 3 Pie Chart showing percentages and Bar Graph showing number of arches by geologic unit 11

NAMING ARCHES Chapter 3 12

    Figure 4 Pie Chart showing percentages and Bar Graph showing number of arches by name origin 13

    Table 1 List of individuals who reported and named the majority of arches 15

DETERMINING AND CLASSIFYING ARCHES Chapter 4 16

    Figure 5 Pie Chart showing percentages and Bar Graph showing number of arches by type 21

    Figure 6 Drawing of front and end view of arch showing how measurements are made . 22

THE ORIGIN AND DEVELOPMENT OF NATURAL ARCHES Chapter 5 25

    Figure 7 Diagram showing development of expanded joints and fins 26

    Figure 8 Pie Chart showing percentages and Bar Graph showing the number of arches in each exposure direction 28

    Figure 9 Pie Chart showing percentages and Bar Graph showing number of arches in each geographic site 29

REGIONAL OVERVIEW Chapter 6 32

    Figure 10 Pie Chart showing percentage and Bar Graph showing the number of arches in each area 32

    Figure 11 Index Map of twelve Park areas 57

    Area Maps showing location of each arch
Figure 14 Eagle Park 33
Figure 17 North Devils Garden 35
Figure 20 South Devils Garden 37
Figure 23 Klondike Bluffs 39
Figure 26 Fiery Furnace 41
Figure 29 Salt Wash 43
Figure 32 Herdina Park 45

Area Maps showing location of each arch (cont.)

Figure 37 Central Area 47
Figure 40 Great Wall. 49
Figure 43 Upper Courthouse Wash 51
Figure 46 Lower Courthouse Wash 53
Figure 49 Southwestern Area. 55

Bar Graphs showing the number of arches by geologic unit

Figure 12 Eagle Park 34
Figure 15 North Devils Garden 36
Figure 18 South Devils Garde. 38
Figure 21 Klondike Bluffs 40
Figure 24 Fiery Furnace 42
Figure 27 Salt Wash. 44
Figure 30 Herdina Park 46
Figure 33 Panorama Bluffs. 48
Figure 35 Windows Section 48
Figure 38 Great Wall 50
Figure 41 Upper Courthouse Wash 52
Figure 44 Lower Courthouse Wash 54
Figure 47 Southwestern Area. 56

Bar Graphs showing the number of arches by type

Figure 13 Eagle Park 34
Figure 16 North Devils Garden 36
Figure 19 South Devils Garden 38
Figure 22 Klondike Bluffs 40
Figure 25 Fiery Furnace 42
Figure 28 Salt Wash. 44
Figure 31 Herdina Park 46
Figure 34 Panorama Bluffs. 48
Figure 36 Windows Section 48
Figure 39 Great Wall 50
Figure 42 Upper Courthouse Wash 52
Figure 45 Lower Courthouse Wash 54
Figure 48 Southwestern Area. 56

PHOTOGRAPHIC PORTRAYAL Chapter 7 58

Eagle Park. 59
North Devils Garden 65
South Devils Garden 75
Klondike Bluffs. 85
Fiery Furnace 87
Salt Wash 93
Herdina Park. 97
Panorama Bluffs 99
Windows Section 101
Great Wall 106
Upper Courthouse Wash 109
Lower Courthouse Wash 112
Southwestern Area. 116

STATISTICAL SUMMARY Chapter 8 123

    Key to Alphabetical List 123

    Table 2   Alphabetical List of all arches showing type, rank size, who and when reported and named, name origin, geographic site, geologic unit, latitude, longitude, map location, exposure and compass alignment of span 127

    Key to Ranking List 146

    Table 3   Listing of all arches by light-opening size rank showing type, year measured, how each measurement was made, light opening length and depth, opening beneath the span width and height, span vertical and horizontal thickness and extent 148

BIBLIOGRAPHIC REFERENCES 167

ADDITIONAL READINGS 167

APPENDIX: A List of New Arches Found Since Original Field Work 169

CHAPTER 1
HISTORY

Most of the arches known today were here long before Arches National Monument was established, long before any Europeans came to the area and even long before any native Americans made this place their home. It is estimated that most of the larger arches in the Park have been in some stage of development for at least tens of thousands of years. This may seem long in terms of our personal involvement with time, but in geologic terms the life span of an arch is rather short.

It is not known who the first humans were to view the large rock openings which are now called arches and bridges, but some Folsom points (leaf-shaped flint projectile points used by a pre-historic group of people who resided in the western part of the Americas) have been found in the area, though not within the Park boundaries. It is possible that these ancient people may have seen some of the arches well over 8000 years ago. Even then there were many arches in this area, perhaps even more than today. About 2,000 years ago much of the Colorado Plateau was occupied by people of the Anasazi and Fremont cultures. Arches National Park is near the boundary of these two cultures and was probably visited by both peoples. They left evidence in the form of rock art and old chipping sites where points for weapons and tools were made. It seems obvious that they were well aware of existing arches. When the first explorers arrived in the area it was inhabited by Utes. It is certain that these native peoples must have observed many of the arches because their chipping sites are scattered throughout the area.

It should not be thought unusual that these early visitors left no indication of having seen any arches, for the Europeans and Americans who came as the initial explorers did not leave much evidence either, for little appears in their diaries or other publications about the existence of natural arches.

Early Spanish explorers made several expeditions from New Mexico to the Colorado River and its tributaries near the present-day Park beginning as early as 1765. They established the Old Spanish Trail to California in 1831 which ran close to what was to become Arches National Park, but there is no evidence that those who used the trail penetrated the area or saw any arches. The first non-Indian known to have been in what is now Arches National Park was Denis Julien, a trapper who must have had a liking for carving his name. He left a number of inscriptions along the Green and Colorado Rivers. Of interest is one dated 1844, inscribed along with his name on a remote rock wall in the Park. It was first reported in 1977 by Park Ranger Jim Stiles. Although Julien most certainly saw arches, he left no indication of having attached any significance to them. It appears that there was just not much fascination with these landform features in those days, or at least there is very little historical information to warrant an opinion one way or another.

The first attempt to establish a permanent settlement in the area occurred in 1855 when the Mormons built a fort called the "Elk Mountain Mission" in Moab Valley. It lasted only a few months, however, because of trouble with the Indians. Twenty years later sporadic prospecting and grazing was begun. In 1877 William Granstaff, better known as "Nigger Bill" (This name was not considered derogatory in this part of the country at that time and is used here only for historical accuracy), and Felippe "Frenchy" Duran had settled in the valley. They were there when other settlers (mostly Mormon) started to occupy the area in 1878. By 1879 a post office was established in Moab. If some of these people saw any arches, they left no written records that have been discovered.

The first settler within the confines of the present-day Park was John Wesley Wolfe, who is said to have been told that he had only a few months to live if he did not move from Ohio to a drier climate. In 1888 he came with his son Fred and settled along Salt Wash, building a cabin and establishing a small farm and ranch. In 1910 he sold the ranch to Tommy Larsen and moved back to Ohio where he died in 1913 at the age of 84. The ranch was sold to J. Marvin Turnbow in 1914, then to Emmitt Alizondo in 1947 who sold it to the federal government in 1948 to become incorporated into the Park. When the ranch became part of Arches National Monument the cabin was known as Turnbow Cabin. In 1971 the name of the old homestead was officially changed to Wolfe Ranch.

During the late 19th and early 20th centuries, Basque sheepherders and cowboys roamed the area and became aware of many of the arches, as is evidenced by dates and names carved in the sandstone nearby. Area residents also knew about some arches, particularly in the Windows Section where names were given before Arches National Monument was established.

The first recorded suggestion to protect any of the area because of its unusual beauty was in 1923 by Alexander Ringhoffer, a prospector, who shared the details of the unique landscape he had observed (in what is today's Klondike Bluffs) with Frank Wadleigh, Passenger Traffic Manager of the Denver and Rio Grande Western Railroad. He referred to the area as "Devils Garden" and left evidence of having been there by carving his name on the rock. Wadleigh visited the locale with Ringhoffer and was so impressed with the scenery that he wrote to Stephen T. Mather, Director of the National Park Service, about the area. Mather supported Wadleigh's contentions and went about working to make it a national monument.

At the request of Mather in 1924 the General Land Office (GLO) made an investigation of the unsurveyed land. An investigator for the GLO, T.W. McKinley recommended withdrawal of the area as a national monument. However, McKinley had inadvertently visited "The Windows" which he had heard about in Moab, and to which he was guided by local resident Heber Christensen. Wadleigh asserted that it was not the place he had been to, and that he had never seen "The Windows". Ringhoffer knew of the site, calling it "Window Castles" and properly located it in relation to his "Devils Garden." Mather notified GLO Commissioner William Spry of Wadleigh's doubt of the mapped location, and the confusion delayed any formal action of the area becoming a national monument.

In 1925, L.M. Gould of the University of Michigan Geology Department visited "The Windows" under the guidance of Marvin Turnbow. In a letter to Utah Senator Reed Smoot, Gould advocated the site be made a national monument. Smoot in turn forwarded the recommendation to Mather. Arthur Demaray, Mather's administrative assistant and a very active supporter of the proposal, confirmed to Wadleigh that the two areas in question were not the same and quoted Gould's suggestion. Wadleigh proposed that the two sites be combined into one monument. The GLO agreed to make another survey and in a June 1925 report, their investigator F.L. Safley recommended that "Devils Garden" and "The Windows" were separate and distinct and that both should be made national monuments. Although Safley had been to present-day Devils Garden, Klondike Bluffs had still not been examined by the GLO.

Other support for the monument's establishment came from Dr. Frank Oastler of New York who had submitted descriptions and photographs of "Devils Garden" and "Window Castles." He had been guided by Ringhoffer in June 1925 to those areas and likewise was in favor of establishing a national monument. In July of the same year Frank Pinkley, Superintendent of Southwest Monuments, visited "Window Castles" and suggested the name "The Arches National Monument" for the area. Political considerations then delayed the proposal. In June 1928 another GLO report by A.D. Ryan stated that "Devils Garden" and "The Windows" were on unsurveyed land and he accurately identified them as they are known today with descriptions and photographs.

Several of the local people were also involved in the establishment of the monument in one way or another. Some, like Marvin Turnbow, had served as guides to the official parties. Moab physician John W. "Doc" Williams had long favored scenic preservation, having discussed it probably even before Ringhoffer contacted Wadleigh. He was aware of many arches, having traveled through what is now the Park by horseback on his regular visits to Thompson and Cisco. He actively supported the L.M. Gould proposal of 1925. Publisher L.L. "Bish" Taylor, who was born in Moab, was another person who was well aware of the scenic character of the area, and he too actively supported proposals to establish the monument. Evidence for this appeared in articles printed in Taylor's newspaper, The Times Independent as early as 1924.

Finally on April 10, 1929 the new Secretary of the Interior, R.L. Wilbur gave the proclamation to President Hoover establishing Arches National Monument of 4,520 acres. The President signed it on April 12 and Arches National Monument was created. The 4520 acres consisted of two detached sections: Devils Garden containing 2600 acres and The Windows making up the remaining 1920 acres (see Figure 1) Klondike Bluffs, which was Ringhoffer's original "Devils Garden" was not included, nor was the present symbol of the park, Delicate Arch. Part of the present Fiery Furnace was contained within Devils Garden. Does it sound confusing? Well it was. Everyone thought they were talking about the same "Devils Garden", but the GLO surveys were of the current Devils Garden. Ringhoffer must have been aware of the current Devils Garden section, since it was across Salt Valley from Klondike Bluffs and he also knew of The Windows. Although his original name prevailed, it was given to an area that he may not have explored. Delicate Arch was not included in the original monument, probably because it was not in the proposed sections and would have required a third area. This arch was probably better known than any others because of its proximity to Salt Wash and Turnbow Cabin (Wolfe Ranch), but somehow escaped being included in the original national monument.

Although the Monument had been established, many of those who knew the area best were not at all satisfied with the boundaries and the obvious omissions of areas that included some very beautiful and well known arches. It was not long until

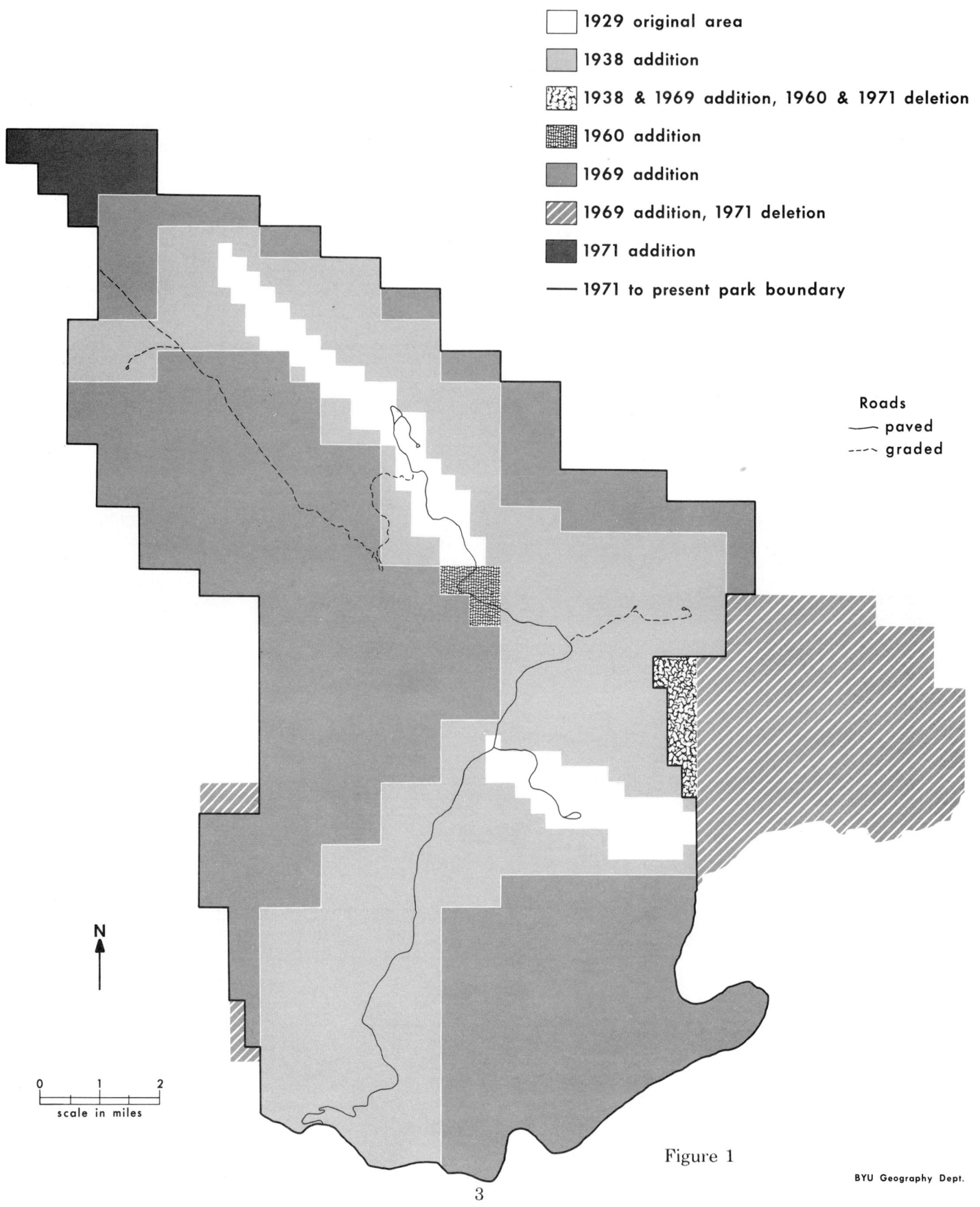
Figure 1

formal attempts were made to enlarge the area of Arches National Monument. Doc Williams and Bish Taylor were credited by the National Park Service for their outstanding efforts in this movement, as well as other local people and the Moab Lions Club. On November 25, 1938 President Roosevelt signed the proclamation enlarging Arches National Monument to 34,250 acres. The boundaries finally included Ringhoffer's "Devils Garden" (part of present-day Klondike Bluffs) and Delicate Arch, along with parts of Salt and Cache Valleys. Also added were Fin Canyon, more of Devils Garden, Courthouse Towers, The Great Wall, part of Petrified Dunes and the area around where the Visitors Center now stands. Although within the new boundaries, Wolfe Ranch (then Turnbow Cabin) was still privately owned and did not actually become a part of the monument until acquired by purchase in 1948.

Another change in the boundaries and size of the Monument was made on July 26, 1960 when President Eisenhower signed a proclamation reducing the size to 34,010 acres. It added the remainder of the Fiery Furnace and deleted a section on the east side of Salt Wash below Cache Valley.

Yet another change occurred on January 21, 1969 by proclamation of President Johnson. The size was more than doubled to 82,953 acres. The Monument had now evolved to approximate its present boundaries by adding the area southwest from The Windows to the Colorado River, part of Upper Courthouse Wash, Herdina Park, Willow Flats, Dry Mesa, and more of Cache Valley, Salt Valley, Devils Garden and Klondike Bluffs. (See the Index map, page 33, to identify these places) There were also some smaller boundary adjustments.

Finally on November 16, 1971 Arches National Monument became a National Park by an Act of Congress and signature of President Nixon. Two major boundary changes occurred, and resulted in a net decrease in its size. Eagle Park was added, but Dry Mesa and two small sections on the southwestern side were deleted leaving the total area within the newly created Park boundaries at 74,234 acres.

THE ARCHES

Historical importance should also be attached to the actual documentation of the known arches since they are the main reason for the existence of Arches National Park. It is difficult to trace information on exactly when the natural arches and bridges were first reported. It is assumed that many of the arches were known to the local people, especially the ranchers who grazed their livestock throughout the area. Doc Williams freely discussed the arches he had seen and Bish Taylor mentioned some in his newspaper. Since 1929 there have been several projects which studied the Park, but were usually concentrated on geology, boundary surveys and general exploration. These studies often mentioned arches, but no lists were included, and no formal recording method was indicated.

The first full-scale effort to scientifically explore the newly created Monument was the "Arches National Monument Scientific Expedition" of 1933 and 1934 led by Frank Beckwith and guided by Arches Custodian Marvin Turnbow. They mentioned some specific arches in their report, but no list or criteria for determining size, shape or other features of an arch were discussed. A report done concurrently in 1933 and 1934, entitled "Geologic Reconnaissance in Arches National Monument" by Joseph C. Anderson, who was a member of that expedition, mentioned a few arches, but no lists were included. Two years later in 1936 a "Report on Arches National Monument" by V.W. Vandiver was done mainly to investigate the boundary situation and mentioned only a few arches. Another report appeared in 1938, titled "Geologic Report on Arches National Monument" by C. N. Gould, who was accompanied in his work by Park Custodian Harry Reed. Although this report mentioned some arches it contained no list, but it did state the "number of arches is not definitely known, but estimates are from 40 to 82 " and "doubtless a systematic count would bring the number to 100 or more". This was indeed a very prophetic statement in view of later developments.

In 1940, Custodian Henry G. Schmidt maintained a list of arches and embarked on a project to place brass markers at each arch. He had completed only eleven arches before he was transferred elsewhere in 1942. Schmidt had accompanied Ross Maxwell for the "Geologic Report, Arches National Monument" in 1941 which stated that "83 arches have been reported" and "also 14 smaller openings referred to as windows." Although there is good evidence that Schmidt had a list of arches, it is unfortunate that his records were apparently lost, along with any criteria he may have used to describe or identify them. It is most likely that his 97 arches and windows are included in the lists of documented arches of this publication. It is interesting to note that in March 1941 Schmidt reported that a large boulder fell from the north end of Landscape Arch, enlarging it from 291 feet to 305 feet. This seems to have been subsequently ignored and the previously quoted size of 291 feet was used until a new measurement was made in 1985 which put the width at 306 feet. There is some controversy about whether this dimension qualifies Landscape Arch to be the largest known arch in the world. The only other contender is Kolob Arch in Zion National Park of southwestern Utah. Until the authors are able to positively verify the actual size of Kolob Arch, this question will not be resolved.

Occasionally, Park records indicated that a new arch was found, but with no further documentation. Doubtless there have been some unofficial (or even official) lists before and since Schmidt's, but no such records have been located. In 1955 Park records mention 88 arches, but there is no available evidence to determine which arches they were or the way they were identified. In April of 1967 a report states that a base map was being compiled of 89 arches that were said to exist, but the locations of many of them were unknown to the Park staff. In 1970 the monument folder stated that there are "nearly 90 arches", but again there is no documentation of which arches were included.

The 1970's might be considered as the great awakening period for awareness of arches in the Park. In 1973 Professor Dale J. Stevens, a geographer at Brigham Young University, included Arches National Park as part of a larger study on the geomorphic importance of arches and bridges in southern Utah. He listed 124 natural rock openings he had been able to identify within the Park boundaries, 90 of which were classified as arches. He also provided substantial data on criteria for determining types and measurements. Stevens' criteria and list of arches then became the record used by the Park. In 1977 Robert R. Vreeland published a book about the arches in the Park containing photographs and other general information on 54 arches and a brief listing of 21 others.

Two other serious arch hunters deserve mention during this time period. Since 1965 Doug Travers from Texas had been visiting the Park about three weeks every year compiling his personal documentation of arches. He located quite a few on his own since there was no Park list when he started. Sometime after Stevens' list came into use, Travers attempted to reconcile it with his records and found that he still had some arches that met all of Stevens' criteria, but were not on the Park list. Since no formal procedure for reporting new arches yet existed, he did nothing further at that time. In 1977 Reuben Scolnik, who had a keen interest in the desert landscape, began his search for known arches. He would stay five to six months each year in the area spending much of the time hiking around the Park taking notes and photographs of any arches he would find. He likewise began to come across arches that were not on the Park (Stevens) record so he found it necessary to make his own list. In 1978 he presented photographs to the Park of most of the arches he had observed. The contribution of these two men caused increased awareness of arches and was very important to subsequent methods of Park recording, resulting in greatly expanded numbers of documented arches. Without their groundwork, including some very helpful suggestions on classification, there would have been little incentive to start this current project. The fact that a number of newly documented arches later became known prompted the authors of this book to pursue an even more in-depth study.

In 1978, Seasonal Ranger Jim Stiles began locating and mapping the arches not shown on the Park (Stevens) list. Then in 1980 the Park began an improved method of recording the information on arches. Using the field work and mapping done by Jim Stiles, the photographs and field work by Reuben Scolnik, and the 1973 criteria of Stevens, more than 115 arches were registered in the Park records by Seasonal Ranger Liz Bellantoni. In 1981 further improvement was made in the Park recording system when Seasonal Park Ranger Ed McCarrick embarked on a part-time project to further document (measure, photograph and locate) listed arches and those which were being reported but were not yet recorded. He located the 200th arch in 1982 and the number seemed to be a milestone. So many had been documented in such a relatively short time that it seemed almost unbelievable. How many more arches could there be? At the time it seemed that there couldn't be too many more, surely not an additional 100; yet by October 1983, 288 arches had been recorded. During this project, McCarrick had substantial assistance from arch hunters Scolnik and Travers, and Seasonal Rangers Jim Stiles and Mike Salamacha. In the Spring of 1984, McCarrick and Scolnik made a personal project to locate at least 12 more arches to see if the magic 300 could be reached. In May of that year they found the 12th arch.

All of this activity concerning arches caused a greater awareness among many Park personnel, which was most helpful in the current project in bringing the total number of documented arches to more than 500. In addition to Scolnik, Travers, Salamacha and Stiles, significant contributions were made by Seasonal Rangers Alice Drogin and Damian Fagan, as well as Chief Ranger Joan Swanson. Without the assistance of these people and several others mentioned in the acknowledgements, the task of locating and sharing the new-found information would have been much more laborious and fewer arches would have been documented.

One of the big problems, other than just incomplete lists and unknown numbers of arches that constantly occurred prior to the 1973 study by Stevens, was the lack of information and agreement as to what an arch really is and what criteria should be used in describing its features. One of the most important of the criteria is that of size. It had been said in the past by some personnel employed by the Park that a ten feet opening was the minimum dimension that should be used to distinguish a true arch, but there is no written record supporting that. If such a size had been used, it must have been only a very general guide, since there are arches in the park with less than a ten feet opening that were recognized as "true" arches. As a matter of fact, the authors believe that some openings previously considered as arches are not large enough to be included in this current project for which the minimum size limit is three feet of light opening in any direction.

Why is a three feet dimension any better than ten feet, or any other value? There are at least three good reasons: (1) The three feet figure has been used by Arches National Park since the 1973 Stevens study and it would be counterproductive to propose a change; (2) it seemed a logical cut-off since it included just about all openings considered to be arches in the past; and (3) it precludes the necessity for interjecting subjectivity into the determination of whether to include or exclude an opening as an arch.

In this study any arches that did not have a light opening of at least three feet were not considered, although many of them were as appealing and attractive as their larger counterparts. If those of smaller size had been included the task would have become monumental, even impossible to complete on a timely basis.

When all the arches listed in this study are grouped by size, it clearly shows the high number of small arches. The list below illustrates that point.

Light Opening	No. of Arches
3 feet or more	527
5 feet or more	367
10 feet or more	200
20 feet or more	96
30 feet or more	66
50 feet or more	29
75 feet or more	10
100 feet or more	6
150 feet or more	2

Light Opening	No. of Arches
5 feet or less	160
10 feet or less	327
20 feet or less	431
30 feet or less	461
50 feet or less	498
75 feet or less	517
100 feet or less	521
150 feet or less	526
306 feet or less	527

Why in such a short time has the number of known arches increased so much? Of course there are not more arches now than before, in fact there may be fewer because of those that have fallen or broken. At least five have fallen since 1977. It is simply a fact that more arches have been sought out and recorded in recent years through the coordinated work of several investigators, and such effort has brought the number to over 500. It should be of some interest to note that since the field work ended in the Spring of 1986, several more arches have been reported that have not been included in this study. A list of some of them can be found in the Appendix.

Like other features of the natural environment, natural arches and bridges are dynamic and ever changing. The large arches have undoubtedly been here for a much longer time than most of the small openings, but size alone is not necessarily the only determinant of age. Once the span of an arch becomes too thin or too long to be supported, it will break and fall. Although slow by our time-reckoning, the processes of weathering and erosion are continually at work creating new openings that will eventually enlarge to spectacular arches similar to those that are so well known today. Those same processes will also lead to the destruction of existing arches. Are there more arches here now than in the past? Will the numbers of standing arches increase in the future? These questions do not have simple answers, but pondering them will help stimulate an interest in these unusual features of nature. The history of arches is much more than just keeping track of the persons who happened to observe an arch and record its location and dimensions. A full understanding of how they form, how they evolve and how they eventually disappear is the topic of another chapter.

CHAPTER 2
GEOLOGY

The geology of Arches National Park is both simple and complex, simple in that it is all exposed and easy to see, complex in its composition and origin. The Park area is a geologic treasure with rock exposures showing the consequence of millions of years of changing geologic activity. It is possible for visitors to see thirteen separate geologic formations as they drive through the Park. In addition to the arches for which the park is well known, a wide range of landform features can be seen such as balanced rocks, pinnacles, monoliths, fins, canyons, alcoves, washes and other distinctive terrain features. The arches of the Park, however, attract most of the attention, and rightfully so, because nowhere else in the world are there so many of them in such a small area. These arches vary widely in size, in shape and in color because of the geologic circumstances and climatic conditions that have combined to create an inviting landscape here.

Arches National Park is located in the northern part of the Paradox Basin of southeastern Utah and southwestern Colorado. This "basin" is only one section of the much larger Colorado Plateau Physiographic Province which covers parts of Utah, Colorado, Arizona and New Mexico. The Paradox Basin is very complex geologically consisting of warped or bent rock formations that display considerable fracturing or breaking. Most of these surface rocks are underlain by large deposits of rock salt. More than anything else, the initial development of the landscapes in the Park area can be attributed to these consolidated salts, which are both plastic (will flow under pressure) and soluble (will dissolve when contacted by water).

The Paradox Basin had its beginnings some 300 million years ago when major northwest-southeast trending faults caused the land to subside (drop down) creating a large depression in the earth's crust. At about the same time, the near-by Uncompaghre Highland was lifted up and flanked most of the north and east sides of the basin. A marine sea had existed when the basin was forming, and as the depression became filled with salt water it developed into an isolated sea separated from the main oceans. In time the warm climate accelerated evaporation from the sea and the dissolved minerals were left behind as deep layers of rock salt. Periodically, sea water drained into the basin and then was cut off, resulting in continual salt buildup. Geologic studies have identified at least 29 such cycles of evaporation which accumulated thousands of feet of salt, consisting of 75 to 90 percent sodium chloride (table salt). The remainder is made up mostly of potassium chloride (potash) and magnesium salts.

The enormous weight of overlying rocks, which were subsequently laid down on top of the salt deposits, exerted pressure on the underlying beds and eventually deformed them into irregular thicknesses with some areas having only thin layers of salt while others were very deep. Many areas buckled up forming anticlines (upfolds), while others fractured and greatly modified the surface of the area. As later formations were laid down, they were thinner over the anticlines and thicker in adjacent lower areas. Thus the thickness of the salt and overlying sediments varied considerably in depth from one location to another. Eventually water entered the buried salt where the overlying rocks were relatively thin or through fractures, and dissolved it away. Where that happened the dissolution ultimately caused a collapse of the anticline's crust, often culminating in the formation of a valley.

The dissolution of the salt also caused faulting to occur, and erosion excavated much of the surface material during periods when deposition was not active. Eventually the cracks or "joints" in the fractured surface became widened by weathering and erosion, and fins or thin slabs of vertically standing rock developed, producing conditions conducive to the creation of natural arches and bridges. Salt Valley in the northwestern part of the Park is a good example of the collapse of an anticline underlain by thick beds of salt. On both sides of this valley fins and arches can be found in large numbers. The thickness of salt beneath Salt Valley is at least 10,000 feet.

The geologic activity in the entire area of the Paradox Basin is more complex than that described above. All salt anticlines did not collapse as is evidenced by some that still remain, while others appear to have no direct relationship to salt domes. There are also several synclines (downfolds), faulted and folded features and of course, the various erosional forms such as canyons, washes, etc.

Deposition of the material which eventually forms the rock of a geologic formation may take millions of years. Sands, muds and other material are carried into an area by some transporting agent such as water or wind where they are then laid down through long periods of time (perhaps as long as 20 million years or more) accumulating into rather deep "deposits". The weight of overlying layers compresses the material and the presence of mineral solutions, such as calcium carbonate, cement the particles together to form rocks such as the sandstones which are so common in the Park. Since the rate of deposition is not always uniform, there are periods when the amount of material accumulating is much greater than others; but it continues unceasingly. There are, of course, times when deposition becomes less active and the erosional forces work at wearing away the surface materials. The landscape that we see today has a complex past that has been modified considerably through time, and will continue to change in the future. Because these changes are normally very negligible in a human lifetime, both the rate and amount of alteration are difficult to observe.

In order to appreciate the magnitude of geologic time and to note its consequence in the natural landscape, an example of a shortened time table of the earth's history may be appropriate. If we consider the entire 4.6 billion years of the earth's geologic history as just a single year, the following events may take on a greater meaning. The first abundant fossil record, which began about 600 million years ago, would be in mid-November. The beginning of the story at Arches National Park (300 million years ago) was about December 7. Entrada Sandstone was completely in place on December 19, and Mancos Shale on the 24th. Dinosaurs appeared on December 16 and disappeared on the 26th, 120 million years later. The LaSal Mountains were formed by December 28 and modern man (Homo Sapiens) showed up on December 31 about 11:55 PM (assuming the date to be approximately 35,000 years ago). Columbus discovered America only three seconds before the year's end. Thus, the entire recorded history of the Americas since 1492 is all within those last three seconds of that momentous year.

The general geologic situation within Arches National Park can be seen in Figure 2. The relationship between time and rock formation (including thickness) helps one to better understand the complexity of the earth's surface here. The remainder of this chapter contains a more detailed discussion of the events that led up to the present landscape. It will add greater significance and perception to anyone who is interested in probing further into the explanations of why the Park exhibits such an unusual array of sights.

The geologic activity that has had the greatest impact on the present-day features of the Park commenced about the middle of the Pennsylvanian Period (320 to 286 million years ago) when the Paradox Basin started to form. At the completion of the 29 cycles of evaporation already mentioned, the basin became more settled and began to fill with sediments covering the salt deposits. Even today the salt does not show at the surface in the Park, but there are small exposures in Salt Valley of the Paradox Formation in the form of a gypsum caprock. Eventually sea water from the west moved in to deposit limestone and dolomite to form the Honaker Trail Formation, which is visible at the U.S. Highway 191 cut near the Arches National Park Visitor Center.

The entire time of the Permian Period (286 to 245 million years ago) was involved in producing and depositing the accumulations that formed the Cutler Formation, a red sandstone derived from sediments consisting mostly of reddish granite eroded from the ancient Uncompaghre Highland. At Arches National Park the Cutler Formation appears as an undifferentiated rock layer, while in other areas it is often subdivided into members. It is exposed within the Park along U.S. Highway 191 north of the Visitor Center.

At the beginning of the Triassic Period (245 to 208 million years ago) the Moenkopi Formation was laid down on tidal flats as the seas retreated. These sediments consisted mainly of brown sand and silt. Some small exposures of this rock are found along the southern slopes of Salt Valley. The next layer of rock that was formed is known as the Chinle Formation, composed mostly of fine grained sand, silt and clay that typically forms slopes in the area. It was deposited in stream flood plains after the sea receded. The best exposures within the Park are along the south flanks of Salt and Cache Valleys and along the Colorado River from Big Bend to the mouth of Salt Wash. The movement of subsurface salt slowed down after the Chinle sediments were formed, enabling subsequent deposits to more completely cover the salt anticlines.

The next formation to develop (still within the Triassic Period) is known as Wingate Sandstone, attributed primarily to wind action during a dry period. Rocks of this formation form definite cliffs in the region. Wingate Sandstone is well exposed at the top of the south escarpments of Salt and Cache Valleys, lower Salt Wash, and along the Colorado River above Big Bend. The succeeding rock layer to accumulate was the Kayenta Formation. It is made principally of sand, but contains some shale and limestone, laid down in shallow lakes or ponds. It forms lavender-red, ledge-filled slopes and is exposed at places on both sides of Salt Valley, at the mouth of Courthouse Wash, and along the Colorado River.

Sediments of Navajo Sandstone began depositing during Triassic Time, but extended well into the Jurassic Period (208 to 144 million years ago). These sands, which eventually hardened into rock, were largely created by wind, often as dunes in a desert-like environment or in some cases near coastal areas. The buff colored rocks often

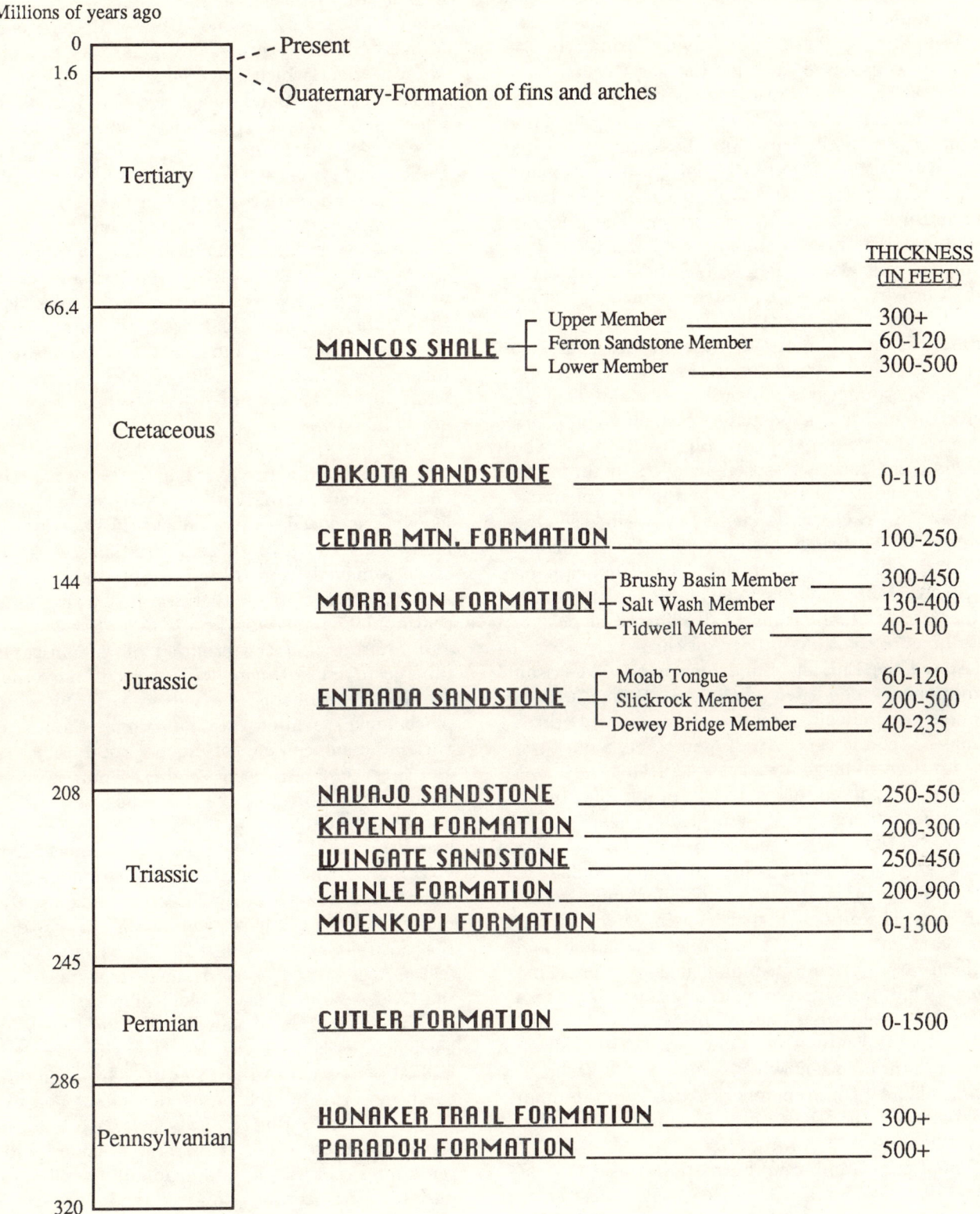

Figure 2

display considerable cross bedding. The Petrified Dunes area of the Park north of Courthouse Wash is an excellent place to see this formation. It is also well exposed on the slopes behind the Visitor Center and in several other areas of the Park. The Wingate, Kayenta, and Navajo formations together are considered the Glen Canyon Group.

The most visible rock formation within the Park is the Entrada, made of sandstones originally laid down in tidal flats and beaches as a sea intruded into the region. Not only is it an obvious formation, it is the best known because it contains more natural arches than any other. The Entrada Sandstone has three members. At the bottom is the oldest, the Dewey Bridge Member, a contorted reddish-brown muddy sandstone which is softer than the members above it. The middle Slickrock Member is a salmon-red, fine-grained massive sandstone which typically forms vertical cliffs. The top or youngest member is the Moab Tongue, a whitish, massive sandstone which often appears as caprock on many of the Slickrock fins. The Entrada Sandstone is exposed along the main paved road throughout the Park. Near the base of many of these Entrada cliffs it is easy to see the crumbly Dewey Bridge member, above which looms the massive Slickrock Member. Aside from capping the Slickrock in such obvious places as the Fiery Furnace, the Moab Tongue also forms slopes on both flanks of the Salt Valley Anticline.

Above the Entrada Sandstone is the Morrison Formation, deposited in tidal flats, stream channels and flood plains. It also has three members. The lower Tidwell Member is a dark red silty unit with large cherty concretions. It was formerly considered to be the Summerville Formation, but was re-identified in 1980. The middle Salt Wash Member is mostly yellow gray, cross-bedded sandstone with some siltstone, mudstone, shale and conglomerate, often forming rough outcrops. The upper Brushy Basin Member contains variegated shale, sandstone, mudstone and conglomerate, often forming slopes with some ledges. The Salt Wash and Brushy Basin Members are well exposed when viewed from the main Park road to the Delicate Arch Viewpoint. The Tidwell Member can be seen when walking the Delicate Arch Trail. All three members show from the main road between the Delicate Arch junction and the Fiery Furnace.

The Cedar Mountain Formation was the first to be laid down in the Cretaceous Period (144 to 66 million years ago) and consists of light variegated mudstone and shale, with ledges of quartzite and conglomerate separating it from the Morrison's Brushy Basin Member, and is exposed in the Park in the same general areas. Dakota Sandstone followed, accumulating on coastal plains and in stream flood plains. Some conglomerate and shale occur with the sandstone of this group. It is rather discontinuous in the Park and is exposed in places as rimrock on the Cedar Mountain Formation. The Lower and Upper Members of the Mancos Shale were laid down as gray mud by the Mancos Sea which covered the area, while the middle Ferron Sandstone Member was deposited when sand was carried in by the sea from the west. All three members are exposed in Cache Valley and lower Salt Valley.

Although more deposits were accumulated after the Mancos Shale, none have remained in the Park to the present time. Formations of the Mesa Verde Group, consisting of lake and coastal plain deposits, are readily seen in the Book Cliffs north of Interstate 70, and probably existed in earlier times in what is now the Park. It has been estimated that more than one mile of rock existed above what we see today, but has since been removed by erosional downwear.

During the first part of the Tertiary Period (66 to 1.6 million years ago) the Wasatch and Green River Formations were deposited, and are likewise exposed in the Book Cliffs. It is very likely that rocks of those formations were among those removed from this area by erosion. Geologic activity did not end with these last formations, but continual change was occurring. Erosion, folding and faulting and the creation of an entire mountain occurred. During this period, movement in the earth (probably caused in part by salt displacement) resulted in the Moab Fault, and a vertical displacement of about 2600 feet ensued, enabling one to see eight separate geologic formations from one vantage point on the road above the Visitor Center. There are not many places on earth where that can be done. Through volcanic intrusions during this same period the LaSal Mountains were pushed up. About 10 or 11 million years ago there was also a general uplift of the entire Colorado Plateau by several thousand feet. Accelerated erosion since then has produced the landscape of today. Most of what we now see in the area has developed in the most recent geologic period known as the Quaternary (1.6 million years ago to the Present). Great amounts of earth material have been carried to the sea by way of the Colorado River. Exposed rock has become worn down by weathering and erosion, with the remaining rock fragments gradually breaking down into sandy soils and isolated sand dunes. Eventually, most loose material will be carried to the Colorado River for further transport downstream.

So, how do all the arches fit into the general sequences described above? Almost all of the arches in the Park occur in rocks that are no more than 230 million years old, but naturally the arches themselves are not so old. Because there is no completely accurate way to date an arch, only estimates can be made on how long some of them may have been in existence. Some of the larger ones like Landscape Arch may have been around for thousands or even tens of thousands of years. Some smaller ones may have had a life span of less than 1000 years. Research is currently underway on techniques which may result in more specific ages for many of the arches. Conditions of rock thickness, hardness and cohesiveness tied into climatic conditions are all responsible for the development of an arch. By examining all the known arches it has been found that the Entrada Formation leads in total numbers, but all formations from Wingate to Morrison have some arches (See Figure 3). An explanation of how these arches form will be discussed more fully in a later chapter.

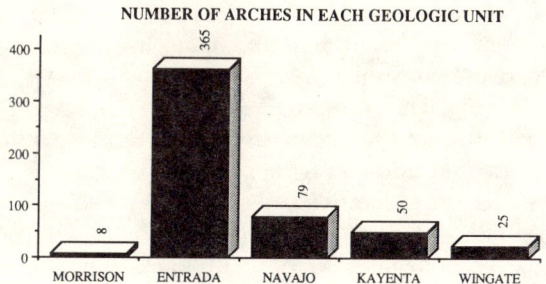
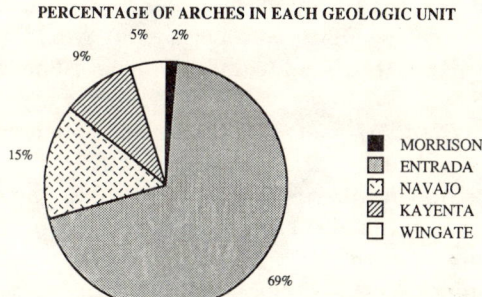

Figure 3

CHAPTER 3
NAMING ARCHES

Names have been used since early in human development to identify different persons, places and things and all possible categories and subdivisions of them. A name has been given to almost everything that is known to exist - animals, rivers, mountains, towns, rocks, chemical elements and just about everything else. Long ago it was also found that numbers often serve a similar function and in some cases were superior to names. One of the early examples is the use of numbers for years and days, but we still use names for months and days of the week, and the Chinese still use names for the years. Numbers, however, are usually far better for record keeping and data manipulation. Although each of us is catalogued by our social security numbers, who would like to be known by that nine digit number? The use of numbers for sequence and statistics is far more efficient than any set of names could ever be, but names are much easier to remember and serve a purpose that numbers cannot accomplish.

So it is with natural arches and bridges. Each one is distinct and different in some way from all others in shape, size, position, or other features. Because of this, names as well as numbers have been given to all the catalogued arches of the Park. This permits greater flexibility in computing statistical information, mapping, and keeping track of the number of listed arches, but it also permits us to remember an arch by its name which is easier and more interesting than a series of digits.

It is difficult to determine exactly when names were first given to the arches in the Park. There is no record to indicate if the native peoples gave any of them names, but there is a high likelihood that they may have named some. It is known that the early settlers gave names to some arches, and in recent times most of the large or unusual arches have been identified by name. As the number of reported arches became increasingly greater, it necessitated a more methodical system of identification that could be used for analysis as well as general recognition.

Several problems arise when an attempt is made to find the commonly accepted names of the earth's natural features. One such problem is deciding which name to use if an arch had been called by more than one name. In most cases, a second or even third name may have been given because inadequate communications resulted in lack of general usage or acceptance. There are also instances where new names were published when an existing name was already known and widely used. That only causes confusion and should be avoided in the interest of authenticity. No attempt was made by the authors to rename any arches that were mentioned by name in Park records, or were generally known by officials or frequent visitors to the Park. The records of Arches National Park show names for most of the 288 that had been catalogued by 1983, so it would be presumptuous and unproductive to rename any of them. Names were given only to those arches newly located or previously unnamed.

Because of the careful and thorough search for arch names, it is hoped that the names used in this publication will become "official" or recognized and thus preclude any conflict in the future. Even where a name may seem "incorrect" or unsuitable, it is best to keep the name that has been widely used in recent times. An example is Tunnel Arch, which is a "free standing" arch type rather than a natural tunnel, but changing the name would be unwarranted and confusing.

A look at some names used in the past will help illustrate the problems. At one time there seems to have been some confusion over the name Box Arch, which was then applied to what is now Elephant Chin Arch. Three separate arches have been known as "Arch in the Making," not at the same time, but all three had all the characteristics of a "true" arch when that name was used. Some previous names shown in Park records are:

Current Name	Previous Name
Delicate Arch	Pants Crotch
Skyline Arch	Arch in the Making
Magic Mystery Arch	Pipeline Arch
North Window	The Spectacles
South Window	The Spectacles
Elephant Chin Arch	Box Arch
Parade of Elephants	Elephant Arch
Double Arch	The Jug Handles
Baby Arch	Arch in the Making
Biceps Arch	Arch in the Making

How is an arch named? Like most everything

else, when an arch was first discovered or reported it was often given a name based on whatever the discoverer's whim may have been. It is interesting to note that only descriptive names were given to the well-known arches by those who first explored the park.

It has long been an unofficial policy among Arches National Park personnel that an arch should not be named after a person, mainly to preclude the possibility of an endless list of such names. There could have been numerous arches named after the person who "found" it, or even honoring someone who may have had little interest or involvement in the arches of the Park. The authors have respected that policy and have continued it in this project. Even though some literature shows personal names for some arches, none of them have any "official" recognition and in every instance previously compiled names found in the Park records show that usage of a non-personal name preceded the attempt to give the arch the name of a person.

There are various reasons for the names that have been applied. Most of them can be determined by examining the nature of the name itself, or in the case of the more recently named arches it is possible to get the information from the person or persons who first used the name. The name might be given because the opening or overall structure resembles or reminds one of some object or concept. Resemblance to an object can depend on how far away or from what angle the arch is viewed.

Nearly one-half of all arches in the park are named after an object. Other categories include names that describe their site, an event that was associated with discovery, being named after something in the vicinity of the arch, and being named after a plant or animal. Others are named because of some feature or characteristic displayed by the arch or for a variety of other reasons that don't quite fit into the groupings listed above. Figure 4 below summarizes the name origins.

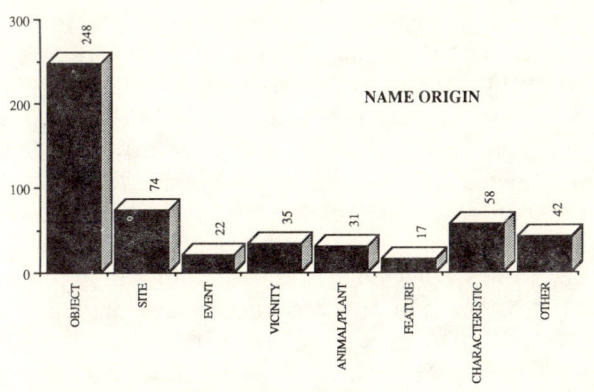

Figure 4

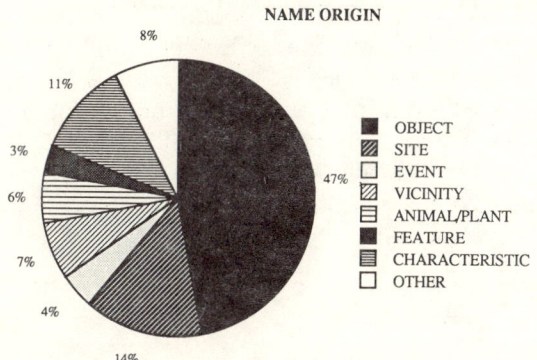

A closer look into the various categories and some samples of each will help to clarify the names of the 527 arches of the Park. The name might be given because the opening or overall structure resembles or reminds someone of an object. Resemblance often depends on how far away or from what angle the arch is viewed. It is in the eye of the beholder - arches may not look the same to everyone. Some descriptive names may not be easy to see, and may require broad imagination. Photographs may not show the resemblance as well as actual viewing. Some of the more easily recognizable arches that resemble something include Indian Head (ND 20), Big Eye (ND 23), Arrow (ND 76), Christmas Tree (WS 19), Fishtail (GW 8), and many others. It might be somewhat difficult to agree with a name such as Ugly Arch (GW 16). Although it may have appeared "ugly" to the person who named it, others may think it to be rather beautiful in its confined setting.

A name is also given in certain instances due to the site or location of the arch. Good examples are Skyline (SD 79), Sand Hill (KB 16), Roadside (FF 13), Salt Wash (SW 2), Wolfe Bluffs (SW 12), Top of the Slope (HP 1), Concealed (HP 15), and West Boundary (UC 15). More difficult to interpret would be Nand and Sand Arches. Nand Arch (SD 19-20) is an acronym for "north arch of north drainage" arm of Fin Canyon. Nearby Sand Arch (SD 21-22) is an acronym for "south arch of north drainage".

Some event or occurrence has also prompted the naming of some arches. Snowy (EP 37) and Thunder (SA 55) were inspired by existing weather; Sunlight (WS 35) was first noticed as light penetrated the opening when viewed from a specific position, while Sunshine (UC 14) could only be proved to be an arch when the sun shone through

13

the opening at a certain time of day. Lost and Found (HP 9) and Regained (GW 5) were relocated, having been previously reported, but almost given up for lost since they were difficult to find again. Forgotten (EP 5) and Neglected (PB 16) were unaccountably ignored for some time. Thanksgiving (WS 26) was documented on Thanksgiving Eve. Some happening suggested Flying Hat (SD 10) and Sit Down (HP 13). Surprise Arch (FF 27) was unknown when a Park Service party found it while exploring for a route through the Fiery Furnace.

Names selected because of something observed in the vicinity of the arch are rather obvious: Big Buck (EP 12), Screech Owl (ND 4), Pine Tree (SD 64), Poison Ivy (UC 1) Quicksand (UC 4) and Running Coyote (UC 8) are but a few examples. The same can be said when names are given for a plant or animal found in the area: Cliffrose (EP 48), Magpie (SD 52-53), Raven (WS 20) and Juniper (SA 22) are but a few. In some instances names came from nearby natural features of the Park that had already been given names. Some examples of these are: Parade of Elephants (WS 21-22), Gossips (SA 6) and Park Avenue (SA 15).

Characteristics of the arch such as color, natural markings, geology, surface conditions, or dimensions can be a reason for the name as in: Filigree (ND 69), Debris (SD 35), White Fin (SD 42), Blue (SW 8) and Brushy Basin (SW 7). One of the best examples where the name fits the characteristic is "The Tunnel" (UC 7), a natural arch that closely resembles a man-made tunnel through solid rock.

There are many other reasons for names. It might be someone's momentary whim. No rules have ever been set down on how to name an arch - and rightfully so- thus there are simply no known explanations for some names. Two Hundred (SA 28) was the 200th arch recorded; similarly identified are Three Hundred (GW 25), Four Hundred (SA 7) and Five Hundred (KB 4). Textbook (ND 1-2) are classic examples of arches that developed from bedding plane openings. Phantom (ND 24) should have been reported when Indian Head (ND 20) was first identified, but it escaped recording at the time. Anniversary (KB 12-13) was located on the wedding anniversary of then Park Ranger Slim Mabery by a visitor in his party. Walk Thru Bridge (FF 45) arches over the trail that is followed on the conducted hike through the Fiery Furnace. Illusion (HP 19) has a deceiving appearance from different angles. Arch of Motion (GW 4) can be noticed best from a moving vehicle as the moving background helps identify its otherwise hard-to-find position. Deception (UC 12) can only be seen from certain places. Baby Arch (SA 5) was so named because it was erroneously thought to be rather small.

It is sometimes difficult to trace when names were first used and to whom credit should be given for deciding on the name, particularly those names that have been in use for a long time. In researching for existing names, the records at Arches National Park were the main source of investigation. Although they may not contain every name ever given to an arch, they are considered to be the best source for names that were recognized. In some instances the first mention in those records indicate that an arch had been known, or a name had been in use, for some time. In such cases only the first reported mention of the arch or its name can be recorded accurately.

A review of old newspapers, local historical data, etc. prior to the establishment of Arches National Monument in 1929 would doubtless reveal other names, but it is most unlikely that any additional arches would be disclosed beyond those shown in this book. No attempt has been made to discover the various names that may have been casually given to some of the more prominent arches.

There may always be some controversy over names of arches, since only a few have been declared official by the Board on Geographic Names. It has been said by some that the names for Delicate (SW 14) and Landscape (SD 56) arches were reversed and applied incorrectly to each arch. Historical records in Arches National Park show, however, that the names were correctly applied. The late Bates Wilson, Superintendent of the Park for more than 20 years, stated in correspondence in 1969 "As far as I can determine, Delicate Arch and Landscape Arch were first named in the early 1930's by a Park Service Field Party photographing the area. Mr. Harry Reed is credited with naming the features." Bates Wilson went on to say that he had spoken with Mr. Reed several times in the past years and that the names were correct and had not been reversed.

The alphabetical list of all the arches (Table 2) on page 127 shows the origin of each name, when and by whom it was named, and when and by whom it was first reported. As new arches were reported, the name used by the finder was considered the "official" name. If no name was suggested, the arch was examined and an appropriate name was decided upon by the individual or persons who mapped, measured, photographed and recorded other information on it. The following list (Table 1) shows the persons who were responsible for naming and reporting the majority of the arches and bridges in the Park.

First Recorded Reporting of Arches

	Number Reported		
	Total	Alone	With Others
Ed McCarrick	168	29	139
Dale Stevens	166	60	106
Reuben Scolnik	162	89	73
Mike Salamacha	40	17	23
Doug Travers	36	25	11
Jim Stiles	32	23	9
Bates Wilson	22	22	0
Carl Horton	18	2	16
Arches NP Historical Records	16	16	0
Alice Drogin	13	8	5
Robert Vreeland	11	11	0
Kelly Nielsen	7	1	6
NPS Expedition 1934	6	6	0
Hank Schmidt	6	6	0
Lewis McKinney	6	6	0
Kay Forsythe	6	2	4
Damian Fagan	6	3	3

First Recorded Naming of Arches

	Number Named		
	Total	Alone	With Others
Ed McCarrick	228	99	129
Dale Stevens	187	92	95
Reuben Scolnik	137	96	41
Mike Salamacha	28	8	20
Doug Travers	20	15	5
Jim Stiles	17	12	5
Bates Wilson	12	10	2
Alice Drogin	10	6	4
Arches NP Historical Records	8	8	0
Kay Forsythe	8	5	3
Carl Horton	8	2	6
Lewis McKinney	6	6	0

Table 1

CHAPTER 4
DETERMINING AND CLASSIFYING ARCHES

When commencing a study of the natural arches and bridges of the earth's surface, it is essential to establish precision in the definition of exactly what an arch or bridge is. The problem of identification is apparent when one reads the literature on natural arches and even more obvious when observing the varied shapes and forms of these features in their natural setting. Some openings in or through rock surfaces would correctly be called caves, alcoves or just holes. Some openings are not necessarily arch-shaped, and may display irregular configurations in both the opening and the spanning rock mass. The commonly used names, "arch," "bridge" and "window" are often used interchangeably and in many cases these names have been formalized with little regard to maintaining consistency with any organized morphological system.

Because phenomena of nature do not always lend themselves easily to classification systems, there may always be some controversy as to how or why the groupings have been organized. This should not detract, however, from the fact that organization fosters understanding and that improvements and refinements are always possible. The definitions or categories herein described were formulated by careful and thorough field investigation and analysis of hundreds of rock openings in Arches National Park and other locations in southern Utah. In other parts of the world where igneous, limestone or other rock types and structures exist, or where coastal wave action or the dissolving of underground rocks by sub-surface water might account for arch development, the classification may be different. The available literature was also carefully searched and many conversations with researchers in the field proved informative and helpful in establishing the categories and divisions used.

Based on the system used in this book, the term "Natural Arch" covers all types of proper openings, including "Natural Bridges" and "Natural Tunnels." An arch-shaped opening is not necessarily required, as the term "arch" is meant to include all natural rock openings that qualify under the conditions established by the authors. Any "natural rock opening" is a legitimate "natural arch" when the four criteria listed below are met. If the criteria are not met, but an opening or hole through the rock exists, it is simply called an "opening."

1- There must be an opening through the rock, regardless of its shape, which has resulted from natural weathering and erosional processes. A cave or alcove without a light opening behind the entrance is not considered an arch even though it may have an arch-shaped ceiling or appearance. The enlargement of an existing opening by rocks falling from that opening is considered part of the natural process of arch formation while an opening created by the repositioning of detached rock is not considered a "natural arch".

2- The natural opening through the rock is always accompanied by a rock span, regardless of its size, shape or orientation. The span's position is typically above or to the side of the opening. In most instances during the formation of the opening, there is no movement or shifting of the span. Where natural weathering processes cause the span to shift or settle slightly without significantly altering the shape or size of the original opening, it is still considered an arch.

3- The opening between the rock span and any nearby rock mass must allow the passage of light along at least three feet of uninterrupted space in at least one direction. In other words a three-feet long rod would pass crosswise through the opening. Because of the shape of some narrow openings, the rod may have to bend somewhat to pass through. Some arches have several in-line light openings with more than one being three feet or longer in length. Even though there may be more than one qualifying light opening, it is not considered a double arch unless the separate light openings are isolated by rock that is an integral part of the main rock mass and not merely blockage by rock or debris that is wedged in the gap. Such a situation is called a "discontinuous light opening".

4- Esthetics can not be a consideration in determining an arch. Some are naturally more beautiful than others, but positive appeal to one person may not be perceived the same way by someone else. Esthetic quality is too subjective and should not be a factor in a scientific study.

CLASSIFICATION OF ROCK OPENINGS

In much of the early literature on natural arches and bridges, a general classification existed where all openings were put into one of three categories: arches, bridges or windows. Such a system is unsatisfactory because there are so many problems and exceptions that must be made when identifying all openings by just three types. The criteria of this simple system are also difficult to explain because of the nonscientific way it originated and came into common acceptance. A more rational system must be based on a thorough examination of all possible openings and one that has utility for the average person who enjoys looking for detail in the varied rock forms encountered.

The natural rock openings in Arches National Park can be categorized into two general groups, those that are considered natural arches and those that are considered just openings. In most cases the processes for both groups may be quite similar, but there are some obvious differences. Natural arches owe their existence and eventual enlargement primarily to weathering processes which include the chemical weakening of cementing agents in rock, the biological action of organisms that are active on the rock, the physical breakup of rock through frost action, differential heating and cooling, repeated wetting and drying, etc. Once the rock becomes weakened or broken up by weathering, the detachment of sand grains and small fragments begins. These smaller particles are carried away by running water or wind and the direct removal by gravity. In other words the opening through the rock must have been formed by natural excavation processes, not by shifting or falling rocks.

The non-arch type of opening is differentiated from the arches described above primarily by size or by origin. Many of them are simply less than three feet and do not qualify under the instituted criteria. Others are not formed directly by weathering, but are created as openings in rock piles that have accumulated from near-by cliffs, or perhaps where a leaning slab of rock broke away and down from a sheer cliff. Shape or esthetic qualities are not used as determining factors in either group. It is possible that an indentation in a cliff face may exhibit an arching shape, but such an alcove is not considered to be either an "arch" or an "opening" if light does not penetrate between the observable span and the adjacent rock. Since there are so many non-arch type openings, no attempt has been made to identify or catalog them. The purpose of this book is to identify those openings that fit within the established definition of a natural arch.

Arches National Park displays openings in rock masses, through fins, on canyon walls, in stream beds, on gently sloping monoliths, on ridge tops and in open flats. Some are in the early stages of development, others are old and near collapse.

Some have developed in joints, others in bedding planes. Some occur in massive sandstone that appears to have uniform resistance to weathering, while others are in weakly cemented rock formations. They are so varied and complex that it seems only logical to divide them into types based purely in descriptive terms. Ten arch and five non-arch categories have been determined as listed below.

Natural Arches
Free Standing Arch (FSA)
Cliff Wall Arch (CWA)
Expanded Crevice Arch (ECA)
Jug Handle Arch (JHA)
Platform Arch (PFA)
Natural Bridge (NB)
Spanned Alcove Arch (SAA)
Pothole Arch (PHA)
Natural Tunnel (NT)
Perforated Alcove Arch (PAA)

Non-Arch Openings
Undersized Opening (Miniature Arch) (UO)
Joint Opening (JO)
Bedding Plane Opening (BPO)
Rock Fall Opening (RFO)
Tunnel Opening (TO)

The classification of an opening may not be permanent, nor is it necessarily something that can be agreed upon by everyone. In time, both the arch and its surroundings are subject to change. If, for example, the rock wall behind a Cliff Wall Arch breaks away and leaves the arch free and isolated from any nearby rock masses, it would then be classified more correctly as a Free Standing Arch. Naturally there can be other transformations from one type to another, but usually the process of change is slow and even within several hundred years there may be no visible change.

In some cases the decision to classify an arch into one of the above categories becomes difficult, not because there is no feasible category, but because it may display features of more than one type. When such a situation arises a judgment must be made regarding which type is most appropriate. Although everyone may not agree with the decision, there were always two or more people who participated in those difficult cases. The classification system was not intended to be applicable to all parts of the world, so in areas outside of the Park where sea arches, lava tubes and different rock formations and environments exist, an arch may not fit into any of the above types. In such cases additional categories may be

17

necessary. In order to clarify the characteristics of each of the types that occur in the Park, a more detailed description follows.

NATURAL ARCHES

<u>Free Standing Arch</u> The free standing arch is distinguished by its relative isolation from surrounding fins, cliffs and other rock masses. It is usually easy to observe because of its independence and isolation from nearby features that normally enables one to see directly through it. The rock span may continue from base to base as an independent mass, but many spans of the free standing type merge into larger rock masses such as the fins in which they are formed.

<u>Cliff Wall Arch</u> The cliff wall arch occurs on the side or adjacent to rock walls or cliffs. Supporting columns of the span may continue to the base of the arch as separate structures, or one or both ends of the span may merge with the near vertical walls on which they are found. The arch span is separated from the main rock mass to the extent that light can show through the opening. The depth of this light opening may be only a few inches from the cliff wall, but the length must be at least three feet. Several of the larger cliff wall arches have discontinuous openings between the span and the cliff. At least one of these openings must meet the minimum length requirements of three feet. Some alcoves in the Park appear to include a span separated from the main rock mass as evidenced by desert varnish stains that begin in a crack near the top of the alcove that flows down the back side. Even though it is quite obvious that rain water has seeped through cracks to form these stains, the feature is not considered an arch unless light can penetrate the crack. Identification of a cliff wall arch is often more difficult than others to determine since the light opening is behind the span at the top or the side, and may be visible only from in or near the arch itself, a place which is sometimes difficult to reach for such an observation.

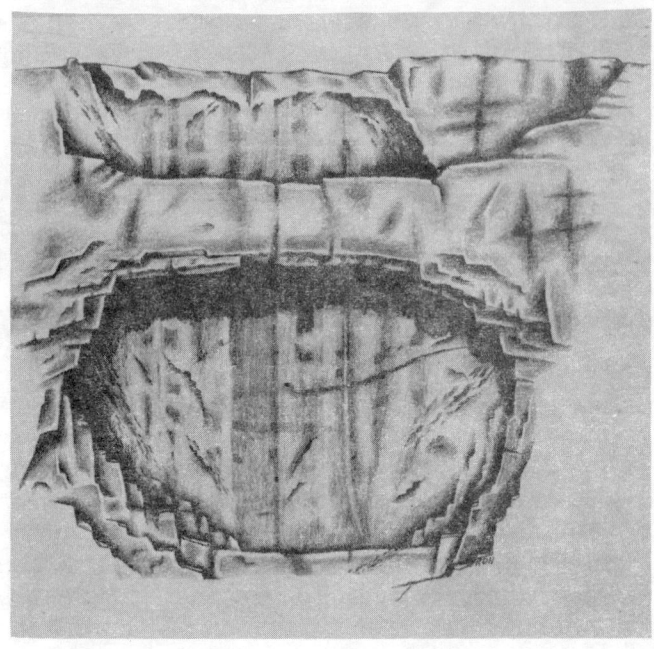

<u>Expanded Crevice Arch</u> The expanded crevice type has its beginnings in a crevice which is usually a bedding plane or joint, then enlarges to where there is a definite light opening. The height of the opening (when occurring in a bedding plane) is still relatively small when compared to the width because of its origin in the weak contact zone between different sedimentary layers or geologic units. In a joint the height would be greater than the width. There is no doubt that many of the large free standing arches in the Park originated as expanded crevice types. The difference between this type and the smaller of the free standing types is in the "slit" shape of the opening where one dimension is very small relative to the other.

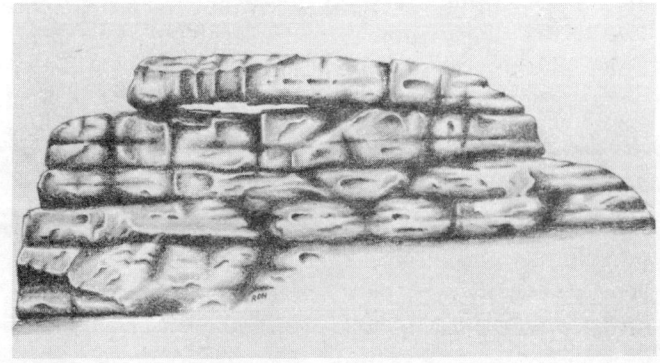

18

Jug Handle Arch The span and the opening on the jug handle arch occur on the sides of rock masses at an angle which is normally closer to vertical than horizontal. The rock span usually displays only a slight curve while the opening is rather narrow and elongated, often resembling the handle of a large jug. The jug handle arch is distinguished from a platform arch, which may also occur on a cliff side, by the narrower light opening and the smaller horizontal span extent of platform arches. Some jug handle arches occur on cliffs where major bedding planes are bridged by the arch span, a situation that does not occur with platform arches.

Platform Arch Platform arches occurs on or near the top of rock masses, usually in open areas where exfoliation is a common weathering process. They sometimes occur on the sides of fins or cliff walls and might be thought of as "hanging platforms." The outer surface is typically smooth with slight indentations. The span closely conforms to the surrounding rock mass, having been formed when an exfoliation slab expanded out and away in the center, but remained attached at both ends, leaving the separated span as a flat or slightly concave roof to the narrow opening. The arch usually has a very limited height, but the width can be substantial. Since the span is usually an ex-foliation slab, the horizontal thickness is much greater than the vertical thickness. Platform arches have often been missed in the past because they are sometimes difficult to see or they are ignored because they are not always impressive looking. They do meet the established criteria, however, and must be considered as arches.

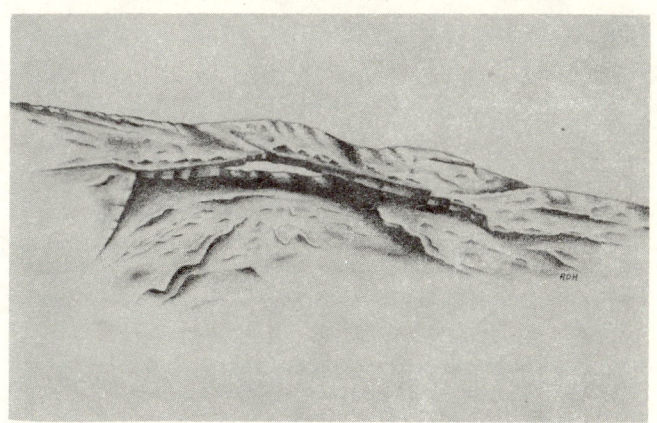

Natural Bridge Although a natural bridge has many of the same characteristics as other arches, it is distinguished from them by its position astride a stream or stream channel even though there may be little evidence of an actual stream. Formation may have been enhanced somewhat by intermittent flowing water, but natural bridges are not normally carved by streams. Like other arches their outward features result primarily from weathering processes, not the hydrologic effects of a stream. None of the bridges in the Park have permanent streams flowing beneath them. Some of the arches which are not called "bridges" may also have an occasional trickle of water flowing under them such as surface flow from a rain storm, but unless there is an obvious drainage course beneath the span, there is no attempt to call them bridges.

Spanned Alcove Arch An alcove in and of itself, without exhibiting a light opening through the rock mass, is not considered a natural arch, although it may be in the initial stage of developing into one. Some alcoves, especially the smaller ones, qualify as arches when they contain a pillar that extends from the outer floor to the outer top of the cave-like opening. This pillar often conforms geometrically to the slope of the rock mass side and usually has a slight outward curve to it. In a few cases the alcove has a horizontal beam across the opening rather than a vertical pillar. The spanned alcove as described above may have been previously called either an "Alcove Pillar" or an "Alcove Beam" type.

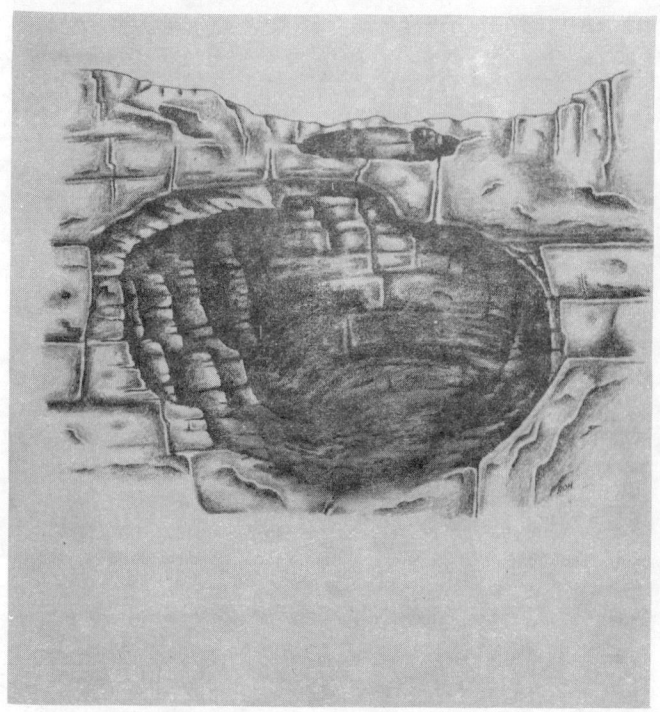

Pothole Arch The pothole arch usually appears as a smooth rounded hole which displays a horizontal opening continuing inward and upward. This occurs because the arch develops where a pothole (small depression) on top of a rock mass merges with an alcove on the sheer rock face. It differs from the cliff wall type in the way it was formed, in its position on the rock mass and in the circular vertical opening that is behind the span. This opening is quite different from the elongated slit that characterizes the opening behind most cliff wall spans. Most pothole arches develop on massive sandstone walls at or near the crest of monoliths which have neither bedding planes nor joints; a condition which typically is not conducive to arch formation. These arches are often the most difficult to measure because of their position high of massive walls which are usually inaccessible to anyone except the experienced climber.

Natural Tunnel The name of this arch type pretty well describes what it is. Only one is listed out of the 527 arches of Arches National Park and it resembles a mine shaft that enters one side of a rock mass and goes to open air on the other side. It differs from the typical rock opening in that it is more of an elongated arching hole or passageway through the rock. To be considered a natural tunnel, the actual length of the passageway (horizontal thickness of the span) must be substantially greater than the height or width, which ever is larger.

Perforated Alcove Arch The perforated alcove type occurs when an alcove in a fin or other narrow rock mass has a distinct opening through its rear or side wall. The opening in most perforated alcove arches is usually angular and quite irregular in shape even though the remainder of the arch might be quite smooth. This is probably due to the relatively recent perforation of the wall by natural forces. Eventually, as the opening enlarges, its significance as an alcove lessens and the opening displays more the characteristics of a free standing arch.

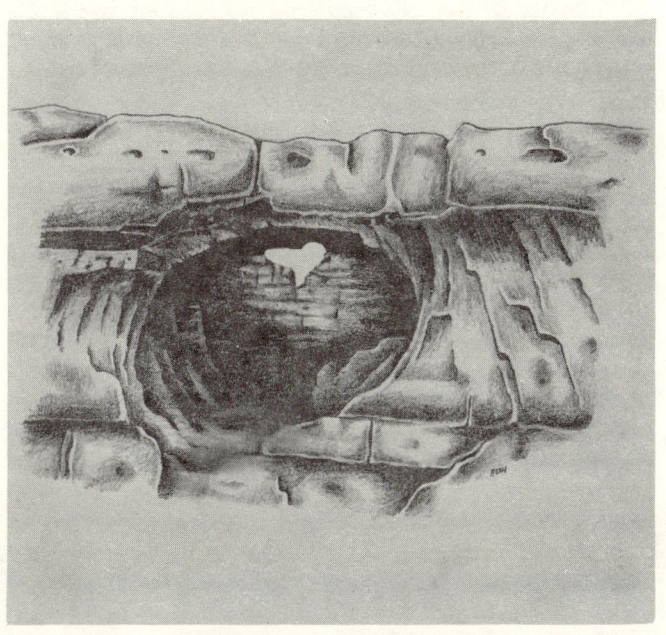

The charts in Figure 5 below show the breakdown of the ten types of arches. Note that combined Free Standing and Cliff Wall Arches account for two-thirds of all openings. Expanded Crevice types are the third most numerous while natural tunnels are the least numerous

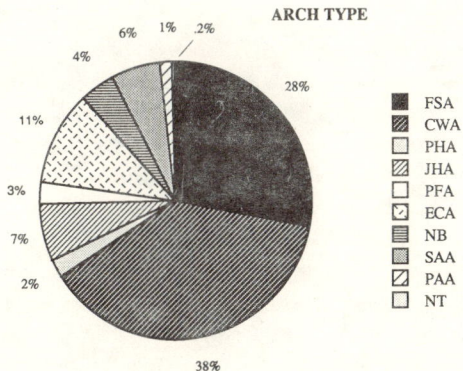

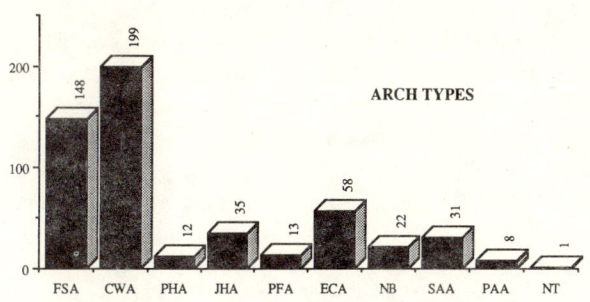

Figure 5

NON-ARCH OPENINGS

Non-arch openings fit nicely into two categories: those that have light openings of less than three feet, and those that have openings greater than three feet, but because of other features do not qualify as being legitimate arches. As might be expected, nearly all the arch types previously discussed can be found in miniature in or near Arches National Park. These smaller (less than three feet) openings are so numerous in the area that some cut-off dimension had to be established as a minimum size for an arch. Those larger non-arch openings are primarily the product of rock falls or advanced weathering that has left the rock encircling the opening without a firm bond of consolidation. Many examples of non-arch openings are found near the main roads and trails of the Park

Undersized Opening (Miniature Arch) Some of the most graceful, interesting and unusual openings in the Park have a light opening of less than three feet. It is difficult to overlook many of them because they are so appealing, but it would be nearly impossible, with any time constraints, to catalog and measure all of them. In some places it is possible to count numerous small openings which are only a few inches in size. Perhaps in the future someone might want to take a closer look at these "miniature arches" that are not considered here. It might be an interesting study. The three feet dimension is not a magic number, but has been in use by Arches National Park since 1973. The original reason for using this dimension was that it was a logical cut-off. (See Chapter 1 on History for further discussion.) Probably thousands of these small openings exist in the Park.

Joint Opening Vertical joints or cracks in the sandstone rock of southeastern Utah are quite common. Often these joints widen to permit the passage of light. These openings always have a greater vertical than horizontal extent and normally do not become too large before developing into widened cracks and isolated pedestals. They are considered openings rather than arches when any of the following conditions are found: 1. The joint continues as a crack for some distance above and below the opening, normally to the top of the rock mass and below to the next bedding plane or geologic unit. 2. The opening is not the major part of the joint, but is only incidental to it. 3. The opening is caused primarily by slippage rather than weathering. 4. Even in those instances where slippage has not occurred, the joint above or below the opening is not completely closed, cemented, or sealed.

Bedding Plane Opening Horizontal bedding planes, which often contain less resistant rocks than those found above and below, provide a convenient place for weathering to occur at a relatively rapid pace. These bedding planes are natural places for openings to develop and they often evolve into some very large arches. Under the following conditions these openings are not considered arches: 1. When there is evidence that significant movement or slippage of the superior rock mass has occurred. 2. The opening is either not completely closed or it lacks obvious cementing or sealing of the two rock masses where they join on either side of the opening.

Tunnel Opening Where joints and bedding planes cross near the surface of rock masses, tunnel openings occasionally develop. They differ from natural tunnels in that the roof of the tunnel is not continuous, but exhibits skylights and loosely cemented cracks. In some instances a part of the Tunnel Opening might qualify as a type of arch.

Rock Fall Opening In many places rocks of varying sizes break away from cliff walls or rock masses and fall to new resting places where their presence results in openings and passageways. Such openings are the result of natural circumstances, but the openings are not considered natural arches because they did not result directly from weathering or erosion, but from falling rock. Another example of a rock fall opening includes a situation where a slab of rock slumps down and partially away from a cliff wall just enough to leave an obvious passage. In other instances large slabs of rock come to rest on top of two or more large boulders much like a man-made lintel. Other examples occur where boulders lodge between two large fins or other large rock outcroppings to produce an opening.

ARCH DIMENSIONS

Arch established dimension may seem like a rather simple thing to determine, but when two different people attempt to measure the same arch the results will often be two different sets of figures. This problem occurs because there are so many variables to consider when measuring an arch. This can be appreciated quite easily when the different types of arches are examined, but it also reinforces the need to have a uniform system of measurements that can be duplicated by those who either wish to measure a newly found arch or verify the dimensions of one that has been previously measured. The measuring points of the typical arch in Arches National Park are illustrated and described below. They include measurements of the light opening, the opening beneath the span, and the rock span itself.

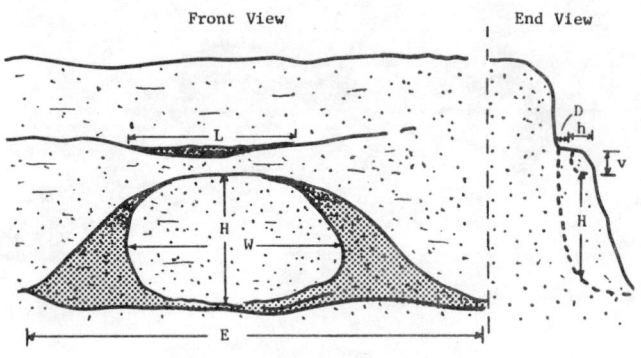

Figure 6

W = width of opening beneath the span
H = height of opening beneath the span
D = depth of light opening
L = length of light opening
h = horizontal thickness of the rock span
v = vertical thickness of rock span
E = extent of rock span

Light Opening Since the light opening dimensions are most critical when determining whether the opening is to be classified as an arch or not, they are considered of utmost importance. On many arches this opening may appear insignificant in its overall appearance, but it is often the factor used to distinguish an arch from a non-arch opening. Most free standing arches and many other types may have the same set of values for the opening beneath the span and the light opening; on others the actual light opening may be smaller than either the width or height of the opening beneath the span. Only if there is a nearby rock mass, or a funnel shaped configuration beneath the span, does it become necessary to make separate light opening and opening beneath the span measurements. The length of the light opening is measured parallel to the span between the extreme ends of the light opening. The depth of the light opening is measured between the span and the adjacent rock mass at the widest place along a plane parallel to the span. If either the depth or length openings between an adjacent rock mass and the span is greater than the actual openings beneath the span, the smaller opening beneath the span is considered the actual light opening. Think of passing that three feet long rod crosswise through the entire opening.

Opening Beneath the Span   Two measurements are made in the opening beneath the span. The width is measured horizontally from the inside of one supporting base to the inside of the opposite supporting base along the longest line that is directly beneath and parallel to the center of the span. The height is measured along the longest line from the underside of the span directly below to the ground or sloping bedrock. This will normally be a vertical line, but the shape of some arches require that the measurements be made along the longest axis of the opening. These measurements are made because they are often the most obvious dimensions that are first noticed.

Rock Span   A span is that segment of rock that bridges or surrounds the upper or outer part of the opening. Obviously, without a span there would be nothing but empty space, and without an opening there would be nothing but rock. Three measurements are made of the span. The horizontal thickness is the length of a horizontal straight line that extends from one side (front) to the reverse side (back) through the center of the free-spanning rock, while the vertical thickness is the top to bottom distance through the rock at right angles to the horizontal thickness. Because many spans are not level, the vertical thickness is not necessarily a vertical (plumb) line. These two measurements are usually made through the span at its narrowest point, which is most frequently near the center of the span. In some high angle spans, however, where the base of the span may have weathered to an exceptionally small pedestal in comparison to the size of the rest of the span, a mid-point measurement is made as it is more representative of the span's cross-sectional size.

The third span measurement is called the extent. It is measured between the discernible inside bases of the span. Many arches, such as those on cliff faces, have a sweeping span that almost always exceeds the width of the opening beneath the span or the length of the light opening. So as not to disregard this visible aspect of many arches the "extent" is measured. In many cases the width of the opening beneath the span, the length of the light opening and the extent of the span are all the same measurement.

MEASURING ARCHES

Measuring an arch may seem like a simple task, but after discovering the varied nature of shape, position and size among the hundreds of arches in the Park, it becomes obvious that a carpenter's tape is not always adequate. Because of all the different shapes and forms exhibited, difficulty of access and other factors, the need for a variety of measuring instruments becomes quite apparent.

Another problem deals with accessing the precise measuring points which are sometimes difficult to reach. Debris often conceals the exact place from which to measure and in some cases, remote measuring points may not allow for direct measurement. The most reliable and accurate means of establishing the true dimensions of each arch often required hours of hiking, climbing and special cooperation of those determining the dimensions. All measurements in this book were made using feet and where applicable, tenths of a foot.

In order of preference the following instruments were employed. A steel tape was used most frequently, especially when the possibility existed to hold both ends of the tape on the exact measuring points. A fiberglass telescoping measuring rod that extended to 37 feet was used primarily to measure the height of light openings or openings beneath the span which could not be reached with the steel tape. Where it was impractical to use either the steel tape or rod because of distance or inaccessibility, a precision range finder was used. It was found that distances of less than 300 feet could be measured with an error of no more than about 1 percent. Range finder accuracy increased with decreased distance.

Inaccessible arches located high on cliff walls or monoliths were measured with a range finder and telefix. The telefix is an instrument held a specific distance from the eye in the line of sight to the object being measured and has a sliding scale that is used to frame the object of unknown dimension. When the distance from the object being measured is known (measured with the range finder) it is possible to calculate the size of the remote object based on the scale of the telefix.

A theodolite (transit) and steel tape were used on only one arch, Landscape Arch. Because of its great width and lack of a line of sight from base to base, it required regular survey techniques and instruments using triangulation procedures.

A very small number of arches could only be viewed from an awkward angle or were so inaccessible that none of the above instruments could be used directly. In those cases one or more of the instruments served as an indirect measuring device for estimating the dimensions.

Organizing, classifying and describing phenomena of the earth's surface have long been tasks that scientists have attempted to do. Among other things, such information provides a good base for further study and analysis and often creates many unanswered questions that stimulate further study. Anyone who is seriously interested in natural arches and bridges will surely want to verify and perhaps add to the information provided in this chapter. We encourage such endeavors.

CHAPTER 5

THE ORIGIN AND DEVELOPMENT OF NATURAL ARCHES

Natural arches and bridges are found throughout the world in a wide variety of rock types and environmental conditions, but nowhere is the density as high as in the southern Utah section of the Colorado Plateau. There are many aspects of each area of the world which account for arches, but in the case of the Colorado Plateau it just so happens that all the proper combination of circumstances exist to have produced the exceptionally large number.

As a general rule arches or bridges will most likely occur where the following conditions are found: There must be sufficient exposed rock to allow openings to develop. This rock must also be strong enough to support its own weight if an opening forms through it. Isolated masses of rock must occur which are massive and relatively free of closely spaced cracks and breaks, so that if holes do develop, they form an arch rather than a cave or just a pile of rock rubble.

Certain climatic and related conditions also favor the development of arches. Some minerals in rocks are much more susceptible to disintegration in humid climates than in dry areas and the reverse is also true. High humidity, large or erratic amounts of precipitation, the presence of streams, the size and type of vegetation and such factors as wind, freezing or extremely hot temperatures all have some influence under the proper circumstances to produce arches.

Probably the most important factor that allows for the development of arches is the condition of the exposed bedrock in its environmental setting. This is especially obvious in places like Hawaii where many arches and "tubes" have developed in lava flows where there are continual volcanic eruptions. Openings within these solidified flows are quite common, especially along some coasts where wave action has helped to isolate and modify the rock into beautiful arches.

In areas where underground water has developed passageways through highly jointed and thickly bedded limestone rock, such as Virginia's Natural Bridge area, natural arches and bridges may also form. Yet in the thickly bedded and parallel jointed sandstones of southern Utah, where the dry climate and rather mild temperatures aid in relatively slow disintegration of the rock, the formation of natural arches and bridges might seem unexpected. A closer look at the conditions and processes that account for this local phenomena will be helpful in gaining an understanding and appreciation of these wonders of nature.

It is interesting to observe that the geologic formations which cover the greatest surface area in the Park all contain arches, but the Slickrock Member of the Entrada Formation stands out as having more than any other. Two conclusions can be drawn from this. The Slickrock Member must have some properties that favor arch development, but other environmental factors must be very important as well, because the other rock formations in this region have many more arches than would normally be found in similar rock in other parts of the world. Upon examining the local variables that play a role in the development of natural arches and bridges, the ones that predominate are as follows: 1- The nature of the exposed rocks in the Park are massive and contain zones of weakness that permit the wearing away or disintegration of the rock to be rapid in some places and slow in others. 2- Tectonic forces have been active in the recent past moving the crust of the earth through domal lifting, seismic fracturing and collapses. 3- The process of weathering is especially important in this environment which not only produces arches, but also the unusual shapes and forms that are seen on all the exposed rocks. 4- Mass wasting, or the movement of earth material directly by gravity, is very important in the arch enlargement process as it contributes to the rapid size increases that are noted in some arches. 5- Running surface water in this environment is erratic and unpredictable, 6- The effect of wind is able to move the surface sediments about freely because of the lack of a dense vegetation cover and the dry sandy surface. 7- The role of some miscellaneous factors should also be included such as: the orientation of major rock outcroppings to the direct radiant heat of the sun, the erosional gradient which has allowed deep canyons to develop thus exposing massive rock faces to degradational effects, and the biological communities including desert varnish that can have an influence on rates of arch development. A closer look at each of these factors will help establish a more complete explanation to the origin and development of natural arches and bridges in southeastern Utah.

EXPOSED BEDROCK All of the consolidated surface materials in the Park including the large monoliths, spires, etc. are clastic sedimentary rock. That is they are made of sand grains, clay particles, etc. which were cemented together in past geologic times by other minerals, especially calcium carbonate, when they were buried deeply beneath the surface of the earth. Large masses of these sedimentary rocks have remained intact with few evidences of having been broken or fractured when internal earth forces modified the area. The result is that today one can observe large masses of rock with hundreds of feet of either vertical or horizontal rock existing with only few signs of cracks or breaks that would be so common in outcroppings of sedimentary bedrock in other localities.

The cracks or layering that one does observe in the rocks are usually quite widely separated from each other typically forming elong-ated parallel breaks. The most obvious feature one would notice if flying over the Park would be the general alignment of rock outcroppings in a northwest-southeast direction. This alignment is due to joints (fractures in the rock with no movement along the fracture) or parallel breaks in the massive sandstones that developed when the area underwent considerable tectonic deformation and dissolution along the anticlinal folds. Because these joints are nearly parallel and many of the exposed rocks have worn down and back more rapidly along these fracture lines, they produce what are commonly called "fins" or the elongated narrow rock slabs that protrude from the sand covered surfaces.

The horizontal lines that one observes on fins or other rock features are called bedding planes. They are simply the contact zones where sand or other rock material accumulated in a layer that was piled up on an earlier deposited layer of sediment. In time these layers of sand became consolidated or solidified into the sandstones, shales, etc. we see today. The depth of these layers of sediment were often very great, exceeding hundreds of feet in some cases.

Three things should now stand out regarding the rocks of Arches National Park. They are all sedimentary; mostly sandstone, they occur in rather large chunks, often as elongated narrow fins; and they have widely spaced bedding planes and vertical joints or cracks which often meet at right angles to each other. Of course, not all parts of the Park fit this general description, but this stereotype is given to illustrate an ideal condition in which many arches develop. Although further discussion will follow to illustrate the importance of the circumstances described above, it should be obvious that if an arch is to form, it will occur where zones of weakness are found. One of the most apparent places for this to occur is where a bedding plane meets a joint in a thin rock fin. In a later part of this chapter more detail will be given to the combined effects of rock and the forces working on it to create natural openings.

TECTONIC FORCES: The crust of the earth is continually under considerable stress and strain that cause it to bend, warp, break or rearrange its structure. As stated in the chapter on geology, one of the significant features in the Park is the elongated anticlinal fold (upwarp) and the subsequent collapse because of the dissolution of the salts that were beneath the upward stressed rock surface. Add to this both minor and major faults or breaks in the crust and the result is a surface that has rather significant irregularities due to the internal forces of the earth. Where massive rock formations such as the Entrada Slickrock are put under such stresses, they tend to retain that massive character with parallel breaks (joints) developing in-line with the axis of the uplift or the collapse. In the case of the Salt Valley Anticline the crest of the uplift is now either buried beneath the sediments of the valley, or eroded away so that the flanks near the edge of the depression display the best examples of jointed sandstone beds. (See Figure 7)

This is not to suggest that all arches form in areas that have been specifically modified by tectonic forces, but there is a higher concentration of arches in those areas where "fins" have evolved along the current crests at either side of the anticlinal fold than in other areas. (Note Devils Garden and Klondike Bluffs.) It should also be noted that the fins did not develop by tectonic force alone, but by gradual enlargement of joints that developed into widened, elongated slots. At the same time similar processes modified the overall outward dimensions of the fins.

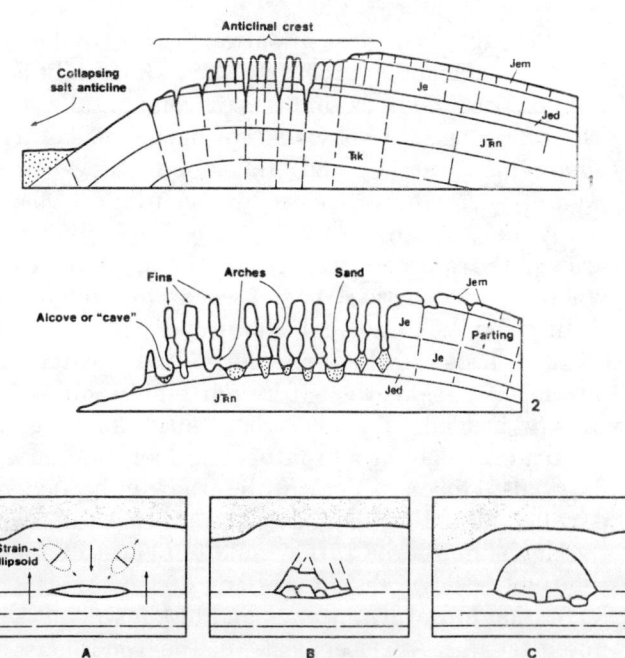

Figure 7. Diagram illustrating expanded joints and the development of fins and arches. (After Doelling, p. 14)

Many of the arches and bridges in the Park are rather fragile and could easily be broken by repeated earthquakes. If the Park were currently in an active seismic area, there would definitely be fewer arches. It is therefore important to note that while tectonic forces were important in creating the proper conditions for the development of arches, the lack of them at the present time has helped preserve them.

WEATHERING AND MASS WASTING: The two processes called weathering and mass wasting are among the most important in arch formation, yet they are the least understood by the average person. The word erosion is often used to denote the general wearing away of the earth's surface, but included within that process are these two sub-processes. If a large mass of rock were to be attacked by running water, a moving glacier, or even blowing wind, the effects of that "erosion" would be negligible unless the rock were first weakened or disintegrated by weathering. In other words, weathering is the process of rotting or breaking down of the rock into individual minerals or a chemically altered derivative. Such a process can be seen in action on old stone monuments or buildings where the exposed surface has become granular or powdery rather than the polished surface it once was.

Weathering can be either chemical or mechanical or both, and the effects of water is the single most important factor contributing to each. As water lays on the surface and seeps into the rock it combines with various minerals, especially the cementing agents of the sandstones, and weathers the rock away. During winter, water freezes and expands in rock cracks resulting in the break up through expansion in a process called mechanical weathering. The rusting of iron or steel is a good example of chemical weathering on man-made objects, while the break-up of asphalt on road surfaces during the winter months is a good example of mechanical weathering. Coupled with weathering in preparing rock to be removed by erosion is "Mass Wasting". Mass Wasting refers to the direct force of gravity to "pull" rock fragments or other material from a higher to a lower position once they have been loosened or freed by weathering. Some of the more common forms of mass wasting are landslides, rockfalls or slumping of unstable slopes.

It should be clear that these two processes work hand in hand. Weathering weakens or fragments the rock and mass wasting removes it from its place of disintegration if the slope is steep enough for it to slide, roll or creep to a lower position. In forming arches, zones of weakness are the prime targets of weathering. Both small and large chunks of rock that have become detached by weathering may then be removed by mass wasting assuming gravity alone is able to apply sufficient force on a steep enough slope to displace the separated rock fragments.

RUNNING WATER: This process is probably the most important in eroding and depositing sediment in most parts of the world, including Arches National Park, but it is only secondary to other processes in the actual formation of natural arches and bridges. Water flowing over any surface will pick up and carry away any loose material that is large enough or light enough to be moved by the frictional effects of the moving water. The corrosive or abrasive effects of running water, on the other hand, are usually much less important in modifying the surface form of exposed rock.

There are excellent examples (though small in size) in the Park where sand being moved along by running water has gouged out or grooved the surface over which it flows, but these features are minor when compared to the washes or gullies that occur in unconsolidated sands, silts and clays that are not attached to bedrock. It should be clear that running water's main role is in removing sands and other small-sized sediments that are already loosened (by weathering) rather than carving any significant forms or openings in the exposed rock.

The work of running water may range from sheet flow over a broad surface to a raging flash flood in one of the larger washes such as Courthouse Wash. Of course any material picked up and carried along by running water will eventually be deposited as some form of alluvial feature such as a sand bar or an alluvial fan. Many of the landforms in the Park are the direct result of either the erosional or the depositional effects of surface water, but the natural arches are not.

WIND: Many of the early writings about arches and bridges attributed them to blowing wind, but with subsequent detailed investigations by many researchers this theory has proved to be untrue. The wind does play a role in removing the loosened weathered sand grains from the rock surfaces, but it has only negligible effects in enlarging or causing a perforation in a rock to develop. There is also evidence to support the idea that blowing sand may pile up at the base of a rock outcropping where it acts as a collector of rain water and a barrier to the evaporation of that water. The net result is a moist condition adjacent to the rock which accelerates the disintegrative effects of weathering.

A common landform feature that can be observed in many parts of the Park is the rounded opening or groups of round holes that occur on rock faces. In some cases they may appear as "honeycomb" surfaces with the individual cavities ranging from less than an inch to over several feet in diameter. These impressions are often thought to have been formed by sand grains being swirled around abrading the surface into ever larger holes and in some cases evolving into a natural arch. Although there may be a slight abrasive effect as described above these circular holes are not the product of wind action. They are another example of differential weathering where either the matrix of the rock or the cementing agent are locally weaker than the surrounding rock and through time have weathered into these depressions.

The wind's role is much less important than that of running water in modifying the surface forms in this area. It picks up or moves sand grains and smaller silt and clay particles from one place to another, but is not directly involved in carving the openings called natural arches and bridges. The most common landforms attributed to wind action are the numerous dunes of varying size found in almost all sections in the Park, the sand having been derived from weathering of the exposed bedrock surfaces.

OTHER FACTORS Mention was made of rock exposure, surface gradient, and biological communities as having some role in the development of natural arches and bridges. A little more insight into each of these will help to explain some of the reasons why arches form and enlarge. The heating of exposed rocks during the long warm days of summer and the cooling of those same rocks during the cool nights and especially the cold winters has a pronounced effect on the rates of weathering. It is known that most chemical reactions double with each 20° F. rise in temperature, thus the rates of chemical weathering in summer, especially when the surface is wet, are fairly rapid. The expansion and contraction of these same rocks with daily heating and cooling also favors the relatively rapid disintegration of rocks which have the greatest exposure to the direct rays of the sun. South and southwest facing rock outcroppings which are at about 40° from a horizontal position are the most vulnerable to both total heating and extremes in temperature. The high weathering rates of these surfaces would typically produce the most arches. Figure 8 illustrates that situation.

Where the slope or gradient of the surface is greatest, the down-cutting effect of surface streams, especially during flash flood conditions can be expected to have the most pronounced effect in producing steep canyon walls which become susceptible to arch formation. This can be noted in the canyons on the east slopes of Devils Garden where gradients are steep and stream erosion is significant.

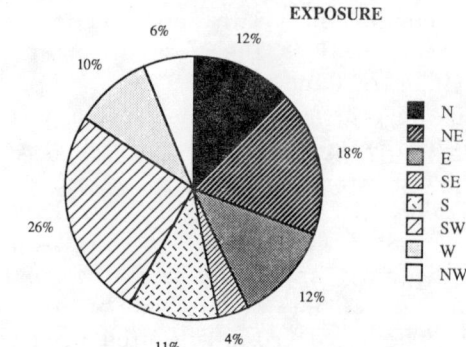

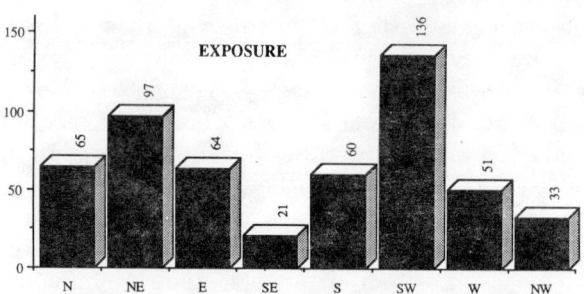

Figure 8

Plant and animal life has little impact on either producing or enlarging natural arches and bridges, although there are probably some examples where root growth may have been partially responsible for the break-up and separation of some rock material from a rock span. Burrowing animals or even larger animals may also have had some role in movement of rock through their physical contact, but it would be negligible in the overall explanation of arch formation.

One rather universal phenomenon throughout the Park and in the Colorado Plateau is the occurrence of desert varnish, a substance that may not account for arch development, but could be a factor in the rate of development. Desert varnish is a thin coating of manganese and iron oxides and hydroxides, clay minerals and other trace elements that adhere to rock surfaces. Although the theories of its origin may not be universally agreed upon, recent studies suggest that it has a biological genesis. Microbial activity is thought to be the main cause of manganese enhancement in the development of desert varnish.

Those rock surfaces that have a firm coating of desert varnish are much less prone to the usual surface weathering than those without it. Thus an arch that is coated with desert varnish is more likely to be in a relatively stable condition when compared to one that has no varnish. There are no definitive studies that have been done on weathering rates and the existence or absence of desert varnish, but manyh arches that do not appear to show significant recent modification by surface weathering often have the usual stains and coating of this interesting material.

When looking at the geographic position of all the arches in the Park the conclusions noted above can be verified. Thirty-five percent of all arches occur on steep slopes or cliffs, while only three percent are found in flat open areas. The existence of steep or moderately steep bedrock slopes favor the development of arches. See Figure 9. Refer to the "key" of the Alphabetical List, page 123 for legend explanation.

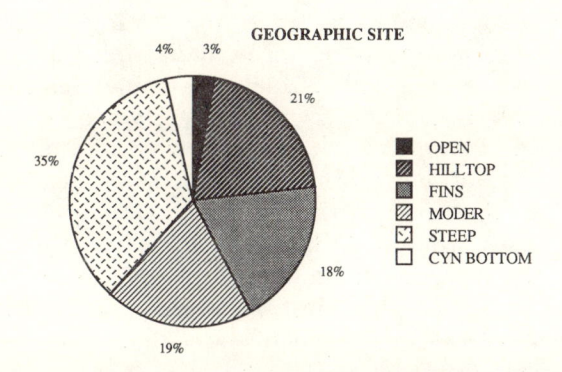

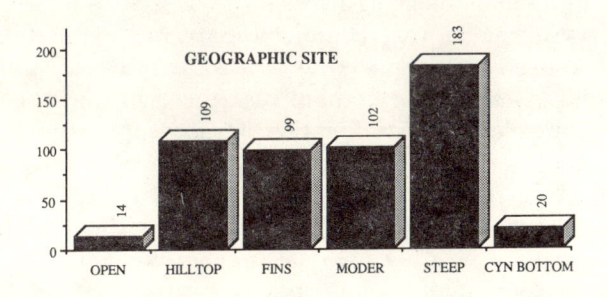

Figure 9

ARCH FORMATION

When all the above criteria are examined there are several which deserve further analysis if the total story of arch development is to be understood. This is best done by examining several different types of arches, for there is not one universal process or group of processes that fits all arch categories.

Cliff Wall Arches are more numerous than any other type within the Park boundaries, the count being 199, or 37.7 % of all arches included in this study. Their position on cliff walls indicates that they occur where either large masses of rock stand out and above the general lay of the land or on canyon walls where downward cutting streams have exposed steep cliff faces. Some Cliff Wall Arches develop parallel to the main rock mass where a narrow vertical slab of rock becomes separated by weathering along a joint (vertical crack) line. Since the vertical slab might be standing alone and be fully or partially separated from the rock mass, weathering can accelerate from both sides, although the most probable place for this to occur is on the inner side where the rock slab merges with the main rock mass. It is here where rain water is most effective in the chemical decomposition of the sandstone. Once an opening has developed through the rock slab, further enlargement can be very rapid because as the opening increases in size through disintegration, stress lines develop from the weight of the overburden creating small fracture lines that eventually cause large segments of rock to become detached from the underside and sides of the opening. A close inspection of the inner surfaces on many of these arches will reveal highly angular forms where rock fragments have broken loose and dropped to the ground.

Other Cliff Wall arches develop in the ceilings of alcoves. The alcove itself is basically a weathered feature, often occurring where seeps or bedding planes produce a zone of weakness in the rock. As the back wall and ceiling of the alcove gradually retreats due to the disintegration of the surface, the outer part of the ceiling comes under considerable stress and often forms a break from the main rock mass. This crack becomes a natural place for rain water to penetrate and soon the crack widens through both physical and chemical weathering and an opening is formed.

The second most common arch type in the Park is the Free Standing variety. Twenty-eight percent of the arches or a total of 148 are in this category. Their formation is not too different from the Cliff Wall type, but their position away from major rock walls or cliffs tends to produce a little more symmetry in their outward appearance. They usually develop where there is a bedding plane or a zone of weakness in a fin or isolated slab of rock.

The most likely situation would be where a bedding plane in a fin is near or slightly below the general ground level. Here water is able to aid considerably in the weathering process, especially in the initial stages, and development of an opening is quite likely. In time the loose surface material that has been weathered free from the main rock mass falls away through the force of gravity, or in some instances is washed or blown away, and an opening through the fin is accomplished. Break-off of angular pieces of rock are quite common on the sides and underside of the span and stress or pressure from the weight of the supported rock builds as the opening enlarges. At the same time the base and top of the span experiences more of a granular disintegration of the solid rock. This results in a smooth top and base, while the inner sides and underside show signs of exfoliation and breakage due to tension from the weight being supported.

Many of these arches display rather close secondary jointing or cracks at both sides of the opening near the base of the span where the stress is greatest. Whereas joint spacing in the typical rocks of the area would most commonly be from three or four feet up to 30 feet or more, these secondary joints, which are formed as the arch enlarges, are often less than an inch apart near the base where the added weight has put considerable strain on the supporting rock. It should be obvious that arches are in a mode of self destruction. As the span becomes thinner, especially at the base, the weight it must carry adds to the rate of eventual disintegration.

In many arches it has been noted that these secondary joints or stress lines appear to be farther apart near the base than they are higher up on the span. This would suggest that as arches enlarge through this process, the curve or arching shape on the underside of the span would flatten out. In other words older arches that have enlarged through break away of rock due to stress line fracture would be much wider (from base to base) than the height from the underside of the span to the solid rock beneath the span.

It should be remembered that within any given type there will be enough variety of forms, shapes and forces that there will be no simple explanations that will totally solve the mystery of their origin. The processes described above for the Free Standing Arch would apply in specific cases to almost all other types as well.

Two other arch types will be discussed to point out some of the additional complexities that exist in the formation of natural arches. The Pothole Arch is fairly common throughout the Colorado Plateau. In the Park it accounts for only slightly over 2 percent of all arches. Nevertheless it has an interesting origin. The word "pothole" is used in this area to describe depressions that occur on top of solid rock masses that become small catchment basins for rain water. In most cases any water which finds its way into the depression will soon evaporate away leaving a thin layer of sand and silt that was either washed in or weathered loose from the base of the pothole.

Like most other features of this environment these potholes are the product of many years of wetting and drying and the accompanying chemical and physical "weathering" of the solid rock. If a pothole were to exist near the edge of a rock mass and if some of the water were to seep into the rock and out the cliff side, the zone of water seepage soon gives away to rock disintegration. When this occurs, the pothole on top of the rock is supplying a longer lasting chemical agent (water) to help in the disintegration of the cliff face below than would occur if non-stored rain water were the only supply. In time an alcove develops on the side of the cliff and eventually the pothole and the alcove merge to form a continuous light opening.

Pothole Arches are not necessarily the product of large potholes and alcoves eventually developing a small opening, with gradual enlarging of that hole. In some cases the merging of the two depressions may occur before the pothole and alcove have a diameter of three feet. Most pothole arches have smooth surfaces, indicating that granular weathering rather than stress-line weathering is mainly responsible for their development.

The Platform Arch has somewhat of a different origin than most other types. It is usually a rather flat arch with the span having a much greater horizontal thickness than vertical thickness and the light opening is almost always much wider than it is high. On first observation the Platform Arch looks like a band of rock that has become detached from the main rock mass along its length, with its ends merging in with the bedrock surface.

Earlier in this chapter the term "exfoliation" was used to denote where a slab of rock would break away from the main rock mass in thin sheets of concave rock. Exfoliation is more properly used in the literature on geomorphology to describe thin sheets of rock breaking away in convex sheets on the outer surfaces of large monoliths. This process of weathering is very common on granite in more humid regions, but it also occurs on the thickly bedded sandstones of the Colorado Plateau. The Platform Arch is a modified version of exfoliation where two ends of the separated rock slab remain firmly connected to bed rock. As the thin sheet of rock becomes detached, it will expand because the bonds to the main rock have been severed and the relief of pressure tied up in the rock are relaxed in the thin slab. In time the cementing agent will also expand as it disintegrates, causing the rock span to bow outward slightly from the rock to which it was once attached.

There are many examples in the Park where this process can be seen in action, but it usually does not produce an arch unless all conditions just happen to be right. Only 13 Platform Arches were found in the Park, making up 2.4 % of all the arches surveyed. This number is probably low, because this arch type is so difficult to see. Many could have been missed in the course of looking for more impressive arches.

The other Arch types not discussed here differ from the ones described mainly in outward appearance rather than in origin or genesis. The Jug Handle Arch is basically a Free Standing Arch that has a span and opening that are more vertical than horizontal. Other than that one characteristic, it has all the outward appearances of having been formed in the same way as the Free Standing Arch. In many cases the zone of weakness where the opening develops is in a joint rather than a bedding plane.

The Expanded Crevice Arch also resembles the Free Standing Arch in processes of formation, but the massive span and the elongated opening have not yet developed to the point where large blocks of rock have been able to break loose and enlarge the opening.

The Spanned Alcove Arch has developed in an unusual setting where a more resistant rock span has not weathered away as fast as the large hole or cave behind the span. In some cases the span may have been in an area where seepage or flow of chemicals in conjunction with the build up of desert varnish helped to form a shaft of rock that deteriorated at a slower rate than the surrounding rock.

The Perforated Alcove Arch forms in a similar way to the Pothole Arch through expansion horizontally of a cave or alcove in a relatively thin rock fin. Most Perforated Alcove Arches develop in or just above bedding planes, and if they are in the latter stages of development they might likely be classified as Free Standing Arches.

The Natural Bridge is not the product of rushing water carving a hole through rock as might be thought, but where a stream flows beneath a natural bridge it will naturally aid in the weathering process to enlarge the opening. There are several examples, however, where a deep pothole may develop in a solid rock stream bed and provide conditions that assist in the formation of a natural bridge. These potholes often contain rounded boulders that grind around when the stream is in flood stage. This abrasive action can eventually result in the perforation of the pothole to form a natural bridge. Even though sand abrasion in streams can wear away a surface, rock weathering is still the chief agent responsible for the creation of this arch form.

Some natural bridges are found where the bedding planes within a rock formations are close together. If water begins to seep or flow from one bedding plane to another, it may isolate a rock span and form a small channel beneath it. In this case it might be said that the stream initiated the development of the Natural Bridge, but the enlargement, especially upward, is due more to weathering than to stream erosion.

A Natural Tunnel, especially the arch known as "The Tunnel" (UC 7) is difficult to explain. The interior of this tunnel is smooth, indicating that granular weathering is currently the active force in enlarging the opening. But why a small tunnel-like opening would develop through such a massive rock is not easily explained. It is possible that during the time the sands were deposited but before they were solidified, a stream, a seepage, tree roots, a fallen tree or even burrowing animals may have altered the structure or displaced the sand grains in an isolated deposit so that when the cementing process occurred, an elongated segment developed with less cohesiveness than the surrounding sandstones.

As later forces of tectonic uplift and erosional downwear cut into these sandstones, a tunnel-like opening developed along the previously weak shaft of sandstone or other material. Other natural tunnel type openings in southern Utah are known where there is an elongated intersection of a bedding plane with a vertical joint. If the bedding plane has a slight slope to it the weathering processes and removal of loose material by running water may account for a natural opening that has the outward appearance of a tunnel. These openings may not meet the criteria for a Natural Tunnel because of joint openings in the ceiling and may be more properly classified as non-arch openings.

It should now be quite clear that the explanation of arch formation is even more complex than any classification system which attempts a description. One thing stands out above all others, however, and that is the importance or role of weathering as the actual "carving" agent. Both chemical and mechanical weathering work together in creating all arches, but other forces such as gravity, running water and wind aid in the removal of the loose rock fragments and sand grains that are weathered from the surfaces of natural arches and bridges. As more geomorphic studies are completed in the Park and other areas of the Colorado Plateau, more detailed explanations will be found. In the meantime a number of unanswered questions will continue to stimulate the experts to further their studies. Such a situation justifies scientific investigation and keeps it active and healthy. May we never come to the point where we think we completely understand everything.

CHAPTER 6
REGIONAL OVERVIEW

The Park has long been divided into well known areas or regions, usually distinguished by some characteristic of the landscape. Most of these different areas, and their subdivisions called sections, have names which were originally given by early cattle ranchers, settlers and others. In dividing up the Park for mapping purposes, not only were these previously named areas used, but in many cases they turned out to include convenient groupings of arches. No attempt has been made to draw definite boundaries around each of the 12 areas used in this study, but by glancing at the index map (Figure 11) and each of the 12 area maps, it is easy to see where the arches are clustered and where none have been found. Each of those areas where arches are found has been designated as an "Arch Region." The detailed regional maps show both density and size category of all arches.

Most Arch Regions, as defined in this book, are approximately equal in size, yet they do not have an equal number of arches. When a list is compiled which shows where the arches are most numerous, Devils Garden leads the list with the greatest concentration. Figure 10 shows both percentage and number of arches in each region. Refer to Chapter 8 (Key to Table 2, page 123) for a reference to the symbols used on these charts. If both North and South Devils Garden are grouped together, one-third of all arches are accounted for. This should not be surprising in view of the discussions in the chapters concerning Geology and Origin of Arches. Areas adjacent to Devils Garden also display rather high numbers.

All references in this chapter to ranking, quantities, percentages, etc. are based on the 527 arches included in this book. Continuing research is being conducted as additional arches are reported. There will undoubtedly be changes in almost all statistical references in the future supplement to this book. See Appendix.

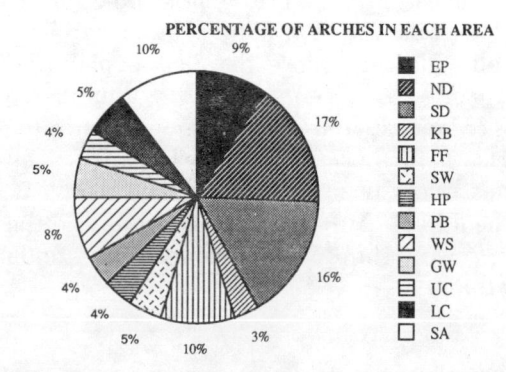

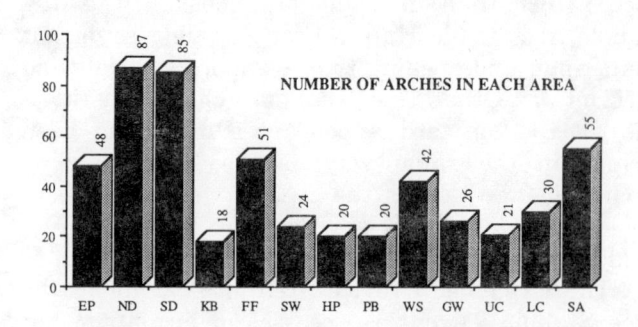

Figure 10

It should be noted that the 12 area maps do not cover all parts of the Park. Salt Valley is such a place, where the lack of bedrock exposure accounts for the absence of arches. The Courthouse Upland in the southeastern region between the southern border and the Windows Section is another area where no arches are listed. This area was not thoroughly explored because at the time the field work was being done there were no indications that anyone had reported any arches there.

It is also interesting to note that there are many arches outside the current Park boundaries. If all areas were included that had at one time been within the confines of the Monument or Park, there would be many more arches to report. Some were so close to the present boundary, that careful check of boundary markers had to be made to determine if they should be included in the total number.

The regional diversity of the arches in the Park can best be made by taking a closer look at each of the Arch Regions. This will be done primarily with the maps and charts that follow. The sequence used will be from the north to the south of the Park. Note the index map (Figure 11) for reference to the location of the area maps and those areas where there is no map coverage. The scale of all regional maps is 1:24,000, or two and a half inches per mile.

It should also be noted that the size of dots on the area maps represent a size category of the opening beneath the span, not the light opening. This variable was used because it is the most obvious dimension that is first noticed on many arches. In order to gain a full understanding of all the measurements that were made, please refer to the tables in chapter 8.

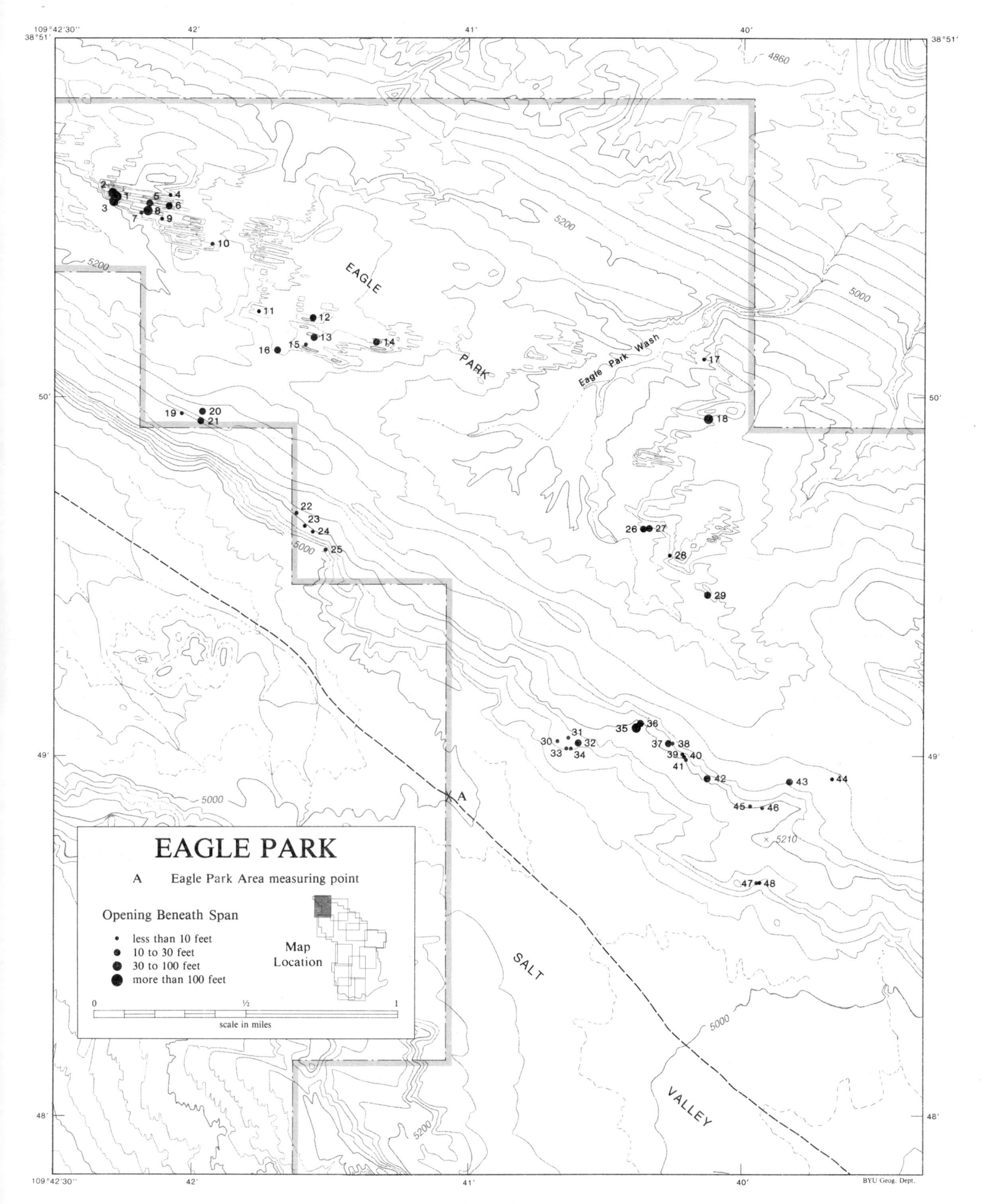

Figure 14

EAGLE PARK

This northern-most region is one of the most remote and secluded in the Park. Vehicle traffic is no longer allowed on the old mining roads which are gradually being overgrown with vegetation, so hikers are able to view a landscape without seeing many other people. Many of the most recently reported arches are in this area. There are several groups of standing fins and monoliths here with areas of open land between them. This area is divided into the following sections: the Salt Valley Slope, the Northwest Fins, and the Southeast Fins. Almost all groups of rock outcroppings have some arches. Most of the arches (67 percent) are in the Slickrock Member and the Kayenta formation. The graph below (Figure 12 shows the distribution according to occurrence in the respective geologic formations.

Cliff Wall Arches are the dominant type in Eagle Park, accounting for 58 percent of the total. Of those arches found in this area, Pot Hole Arches, Natural Bridges and Natural Tunnels are absent here. Many of the arches are some what difficult to find as they are not in plain view to the casual hiker. The largest arch is Sibling Arch Center (EP 1) which has a light opening of 55.2 feet. Figure 13 gives a graphic picture of the numbers and types of arches in the Eagle Park area.

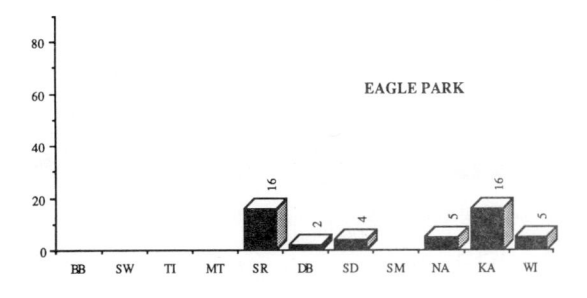

Figure 12

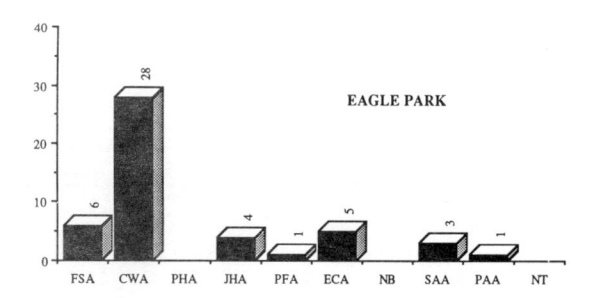

Figure 13

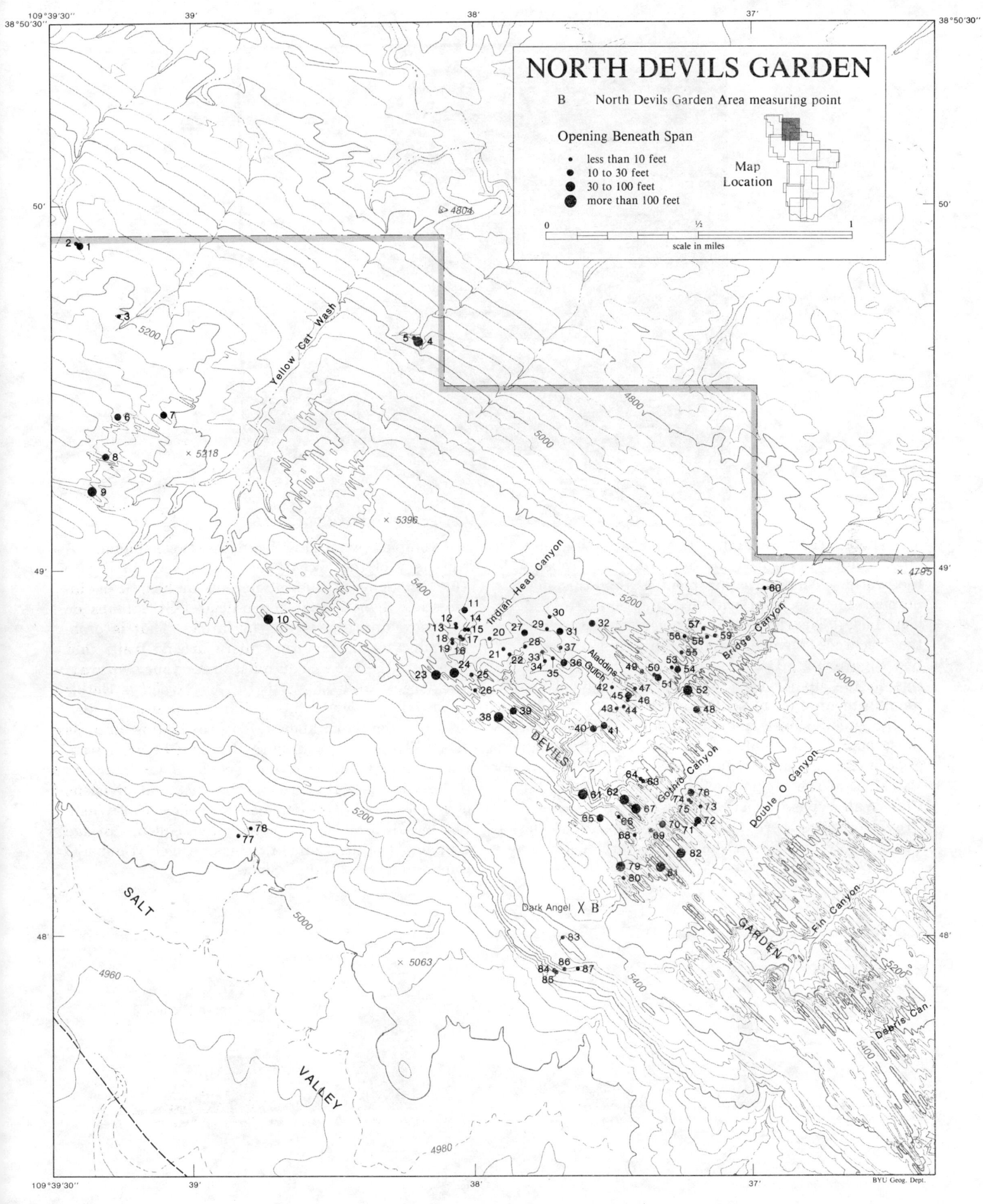

Figure 17

NORTH DEVILS GARDEN

There are more arches in this area than any other comparable area in the Park and probably the world. An interesting point is that this high number is associated with a rather uniform geologic base. Nearly 90 percent of all arches are in the Slickrock Member of the Entrada Formation. See Figure 15. The area is typified by elongated fins in the higher area with several canyons extending in an east to southeast direction. Because of the steep slopes and deep nature of many of these canyons it is difficult to hike around without a lot of climbing and scrambling.

Most of the arches are either Free Standing or Cliff Wall types. There are also more Expanded Crevice arches here that in other parts of the Park. Only Pot Hole Arches and Natural Tunnels are completely missing from the types found. A summary of the arch types can be seen in Figure 16. In spite of the numerous arches, it is interesting to note that the official USGS maps do not show any arches for this area. That is probably due to the fact that there are no trails that penetrate the area. You must make your own way. The largest arch of North Devils Garden is Gothic Arch (ND 67) which has a light opening of 58 feet. Perhaps the best known feature of this area is "Dark Angel", a rock spire that can be seen from miles around and is often used as a landmark to those who hike the area. The sectional divisions of North Devils Garden include Yellow Cat Wash, Indian Head Canyon, Aladdins Gulch, Bridge Canyon, Gothic Canyon, Dark Angel, Double-O Canyon and Salt Valley Slope.

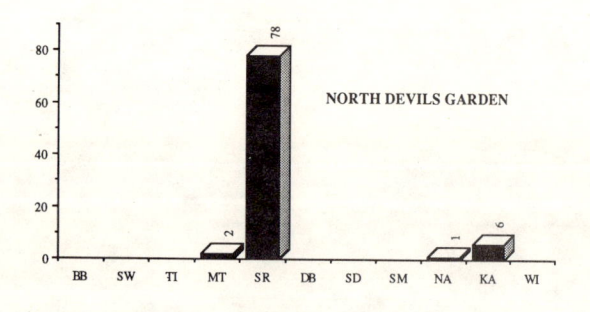

Figure 15

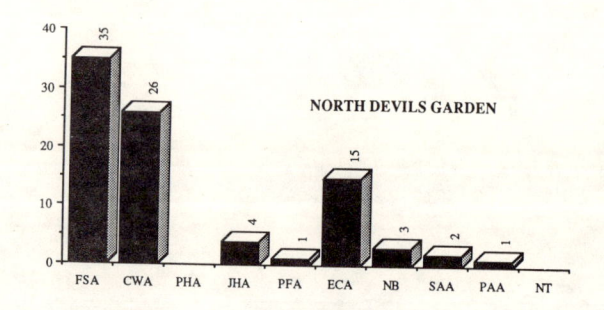

Figure 16

Figure 20

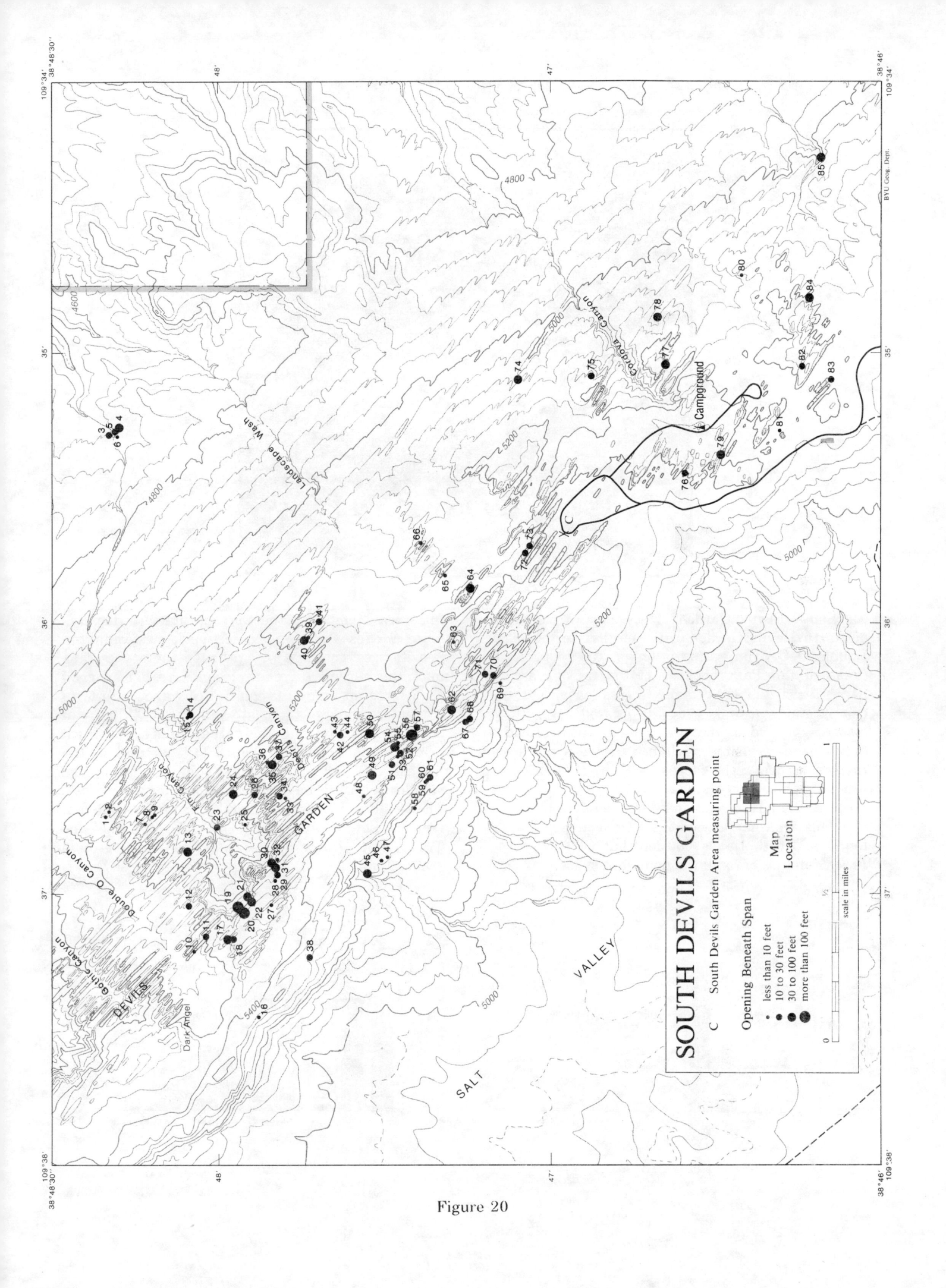

SOUTH DEVILS GARDEN

South Devils Garden is actually an extension of North Devils Garden with the division being at Double O Canyon. This is one of the best known areas of the Park because of the famous arches here, the trails that make access easy and the campground facilities that are located here. It is also at the end of the paved road which provides even the day visitor a chance to see some spectacular arches. The largest arch in the Park and probably the world, Landscape Arch, is just a mile north of the paved road on an excellent trail.

This area has a wider variety of arches than is found in North Devils Garden, but Cliff Wall and Free Standing are still the dominant types. The Slickrock Member of the Entrada likewise displays more arches than any other geologic formation. See Figures 18 and 19). Although there are trails into this area, there are some rather rugged sections that require some skill and effort to traverse. Some of the best examples of "Fins" can be found throughout this area, many of which display arches. There are 12 (48 percent) of the largest 25 arches in the Park in this area, the smallest of them having a light opening of 53 feet. The sections include Double O Canyon, Fin Canyon, Crystal, Lower Fin Canyon, Upper Trail, Landscape Trail, Salt Valley Slope, and the Campground section.

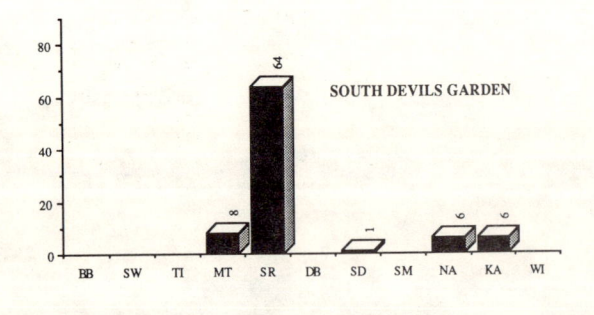

Figure 18

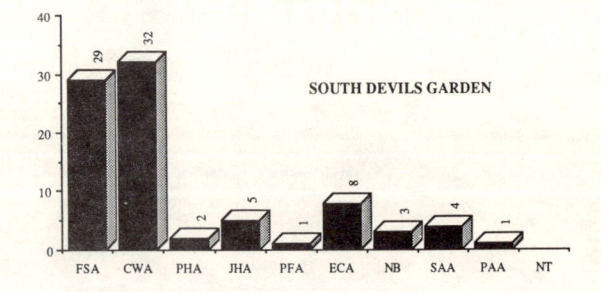

Figure 19

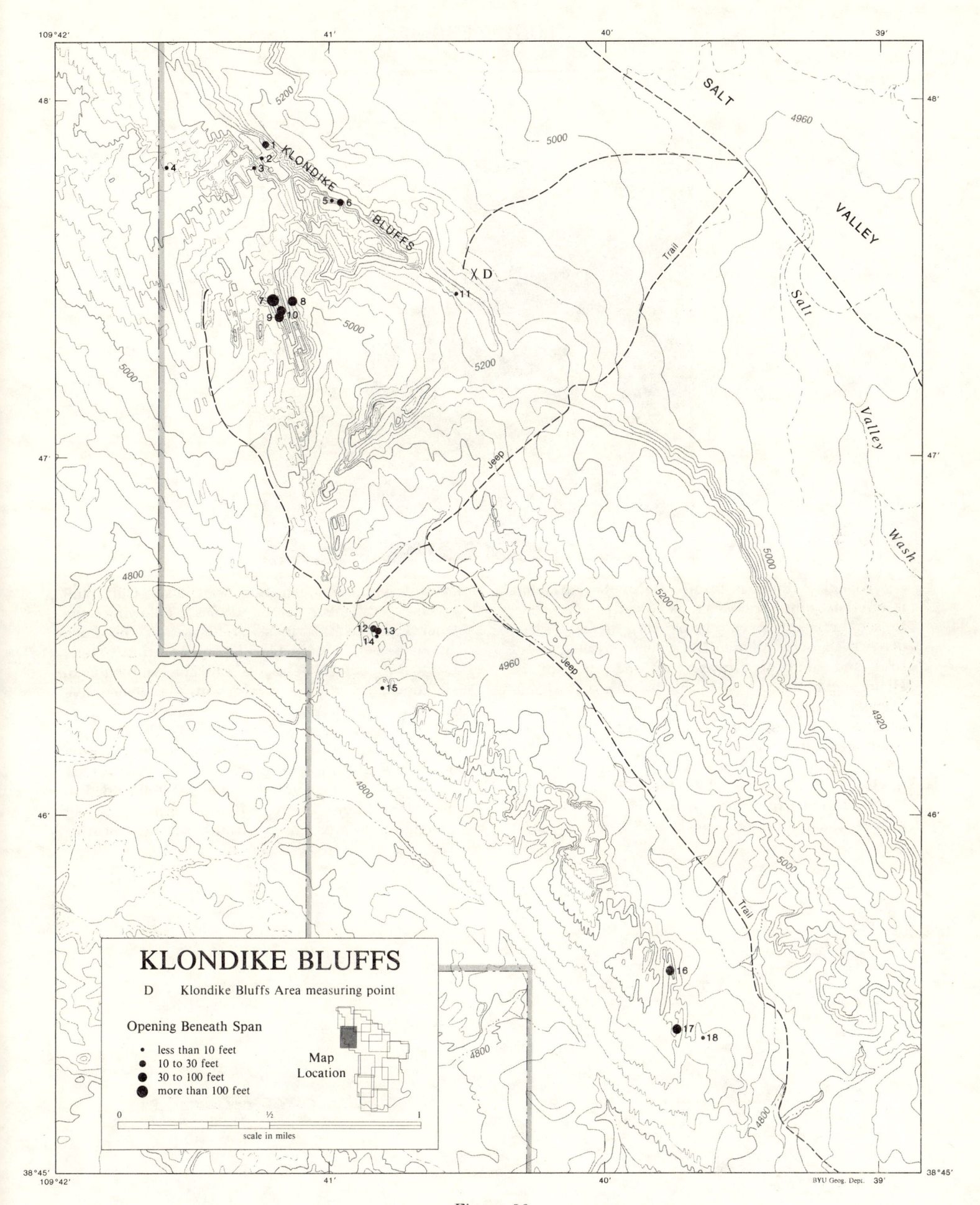

Figure 23

KLONDIKE BLUFFS

Klondike Bluffs is in an area of the Park that is off the beaten track, but is still a popular place to see arches. It can be reached by a 4-wheel drive road or a hiking trail to view some beautiful and unusual arches. As indicated in the History chapter, Klondike Bluffs was the original "Devils Garden" proposed for preservation, but because of its relatively remote location it has not been as well explored for arches as most other areas. Klondike Bluffs has the distinction of having only 18 of the 527 arches described in this book. Recent exploration in the area, however has proved that there are several arches not included in the original eighteen (See Appendix). Cliff Wall Arches outnumber other types, following the general pattern for most areas within the Park boundaries. The only rock formations that extend above the surface here are Entrada and Navajo. All known arches are in the Entrada; none have been found in the Navajo.

One of the first publicized arches, Tower Arch (KB 7) is located here. It is the sixth largest arch in the Park having a light opening of 95 feet. Also one of the last arches found to be included in this book, Chunk Arch (KB 17) with a 65 feet opening is located in the southern part of this area.

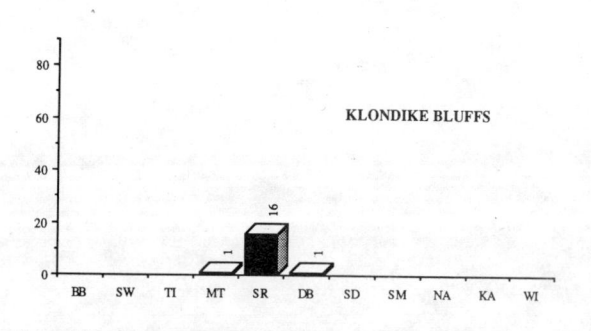

Figure 21

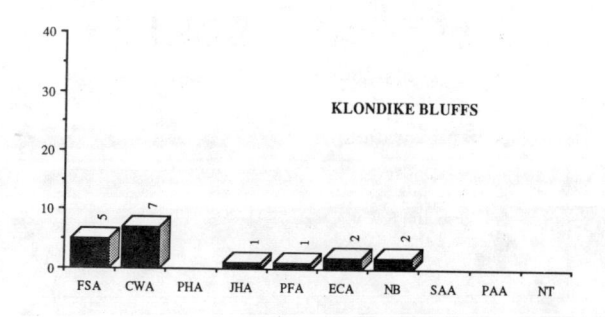

Figure 22

40

Figure 26

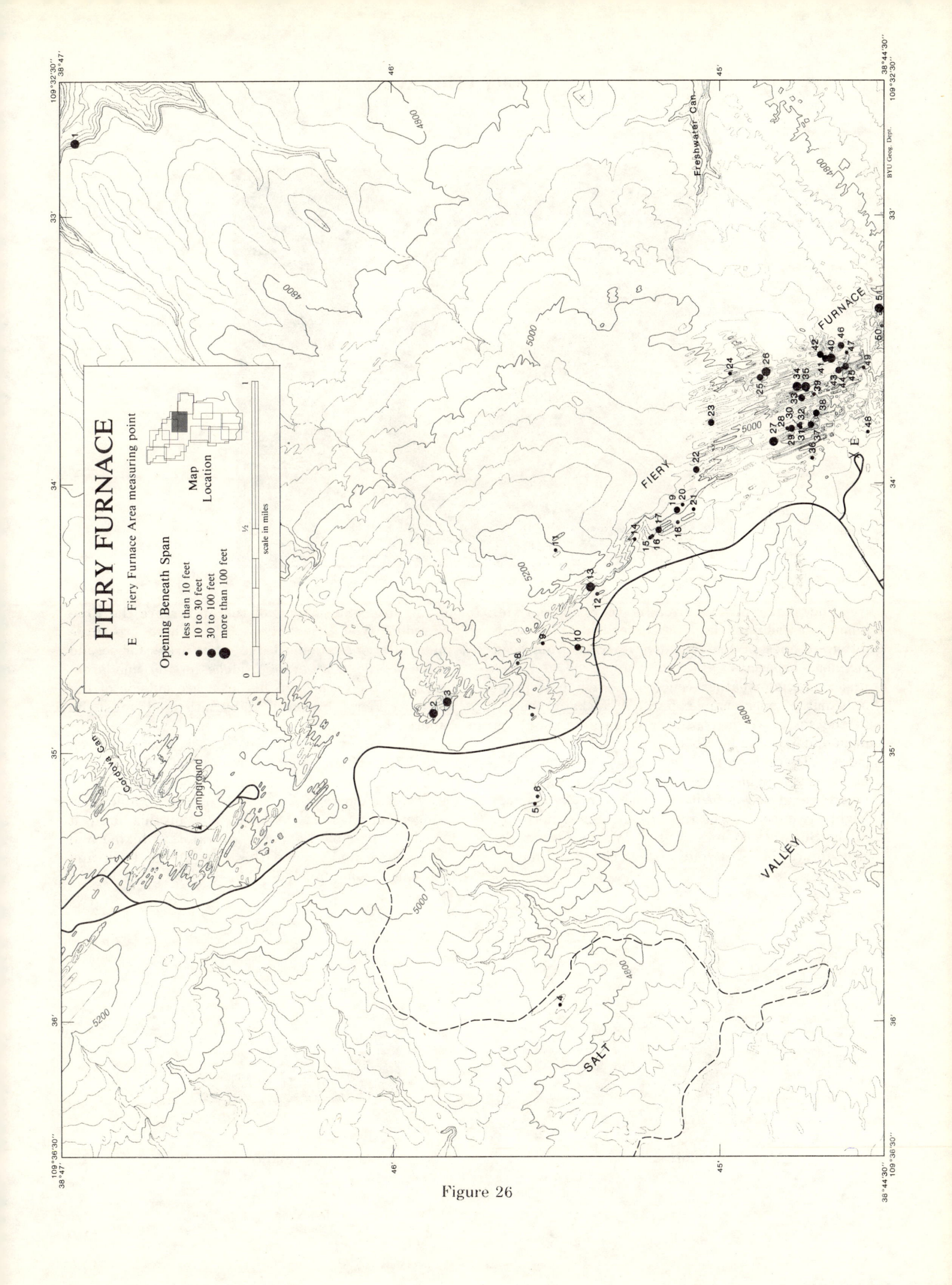

FIERY FURNACE

The name of this area is very appropriate, when describing the large vertical fins with different hues of red reaching skyward from deep ravines, especially at certain times of the day under special weather conditions. There is probably not a more complex maze of rocks anywhere in the Park. It is possible to hike into countless dead-end passages with towering rock walls on all sides. There is a trail into and out of this area, but it is advisable to go with an experienced guide when regularly scheduled hikes are conducted. Eighty-two percent of the known arches here are in the Slickrock Member of the Entrada Formation. See Figure 24. In spite of the "closed in" nature of the area, 39 percent of the arches are the Free Standing type. See Figure 25. There are three natural bridges, tieing three other areas for second place in the number of bridges in any one area. Many of the arches in this area are outside of the actual "Fiery Furnace" labyrinth and must be approached from peripheral routes.

The largest arch in this area is Surprise Arch (FF 27). It has a light opening of 63 feet and is located in a unique setting surrounded by near-by walls of sandstone. Because of the complex arrangement of fins, canyons, etc. in this area it would be possible to spend several days hiking and climbing in and around this part of the Park and still miss seeing much of what is there.

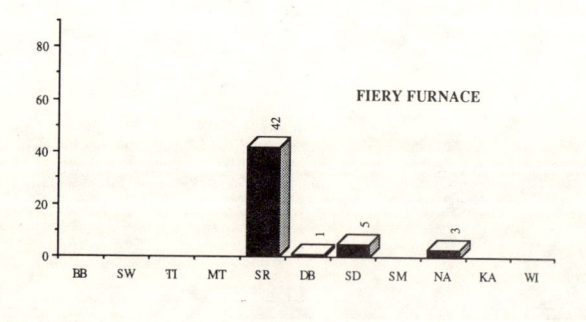

Figure 24

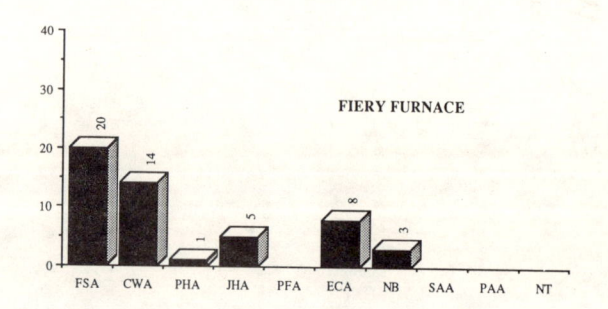

Figure 25

Figure 29

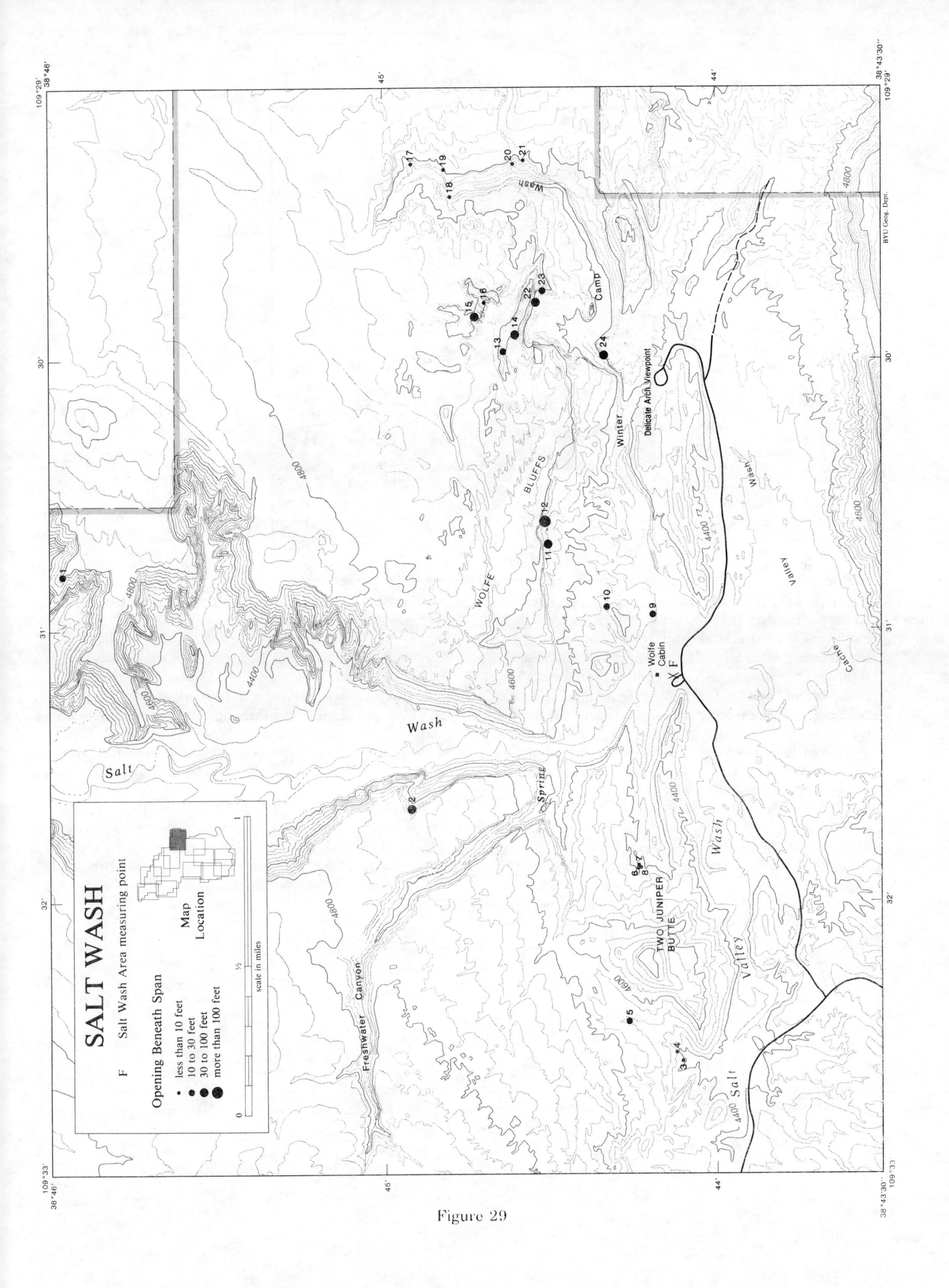

SALT WASH

The best known arch in the world, Delicate Arch, is located in this area. It has come to be the symbol of the Park and is often used in travel magazines, etc. as a "trademark" of southeastern Utah. The geology is very complex because of the collapse of the Salt Valley anticline and the faulting that has occurred here. Salt Wash itself normally has a small stream in it throughout the year and because of that water supply, it was the location of Wolfe Cabin which still stands near the parking area trailhead to Delicate Arch.

This is the only area in the Park where arches are found in the Morrison Formation, but like other areas there are more arches in the Slickrock Member of the Entrada Formation. Figure 27 illustrates the distribution of arches among the various geologic formations.

One of the unusual features here is the relatively high number of natural bridges that occur, most of which are in the Morrison Formation. Cliff Wall Arches outnumber all other types, however, with Free Standing Arches coming in second. The largest arch is Wolfe Bluffs Arch (SW 12), a cliff wall arch having a light opening of 141 feet. Delicate Arch is the second largest, but its light opening is a mere 46 feet. Its fame is due more to its beauty and surroundings than to its size. Note Figure 28 below to see the distribution of arch types in this area. The main subdivisions of this area are Upper Salt Wash, Two-Juniper Butte, Delicate, and Winter Camp Wash.

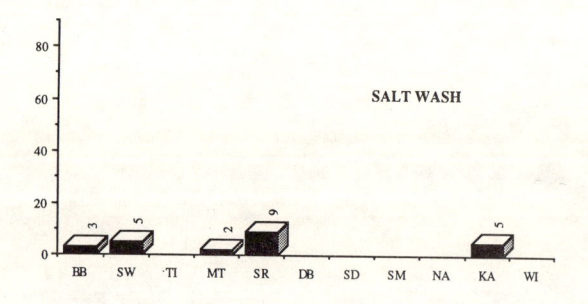

Figure 27

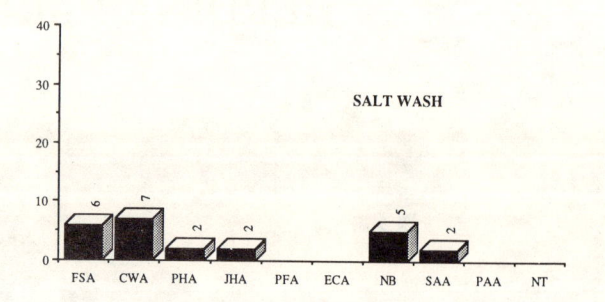

Figure 28

HERDINA PARK

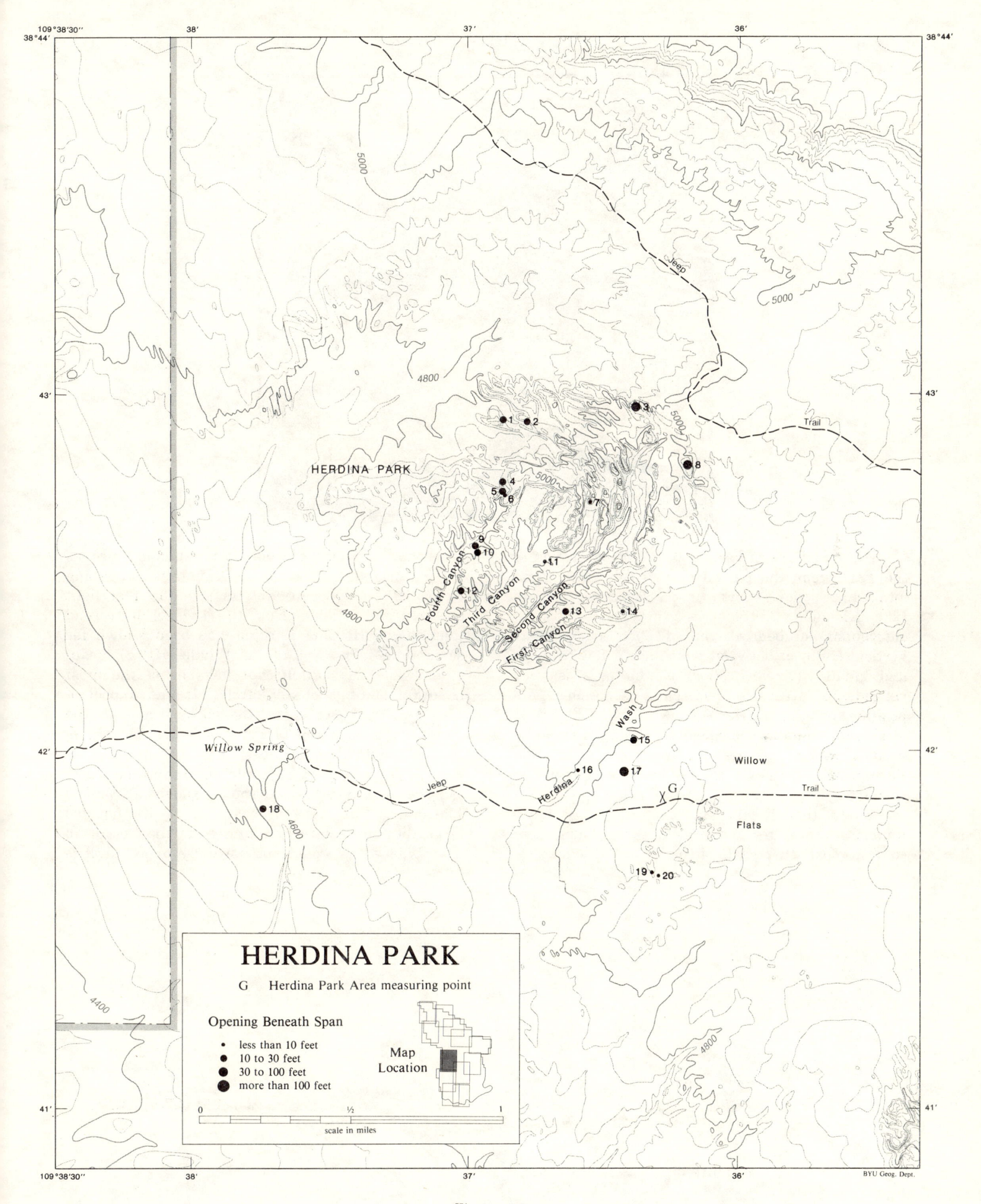

G   Herdina Park Area measuring point

Opening Beneath Span
- · less than 10 feet
- • 10 to 30 feet
- ● 30 to 100 feet
- ⬤ more than 100 feet

Map Location

scale in miles 0 ½ 1

Figure 32

HERDINA PARK

Herdina Park is located in the western part of the Park near the old entrance road which came into what is now known as the Windows Section. Like Klondike Bluffs it is characterized by an outcropping of bedrock that displays many near-vertical cliffs, in between which are a few canyons and small ravines. Much of the area is very rugged, but access to most parts is possible. Its position on the western edge of Salt Valley is somewhat similar geologically to Klondike Bluffs, with all known arches occurring in the Entrada Formation. Only 20 arches have been found in this area.

Even though the geology may be fairly uniform, there are more arch types found here than in most other parts of the Park. The only types not occurring are pot holes, spanned alcoves and natural tunnels. The largest arch is Leaping Arch (HP 3). Because of its size (50 feet light opening) and visibility from the 4-wheel drive road that passes Herdina Park, it has been known for some time. The Eye of the Whale (HP 8) is another well known arch that has one of the most beautiful settings of any arch. It has a pool of water at its base during the cooler times of the year and a backdrop of grasses and other plants that add to its attractiveness.

Other than the rocky outcrop of Herdina Park, the area to the west and south, known as Willow Flats, also has some arches. They are not too large, but are interesting to see as they occur in sites where one would not normally expect arches to be.

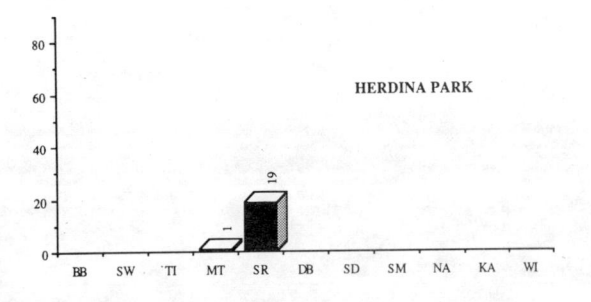

Figure 30

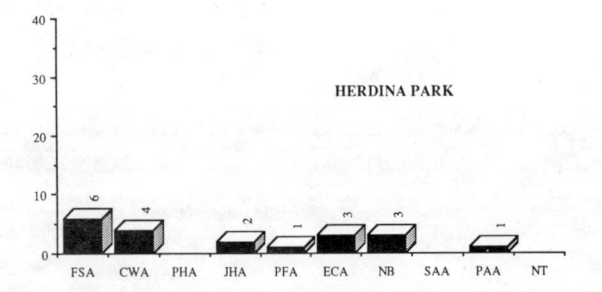

Figure 31

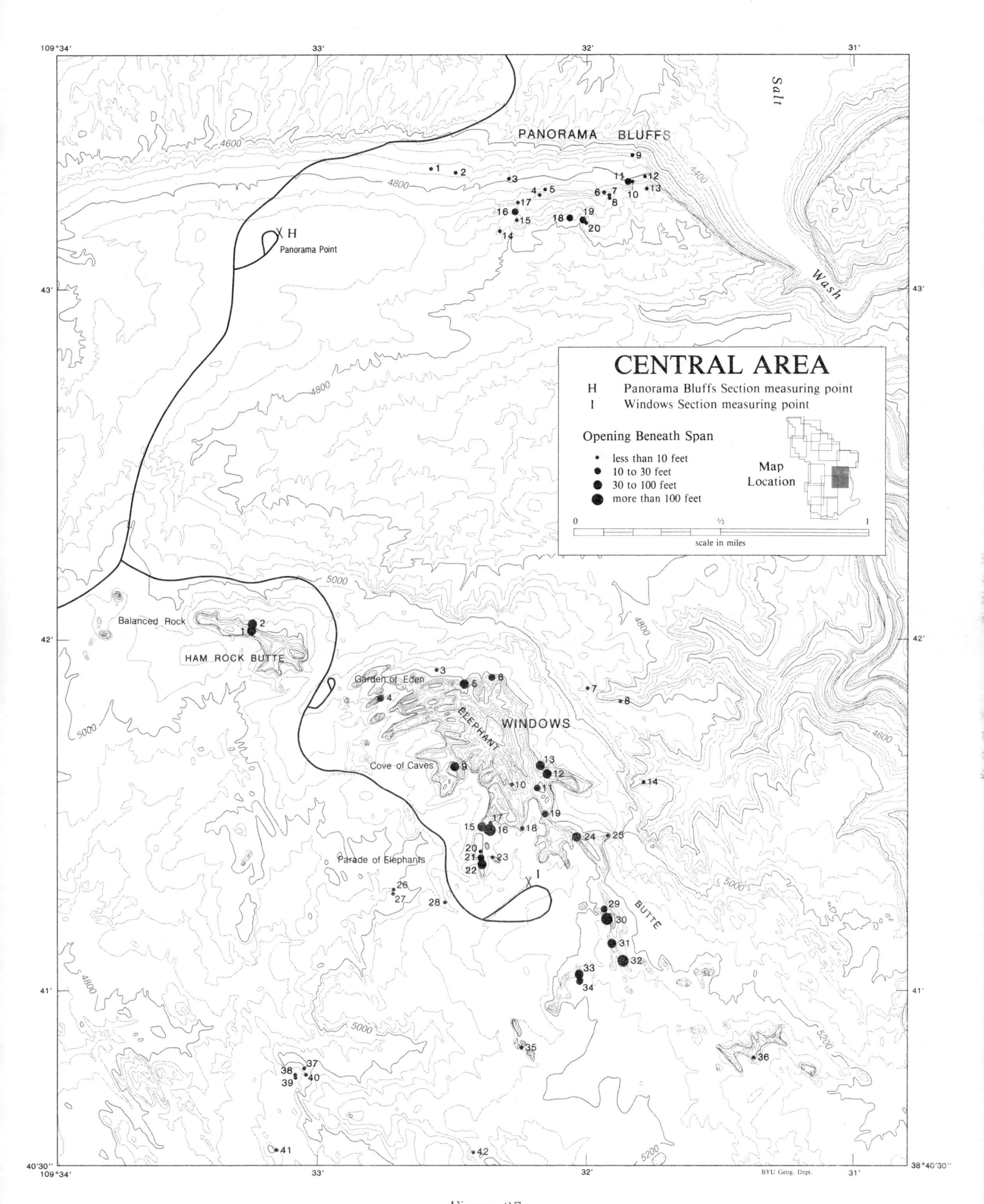

Figure 37

CENTRAL AREA

There are two well known sections in this area, Panorama Bluffs and Windows. Because they are so familiar to those who know the Park, the numbering system of arches in these sections are separate (See Figure 35). The Windows Section is not only centrally located, but it has long been the focal point for visitors since it has been known for such a long time. The first campground for visitors was established near here and the old access road terminated here.

There is no other place in the Park where there are so many "grand" arches. Five of the top ten arches by size of light opening are found in the Windows Section. They include Double Arch (WS 15 & 16), North & South Window (WS 31 & 32), and Biceps Arch (WS 30), The average light opening dimension of the above five is 106 feet. On the other hand Panorama Bluffs is characterized by relatively small arches. The largest here is Flame Arch (PB 19) which has a light opening of 14.2 feet. The differences can be attributed primarily to the exposed geologic formations. The arches of the Windows section are concentrated in Entrada while those in Panorama Bluffs are mostly in Wingate. The closer spacing of bedding planes and joints in the Wingate Formation helps explain why large arches would not develop as easily. See Figure 33.

Another feature of the Windows Section is the existence of a high percentage of Free Standing Arches. Over 40 percent fit this category. For comparison, only one arch is a free standing type in the Panorama Bluffs Section, but Spanned Alcove Arches are best represented in this Section where seven are known to occur, making up 35 percent of the arches there. Compare the graphs below (Figures 33-36) to note the contrasting features of this area.

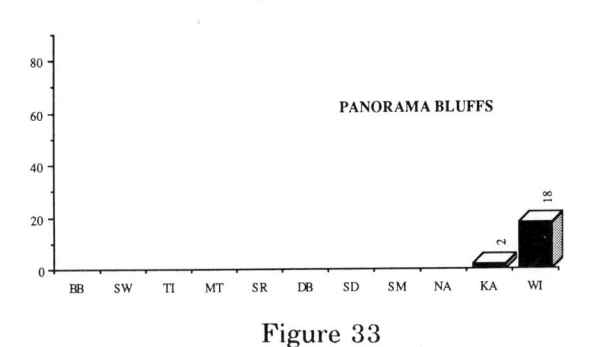

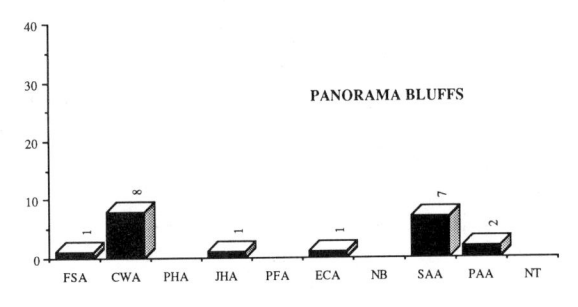

Figure 33

Figure 34

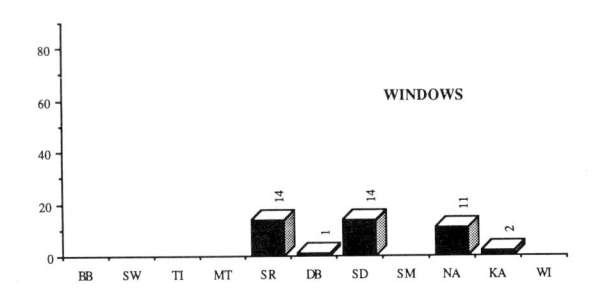

Figure 35

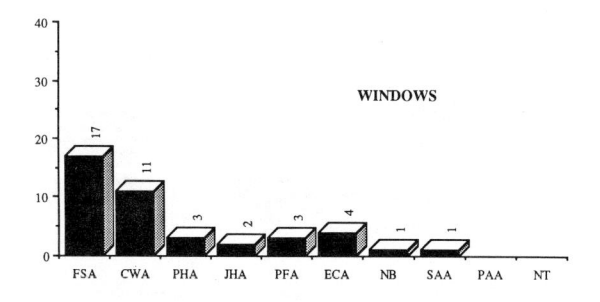

Figure 36

48

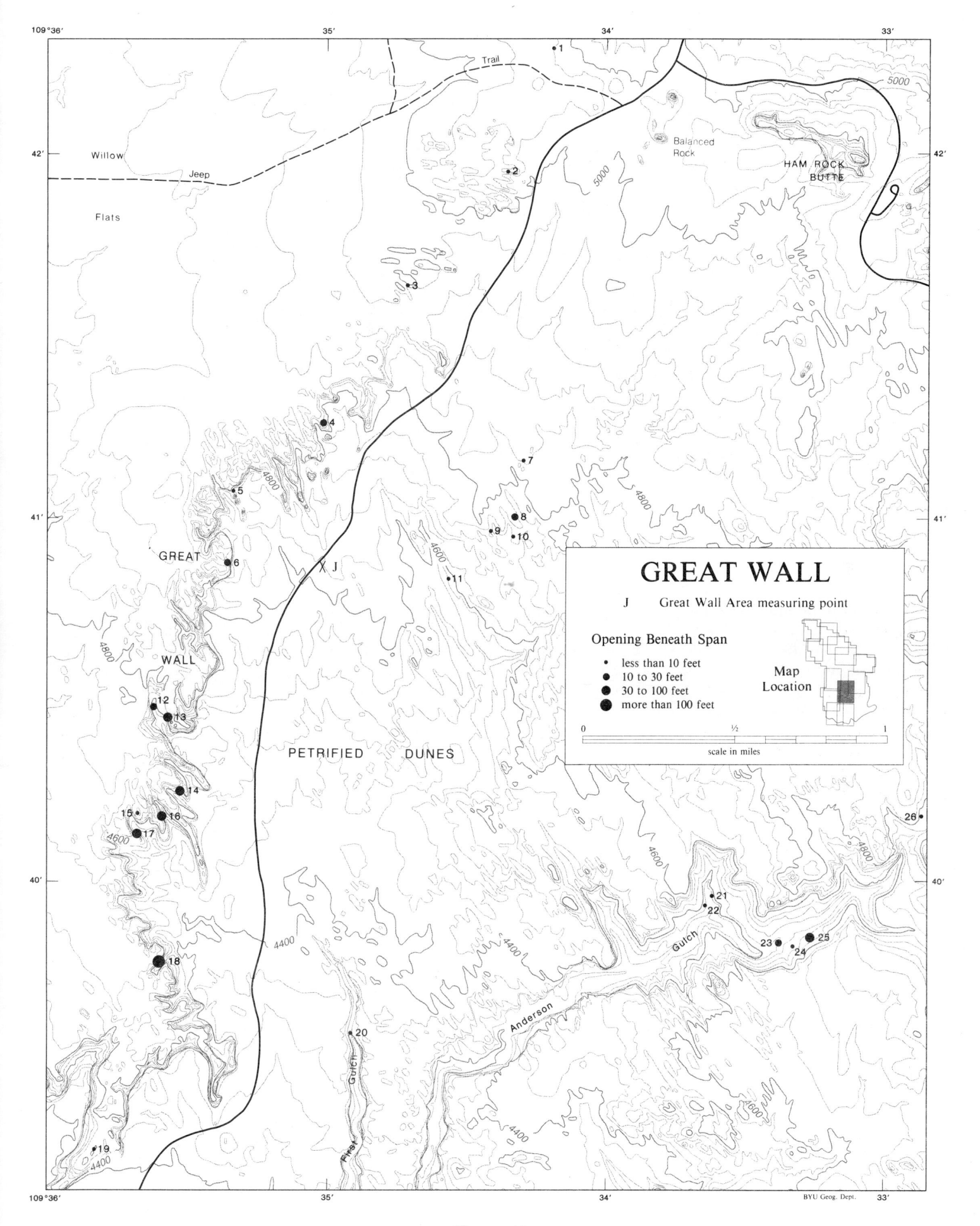

Figure 40

GREAT WALL

Several landmarks within the Park are found in the Great Wall area. Among them are some of the better known features such as "Balanced Rock" near the entrance to the Windows Section, The "Petrified Dunes" which is an extensive area of Navajo sandstone and the "Great Wall" which begins in Courthouse Wash and extends northward to where the road levels off near the turn-off to Herdina Park. At the southern part of this area there are several deep side-canyons which are tributaries to Courthouse Wash. Fifty percent of the 26 arches in this area are in the Entrada Formation while 25 percent are in Navajo and 25 percent in Kayenta. See Figure 38.

Most arches here are Cliff Wall Arches (42 percent), while fifteen percent are Spanned Alcove Arches. Figure 39 illustrates the numbers of each arch type. The largest arch here is Little Gothic Arch (GW 18) which has a light opening of 53 feet, only five feet less than the 58 feet Gothic Arch (ND 67) found in North Devils Garden. Its size is deceiving because most view it from a distance as it is rather difficult to climb to its base. Some other interesting arches here are Arch of Motion (GW 4), Bean Pot Arch (GW 6) and Owl Eye Arch (GW 20).

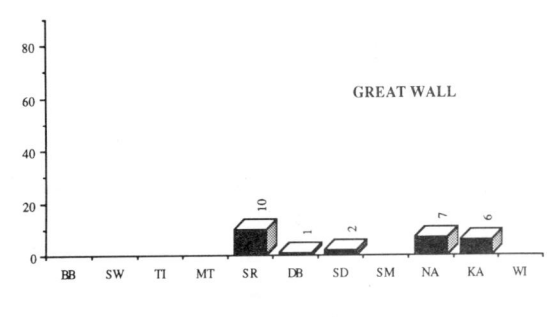

Figure 38

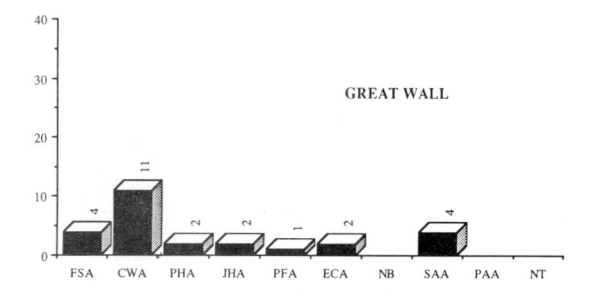

Figure 39

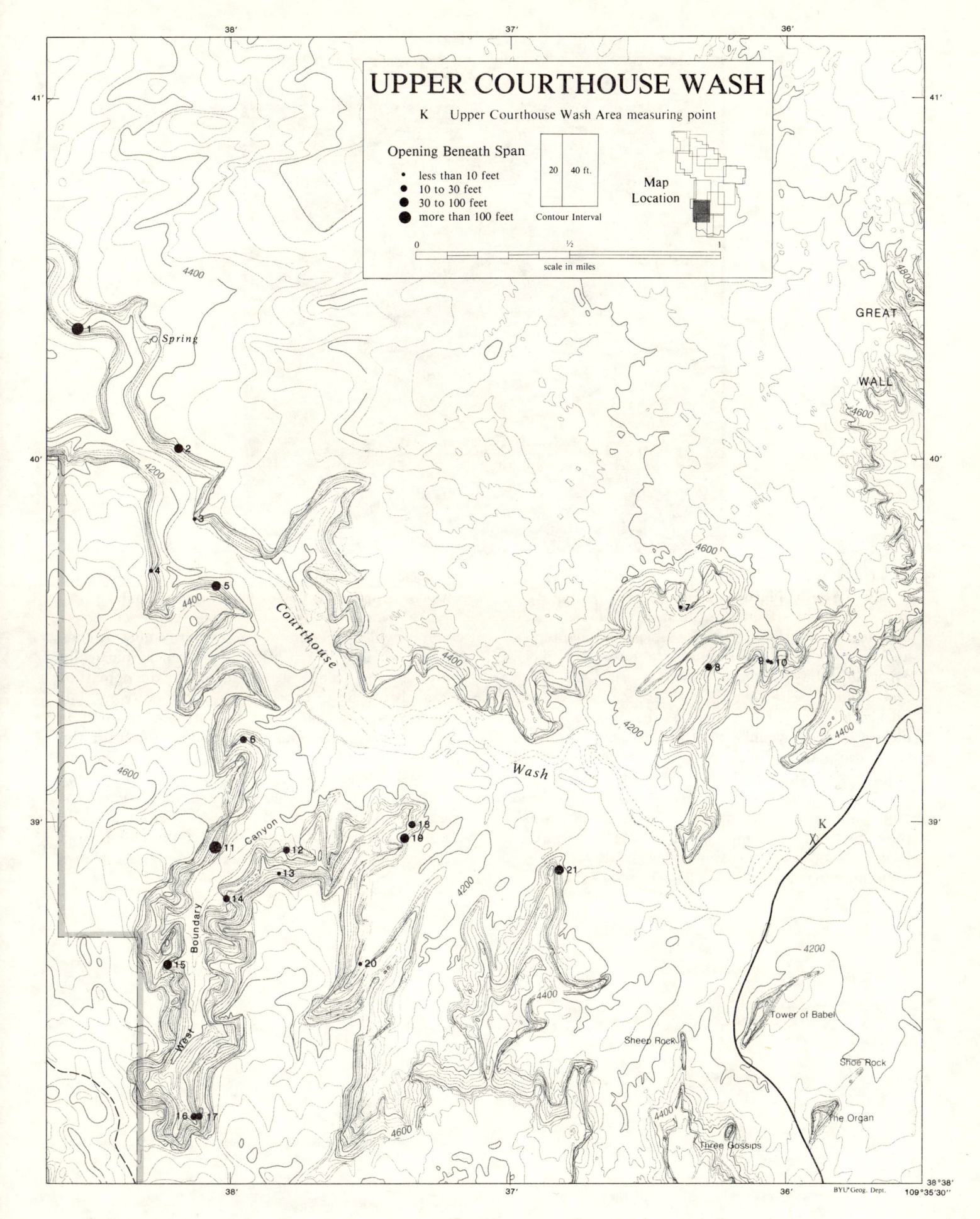

Figure 43

UPPER COURTHOUSE WASH

There are two unusual things about this area; it has the only Natural Tunnel found in the Park and all arches are in the Slickrock Member of the Entrada Formation. The discussions in chapters 4 and 5 give some background to natural tunnels, especially the one here which is very distinctive and unique. The fact that all arches occur in the Slickrock Member is due to the deeply eroded nature of the "wash" into the Entrada Formation, while the plateau uplands on all sides are composed of other geologic units less likely to have arches.

The canyon of Courthouse Wash broadens and levels out where the main road crosses the wash then narrows back into a rather deep canyon before it empties into the Colorado River. For mapping purposes and for physiographic reasons the road in this open area forms the boundaries between Upper and Lower Courthouse Wash.

As would be expected the cliffs of these canyon walls are the places where most arches would be found. Cliff Wall arches naturally dominate the scene. It is interesting to note that there are no natural bridges in these canyons, but that is not unusual since the stream channel is choked with sands and other sediments from the perennial stream that meanders along the floor of the wash. The largest arch here, with an opening of 52 feet, is West Boundary Arch, an excellent example of a Cliff Wall Arch that would easily qualify as a Free Standing Arch if the cliff behind the opening were just not there. Figure 42 shows how the arches were classified into types.

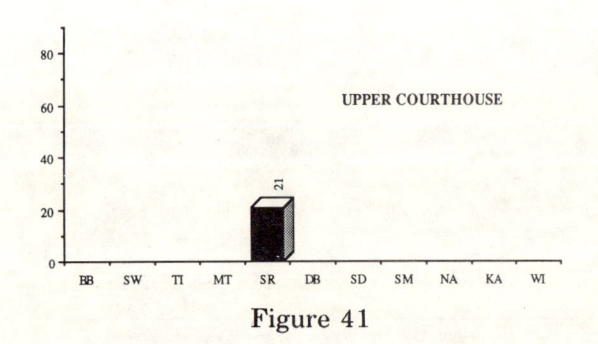

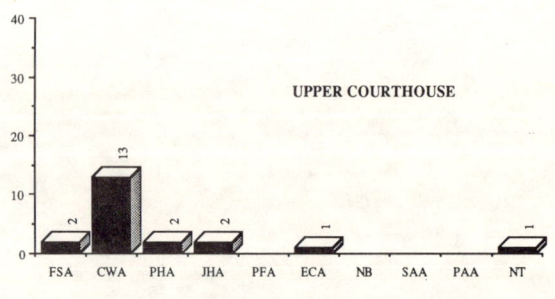

Figure 41

Figure 42

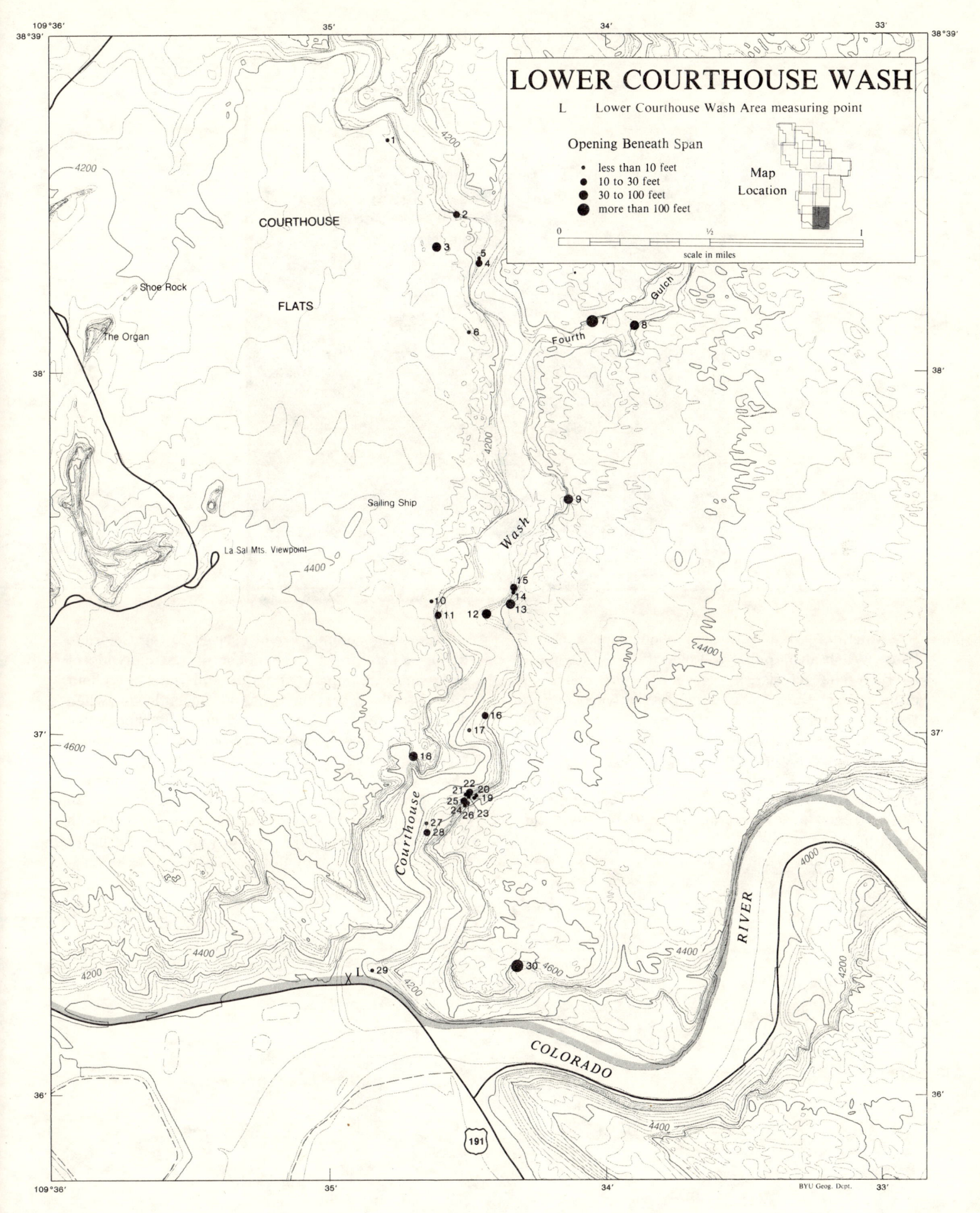

Figure 46

LOWER COURTHOUSE WASH

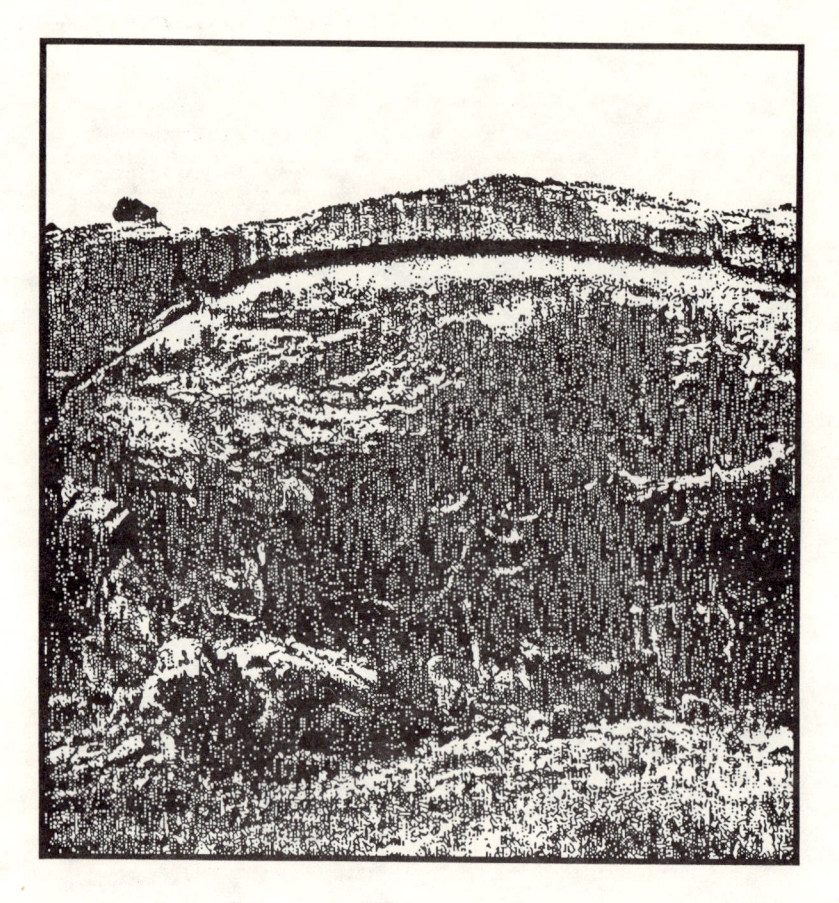

Much of what was said about Upper Courthouse Wash also applies to Lower Courthouse Wash as their characteristics are very similar. The big difference is that the channel has cut deeper into the rock layers and all arches here are in the older Navajo and Kayenta Formations. See Figure 44. These rocks often display a high proportion of Spanned Alcove Arches and Perforated Alcove Arches. Because of the steep canyon walls, Cliff Wall Arches are more numerous than any other type, however.

Courthouse Wash drains a fairly large surface area and the sediment load carried to the Colorado River is significant. The floor of the canyons of this wash are sandy and flat and make excellent hiking trails except in times of flash floods, when it becomes a raging river. Even in earlier times this was a major route from Spanish Valley where Moab is located to the valleys northward. It was also used for cattle drives until fairly recent times.

Streaked Arch (LC 44) is the largest arch in the canyon. It is ranked as the 44th largest arch in the Park, indicating that its light opening of 41 feet is nothing exceptional.

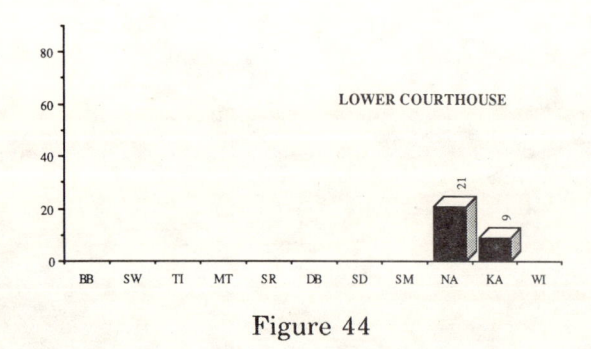

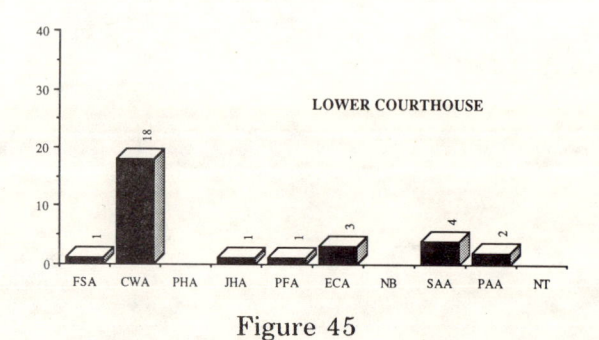

Figure 44

Figure 45

54

SOUTHWESTERN AREA

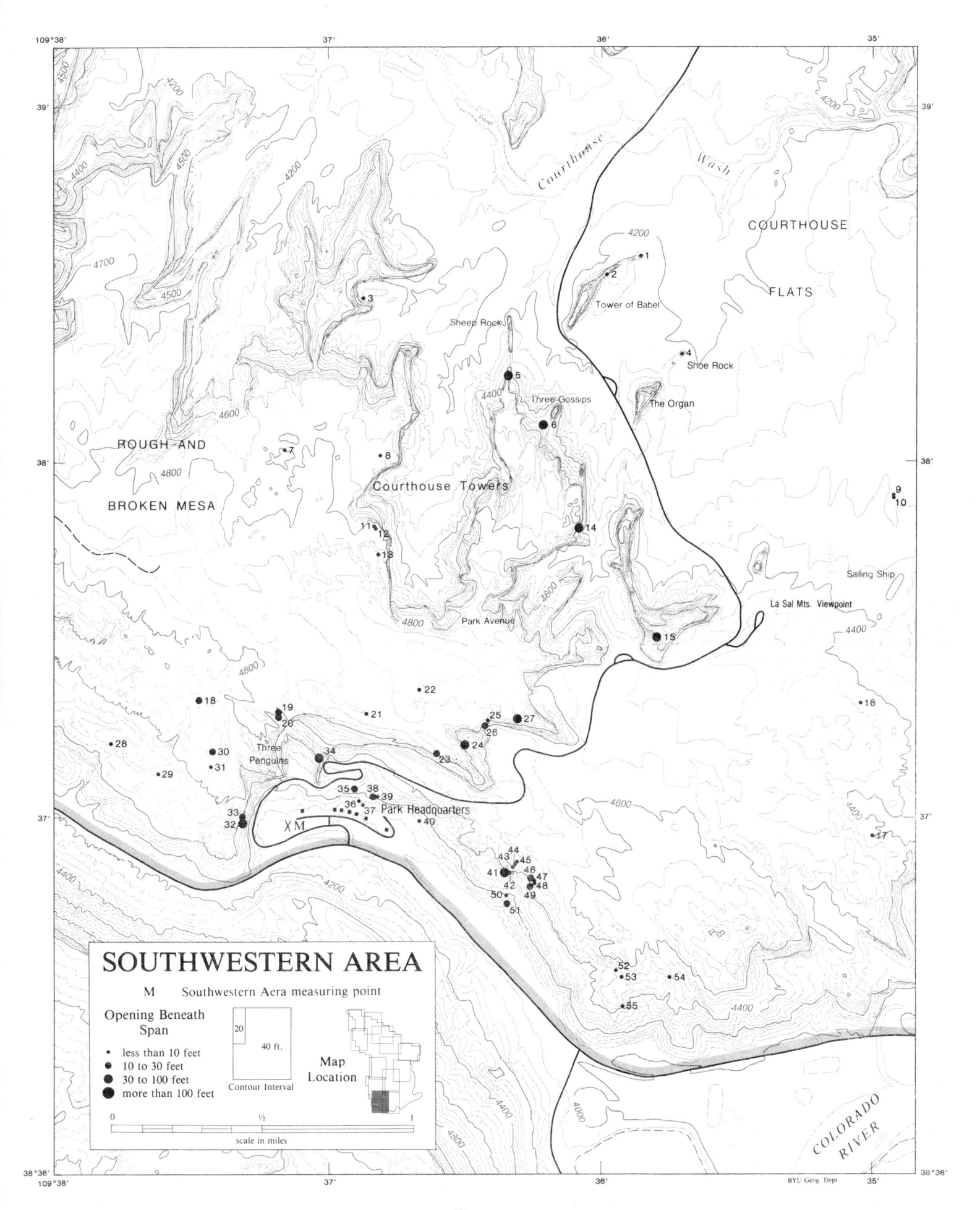

M   Southwestern Aera measuring point

Opening Beneath Span

- · less than 10 feet
- • 10 to 30 feet
- ● 30 to 100 feet
- ⬤ more than 100 feet

Contour Interval: 20 / 40 ft.

Map Location

scale in miles: 0 — ½ — 1

BYU Geog. Dept.

Figure 49

SOUTHWESTERN AREA

As one approaches the main Park entrance and views the massive cliffs of solid rock, there appear to be no arches in plain view, but there are several. A few are visible from the visitor center or from the road if one has a trained eye and a knowledge of arches, but visitors are usually so concerned about the winding highway and getting to the main areas of the Park that they are unaware of any arches. The steep slopes extend upward to well over 600 feet from the visitors center near US Highway 191 and include several thick layers of the major geologic formations found in the Park. In spite of this, all arches here are found in either the Entrada or Navajo Formations. This area ranks third in total arches with 55 listed, 20 of which are classified as Cliff Wall Arches. The types that do not occur are Pot Hole Arches, Perforated Alcove Arches and Natural Tunnels. Figure 48 gives a breakdown of the numbers in each of the categories.

This area is about as diverse as any in the Park, having four different sections. They include: the Southern Border near the visitor center, while farther into the Park can be found Courthouse Towers, Courthouse Flats and the upland region in the southwestern corner known as Rough and Broken Mesa.

There are no large nor impressive arches here, but many of them have unusual shapes and positions. The largest is Split Bottom Arch (SA 24) which has a light opening of 32 feet. The third largest is Baby Arch (SA 5) at 24.5 feet which is usually the first arch visitors see. The amount of rock above this opening is so great it has the appearance of a relatively small arch.

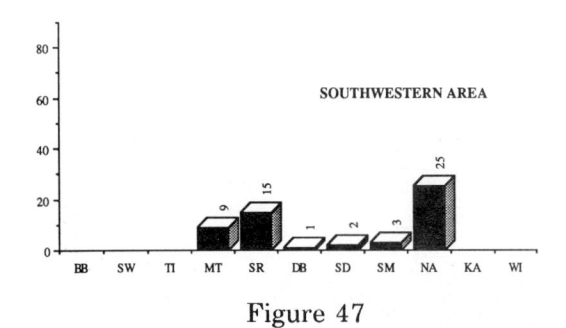

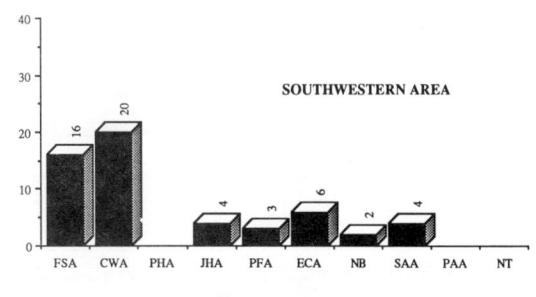

Figure 47

Figure 48

ARCHES NATIONAL PARK
Index to Area Maps

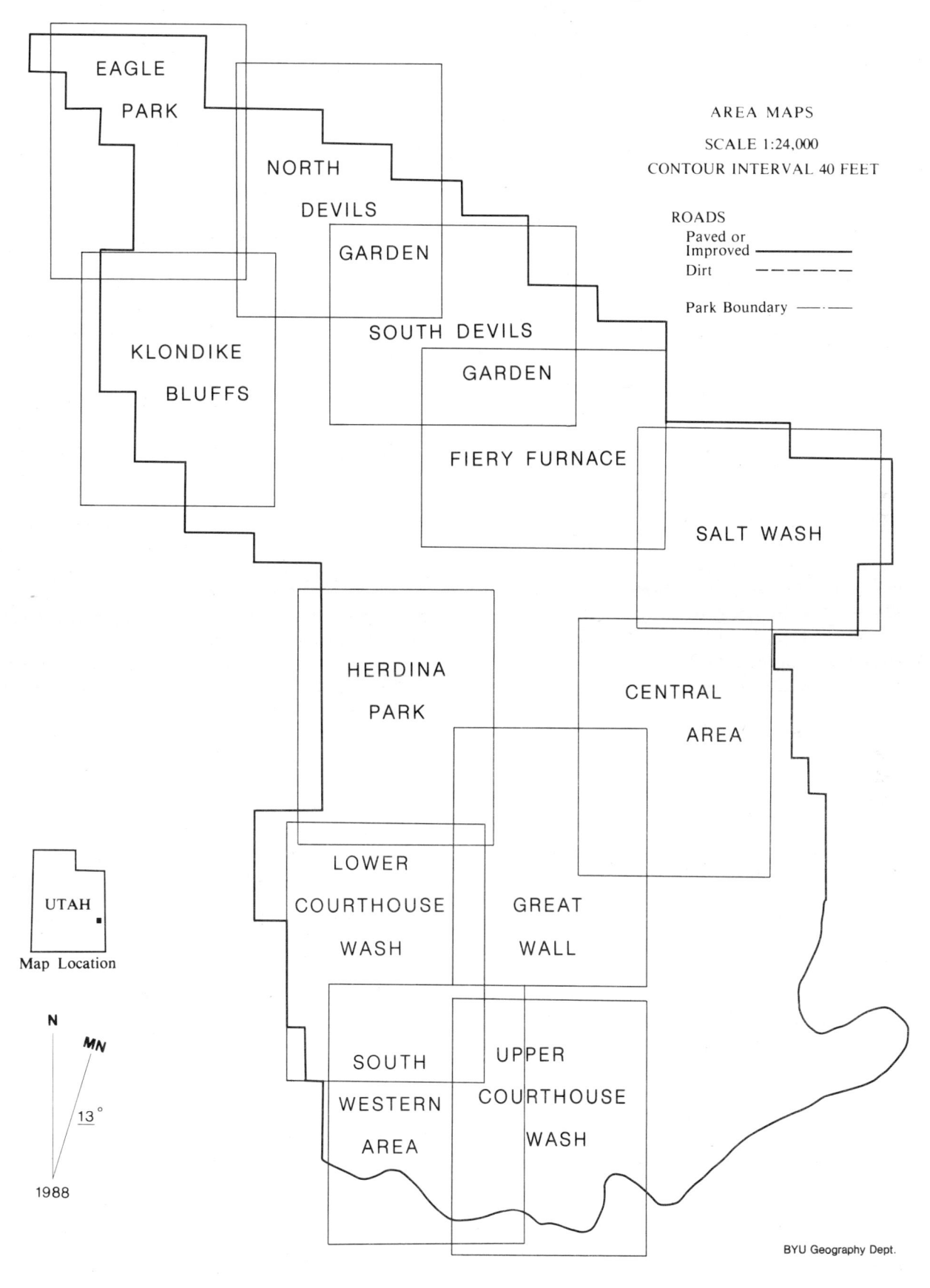

Figure 11

CHAPTER 7
PHOTOGRAPHIC PORTRAYAL

Any discussion on the arches of Arches National Park without photographs can only be partially complete, since the outward appearance and size of an arch is usually its most interesting characteristic. All of the 527 arches discussed in this book were photographed and are included in this chapter. In those instances where arches are close together or where they are double, more than one may be included in a photograph. Where this is done there is full explanation as to proper identification of each individual arch. The photographs are arranged numerically by area starting with Eagle Park and ending with the Southwestern Area. Cross references can be made quite easily with both the alphabetical and the ranking lists (Tables 2 and 3 in Chapter 8) since the photographs of this chapter and the two lists all contain Name, Area and Identification Number.

Besides name and Park area identification number, some key statistical information is included with each photograph. Arch type is designated by the symbols used throughout the book. For convenience, arch types can be identified from the list below.

      FSA = Free Standing Arch
      CWA = Cliff Wall Arch
      ECA = Expanded Crevice Arch
      JHA = Jug Handle Arch
      PFA = Platform Arch
      NB   = Natural Bridge
      SAA = Spanned Alcove Arch
      PHA = Pothole Arch
      NT   = Natural Tunnel
      PAA = Perforated Alcove Arch

The legend for the other symbols used beneath each photograph is summarized below.

      LO = Length and Depth of Light
             Opening
      OB = Width and Height of Opening
             Beneath the Span
      SP = Span's Horizontal and Vertical
             Thickness and Extent

All of these dimensions are in feet and in tenths of a foot. As mentioned in chapter 4, the Light Opening measurements are most critical because they determine the three feet dimension for qualification as an arch. However, the Opening Beneath the Span may be the first view that indicates the possibility of an arch. Refer to Chapter 4 for a more complete explanation of the terminology used and the details of their respective measurements.

It is apparent that some photographs were not made under ideal conditions of lighting and that, along with the angle of view may present difficulties when specific identification of unique characteristics are attempted. In many cases arrows are used on the photo to help in identification. In other cases it was assumed that most readers would study the photograph if the arch were not obvious to them at first glance.

The photos were all taken by the authors in the course of their regular field work at the same time measurements and other data were collected. To photograph each arch under ideal conditions of weather, lighting, position, etc. would have taken years of effort.

In using black and white film, prints turn out best when conditions include an overcast sky with no direct shadows. Obviously, we did not have such ideal lighting for every arch. The normal lighting conditions in this area cause high contrast between the shadow and the bright reflection from the bare rock. This results in over exposure on part of the photograph and under exposure on other parts. Sometimes the only solution is a compromise in exposure which may not produce an entirely satisfactory print.

Color film can usually produce more acceptable results with proper adjustments, even considering the high light contrast. The use of color in this book would have made the cost prohibitive so it was decided to go with black and white film in order to keep the price within the reach of the average person.

Since every attempt was made to include the arch and exclude as much landscape as possible, the scale of each photograph varies considerably. In viewing each photograph, a glance at the dimensions will help to establish scale. The reader will also notice that there are no people in any of the photographs. This was purposely done to avoid having many pictures of the same people.

Although not included in this book, each photograph was documented as to lens, distance and direction the camera was from the arch. The date each photograph was taken was also recorded.

All photographs are arranged by area beginning in Eagle Park in the northwestern part of the Park then continuing southward to the Southwestern Area where the Visitor Center is located. Any arch can be correlated easily with the maps in chapter 6 or with the tables in chapter 8 as all three list name and number.

Sibling Ar Center EP 1
CWA LO- 55.2 X 5.9 ft.
OB- 55.2 X 16.0 ft.
SP- 4.0 X 11.0 X 70.0 ft.

Sibling Ar North EP 2
CWA LO- 13.0 X .9 ft.
OB- 55.2 X 15.0 ft.
SP- 8.0 X 11.0 X 70.0 ft.

Sibling Ar South EP 3
PAA LO- 5.2 X .1 ft.
OB- 41.0 X 11.0 ft.
SP- 12.0 X 22.0 X 50.0 ft.

Eagle Arch EP 4
CWA LO- 8.0 X 1.0 ft.
OB- 8.0 X 1.0 ft.
SP- 8.0 X 9.0 X NA ft.

Forgotten Arch EP 5
FSA LO- 14.6 X 5.2 ft.
OB- 14.6 X 5.2 ft.
SP- 5.8 X 6.0 X NA ft.

Belly Arch EP 6
ECA LO- 1.1 X 11.2 ft.
OB- 1.1 X 11.2 ft.
SP- 13.0 X 13.4 X 37.0 ft.

Hip Joint Arch EP 7
CWA LO- 3.5 X 6.0 ft.
OB- 3.5 X 6.0 ft.
SP- 4.0 X 2.0 X NA ft.

Crow Arch EP 8
CWA LO- 44.0 X .5 ft.
OB- 44.0 X 20.8 ft.
SP- 13.0 X 7.8 X NA ft.

Five Twelve Arch EP 9
CWA LO- 6.3 X .9 ft.
OB- 6.3 X 3.1 ft.
SP- .7 X .3 X 8.2 ft.

Festoon Arch   EP 10
CWA LO- 3.1 X 2.3 ft.
OB- 3.1 X 2.3 ft.
SP- 1.3 X 1.4 X 3.3 ft.

Hammer Arch   EP 11
FSA LO- 3.9 X 3.6 ft.
OB- 3.9 X 3.6 ft.
SP- .8 X .4 X NA ft.

Big Buck Arch   EP 12
CWA LO- 18.5 X 2.0 ft.
OB- 21.0 X 28.0 ft.
SP- 1.6 X 1.1 X 21.0 ft.

Salamander Arch   EP 13
CWA LO- 15.0 X .8 ft.
OB- 15.0 X 22.5 ft.
SP- 2.5 X 3.4 X 15.0 ft.

All The Way Arch   EP 14
CWA LO- 19.0 X 1.0 ft.
OB- 22.0 X 11.0 ft.
SP- 3.0 X 4.0 X 31.0 ft.

Layer Arch   EP 15
ECA LO- 3.9 X .3 ft.
OB- 7.5 X .6 ft.
SP- 4.0 X 1.3 X 7.5ft.

Spider Arch   EP 16
CWA LO- 7.5 X 1.8 ft.
OB- 13.5 X 2.5 ft.
SP- .9 X .5 X 13.5 ft.

Duck Arch   EP 17
CWA LO- 5.3 X .6 ft.
OB- 5.3 X 3.2 ft.
SP- 8.0 X 3.5 X 13.0 ft.

Peephole Arch   EP 18
CWA LO- 23.0 X .6 ft.
OB- 41.0 X 37.0 ft.
SP- 7.0 X 7.0 X 58.0 ft.

Scoop Arch EP 19
CWA LO- 7.2 X .8 ft.
OB- 7.2 X 3.5 ft.
SP- 3.0 X 6.5 X 9.5 ft.

Clinging Arch EP 20
CWA LO- 10.5 X .1 ft.
OB- 23.0 X 2.6 ft.
SP- 1.9 X 2.0 X 28.0 ft.

Swan Arch EP 21
FSA LO- 15.0 X 6.0 ft.
OB- 15.0 X 10.5 ft.
SP- 8.5 X 10.0 X 18.0 ft.

On the Money Arch EP 22
CWA LO- 4.3 X .3 ft.
OB- 9.2 X 2.6 ft.
SP- 1.5 X 1.7 X 12.0 ft.

Superstition Arch EP 23
SAA LO- 3.5 X .3 ft.
OB- 3.5 X 3.4 ft.
SP- 1.1 X 1.0 X 7.0 ft.

Sea Shell Arch EP 24
ECA LO- 3.3 X 1.5 ft.
OB- 3.3 X 1.5 ft.
SP- 5.0 X 3.0 X 7.0 ft.

Cougar Arch EP 25
JHA LO- .5 X 3.4 ft.
OB- .5 X 3.4 ft.
SP- .9 X .4 X 12.0 ft.

Hourglass Arch EP 26
FSA LO- 9.0 X 12.5 ft.
OB- 9.0 X 12.5 ft.
SP- 1.9 X 1.8 X 24.3 ft.

Cracker Jack Arch EP 27
CWA LO- 12.0 X .1 ft.
OB- 16.0 X 4.2 ft.
SP- 2.0 X 2.2 X 21.0 ft.

Lean to Arch EP 28
JHA LO- 1.6 X 3.0 ft.
OB- 1.6 X 3.0 ft.
SP- 4.0 X 2.6 X 7.0 ft.

Hanging Arch EP 29
JHA LO- 2.1 X 10.0 ft.
OB- 2.1 X 10.0 ft.
SP- 6.5 X 3.0 X 12.0 ft.

Weeping Arch EP 30
CWA LO- 3.0 X .5 ft.
OB- 3.0 X .5 ft.
SP- 2.4 X 1.3 X 7.0 ft.

Tortoise Arch EP 31
CWA LO- 4.0 X .5 ft.
OB- 4.5 X .5 ft.
SP- 2.6 X .8 X 6.3 ft.

Pack Rat Arch EP 32
CWA LO- 5.4 X 2.0 ft.
OB- 10.0 X 5.0 ft.
SP- 7.0 X 5.0 X 11.5 ft.

Sleeping Arch EP 33
CWA LO- 3.7 X 1.5 ft.
OB- 9.5 X 3.2 ft.
SP- 1.8 X 6.0 X 16.0 ft.

Cracker Arch EP 34
SAA LO- 4.0 X 3.7 ft.
OB- 4.0 X 3.7 ft.
SP- 3.5 X 1.2 X 11.0 ft.

Inside Out Ar Out EP 35
CWA LO- 31.0 X 5.0 ft.
OB- 31.5 X 15.0 ft.
SP- 3.5 X 7.8 X 47.0 ft.

See Preceding Photo

The "Inner" arch is not obvious on the photo as it is behind and parallel to the "Outer" arch.

Inside Out Ar In EP 36
CWA LO- 13.0 X .5 ft.
OB- 13.0 X 12.5 ft.
SP- 4.5 X 7.5 X 20.0 ft.

Snowy Arch EP 37
CWA LO- 16.0 X .7 ft.
OB- 16.0 X 7.0 ft.
SP- 4.0 X 5.0 X 19.0 ft.

Twig Arch EP 38
CWA LO- 3.4 X .2 ft.
OB- 3.4 X 2.8 ft.
SP- 1.6 X 1.6 X NA ft.

Tornado Arch EP 39
JHA LO- 5.5 X 1.4 ft.
OB- 5.5 X 1.4 ft.
SP- 1.1 X .4 X 6.6 ft.

Pellet Arch EP 40
FSA LO- 3.9 X 3.0 ft.
OB- 3.9 X 3.0 ft.
SP- 7.0 X 2.8 X 8.0 ft.

Valley View Arch EP 41
SAA LO- 3.5 X 1.3 ft.
OB- 3.5 X 1.3 ft.
SP- .5 X .4 X NA ft.

Cry Baby Arch EP 42
CWA LO- 4.5 X .9 ft.
OB- 14.0 X 6.2 ft.
SP- 6.2 X 3.0 X 15.0 ft.

Traverse Arch EP 43
CWA LO- 15.0 X 2.0 ft.
OB- 19.0 X 3.0 ft.
SP- 4.2 X 2.4 X 20.0 ft.

Wimpy Arch EP 44
PFA LO- 5.0 X .7 ft.
OB- 7.3 X .7 ft.
SP- .8 X .3 X 9.0 ft.

Carling Arch EP 45
CWA LO- 5.9 X .5 ft.
OB- 5.9 X 3.6 ft.
SP- 4.5 X 4.0 X 8.0 ft.

Greasewood Arch EP 46
FSA LC 3.1 X 1.5 ft.
OB- 3.7 X 3.7 ft.
SP- 6.5 X 2.2 X NA ft.

Saltbush Arch EP 47
ECA LO- 5.0 X .6 ft.
OB- 5.0 X .6 ft.
SP- .9 X 1.1 X 6.0 ft.

Cliffrose Arch EP 48
ECA LO- 3.2 X .4 ft.
OB- 4.0 X .4 ft.
SP- 1.2 X 1.3 X NA ft.

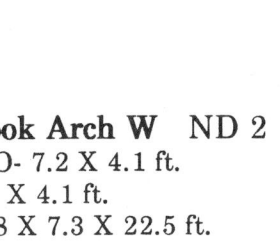

Textbook Arch E   ND 1
FSA LO- 16.0 X 6.0 ft.
OB- 19.0 X 6.0 ft.
SP- 5.2 X 4.7 X 22.5 ft.

See Preceding Photo

The left arrow points to "Text Book Arch West".

Textbook Arch W   ND 2
FSA LO- 7.2 X 4.1 ft.
OB- 7.2 X 4.1 ft.
SP- 10.8 X 7.3 X 22.5 ft.

Flapjack Arch   ND 3
ECA LO- 5.0 X 1.5 ft.
OB- 5.0 X 1.5 ft.
SP- 1.4 X .4 X NA ft.

Screech Owl Arch   ND 4
CWA LO- 32.0 X 4.0 ft.
OB- 32.0 X 16.1 ft.
SP- 9.0 X 10.0 X NA ft.

See Preceding Photo

The right arrow points to "Fledgling Arch".

Fledgling Arch   ND 5
CWA LO- 8.0 X 3.0 ft.
OB- 8.0 X 3.0 ft.
SP- 9.2 X 19.5 X NA ft.

Theory Arch   ND 6
CWA LO- 5.0 X .1 ft.
OB- 11.0 X 3.5 ft.
SP- 2.0 X 1.1 X 14.0 ft.

Far Out Arch   ND 7
FSA LO- 28.0 X 11.5 ft
OB- 30.0 X 27.0 ft.
SP- 16.0 X 29.0 X 44.0 ft.

Shield Arch   ND 8
FSA LO- 10.2 X 9.0 ft.
OB- 10.2 X 11.0 ft.
SP- 5.3 X 9.2 X 26.0 ft.

Postulation Arch   ND 9
CWA LO- 35.0 X .8 ft.
OB- 44.0 X 8.0 ft.
SP- 1.2 X 4.5 X 64.0 ft.

Flying Hat Arch ND 10
CWA LO- 29.0 X 4.0 ft.
OB- 69.0 X 43.0 ft.
SP- 35.0 X 72.0 X 170.0 ft.

Shelter Arch ND 11
FSA LO- 6.0 X 3.7 ft.
OB- 15.0 X 6.0 ft.
SP- 16.0 X 29.0 X 35.0 ft.

Tub Arch ND 12
ECA LO- 8.6 X 1.7 ft.
OB- 8.6 X 1.7 ft.
SP- 7.0 X 5.0 X NA ft.

See Preceding Photo

"Twin Spans Arch East" is the lower and smaller of the two openings in the photo.

Wash Basin Arch ND 13
ECA LO- 3.2 X .4 ft.
OB- 3.2 X .4 ft.
SP- 5.0 X 1.7 X 5.5 ft.

Twin Spans West ND 14
FSA LO- 4.1 X 2.8 ft.
OB- 4.1 X 2.8 ft.
SP- 2.5 X .8 X 6.2 ft.

Twin Spans East ND 15
FSA LO- 5.2 X 4.0 ft.
OB- 5.2 X 4.0 ft.
SP- 8.0 X 2.7 X 10.0 ft.

See Preceding Photo

The arrow on the right points to "Camouflage Twins Arch South".

Camouflage Tw No ND 16
FSA LO- 9.0 X 2.7 ft.
OB- 9.0 X 2.7 ft.
SP- 21.0 X 30.0 X 14.0 ft.

Camouflage Tw So ND 17
ECA LO- 4.3 X 1.7 ft.
OB- 4.3 X 1.7 ft.
SP- 21.0 X 30.0 X 9.0 ft.

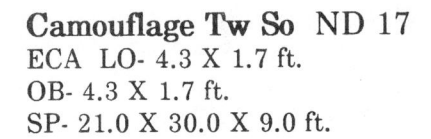

Chamber Arch No ND 18
ECA LO- 6.5 X 1.5 ft.
OB- 6.5 X 1.5 ft.
SP- 9.0 X 4.0 X 10.0 ft.

See Preceding Photo

The opening on the right, beneath the cave-like feature is "Chamber Arch South"

Chamber Arch So   ND 19
ECA LO- 3.7 X 1.8 ft.
OB- 3.7 X 1.8 ft.
SP- 9.0 X 4.0 X 10.0 ft.

Indian Head Arch   ND 20
FSA LO- 3.9 X 4.4 ft.
OB- 3.9 X 4.4 ft.
SP- 2.9 X 3.7 X NA ft.

Hamburger Arch   ND 21
ECA LO- 4.0 X .5 ft.
OB- 6.0 X .5 ft.
SP- 6.0 X 1.0 X 6.0 ft.

Coffin Arch   ND 22
FSA LO- 6.5 X 2.8 ft.
OB- 6.5 X 2.8 ft.
SP- 5.0 X 2.8 X 14.0 ft.

Big Eye Arch   ND 23
FSA LO- 31.5 X 5.5 ft.
OB- 31.5 X 5.5 ft.
SP- 16.0 X 53.0 X 50.0 ft.

Phantom Arch   ND 24
CWA LO- 42.0 X 6.0 ft.
OB- 56.0 X 16.0 ft.
SP- 7.0 X 3.0 X 88.0 ft.

Mushroom Arch   ND 25
FSA LO- 3.5 X 1.0 ft.
OB- 3.5 X 1.0 ft.
SP- .7 X .5 X 7.0 ft.

Keyhole Arch   ND 26
ECA LO- 1.5 X 5.0 ft.
OB- 1.5 X 5.0 ft.
SP- 8.0 X 1.3 X 8.0 ft.

Window Arch   ND 27
FSA LO- 10.0 X 7.0 ft.
OB- 10.0 X 7.0 ft.
SP- 8.0 X 21.0 X 30.0 ft.

Emblem Arch ND 28
FSA LO- 3.9 X 3.0 ft.
OB- 3.9 X 3.0 ft.
SP- 9.0 X 4.0 X 10.5 ft.

Bow Jughandle ND 29
JHA LO- 1.0 X 12.0 ft.
OB- 1.0 X 12.0 ft.
SP- 2.0 X 5.0 X NA ft.

Holey Arch ND 30
ECA LO- 3.2 X .7 ft.
OB- 3.2 X .7 ft.
SP- 1.6 X .8 X 4.0 ft.

One Block Arch ND 31
FSA LO- 10.7 X 5.4 ft.
OB- 10.7 X 5.4 ft.
SP- 6.5 X 7.0 X 12.0 ft.

Piano Leg Arch ND 32
FSA LO- 10.0 X 3.0 ft.
OB- 10.0 X 5.9 ft.
SP- 1.2 X .3 X 17.8 ft.

Turban Head Arch ND 33
FSA LO- 7.8 X 3.0 ft.
OB- 7.8 X 3.0 ft.
SP- 3.3 X 2.4 X 11.0 ft.

Falling Rock Arch ND 34
FSA LO- 7.3 X 4.3 ft.
OB- 7.3 X 4.3 ft.
SP- 2.5 X 3.5 X 9.0 ft.

Aladdins Bridge ND 35
NB LO- 5.9 X .4 ft.
OB- 5.9 X .4 ft.
SP- 1.5 X .2 X 6.0 ft.

Aladdins Lamp ND 36
FSA LO- 14.0 X 5.0 ft.
OB- 14.0 X 5.0 ft.
SP- 7.0 X 9.3 X NA ft.

Hug Arch ND 37
PFA LO- 5.0 X .1 ft.
OB- 5.0 X .1 ft.
SP- .7 X .1 X 6.0 ft.

Cat Eye Arch ND 38
CWA LO- 16.0 X 2.0 ft.
OB- 18.9 X 31.5 ft.
SP- 12.3 X 8.5 X 82.0 ft.

Eyeball Arch ND 39
JHA LO- .7 X 22.0 ft.
OB- .7 X 22.0 ft.
SP- 7.0 X 4.5 X 50.0 ft.

Overhang Arch ND 40
SAA LO- 12.5 X 2.5 ft.
OB- 12.5 X 2.5 ft.
SP- 1.7 X 1.9 X 23.5 ft.

Side Fin Arch ND 41
FSA LO- 24.0 X 12.0 ft.
OB- 24.0 X 12.0 ft.
SP- 10.0 X 80.0 X 29.0 ft.

Canyon Wren Br ND 42
NB LO- 6.4 X .1 ft.
OB- 8.0 X 2.0 ft.
SP- 1.2 X 1.7 X 9.0 ft.

Funnel Arch ND 43
FSA LO- 7.5 X 8.3 ft.
OB- 7.5 X 8.3 ft.
SP- 10.0 X 23.5 X 12.0 ft.

Cat Head Arch ND 44
FSA LO- 2.0 X 3.0 ft.
OB- 2.0 X 3.0 ft.
SP- 1.4 X 16.0 X NA ft.

Dumbbell A Upper ND 45
CWA LO- 5.0 X .4 ft.
OB- 10.2 X 2.5 ft.
SP- .7 X .4 X 10.2 ft.

See Preceding Photo

The "Upper" span is near the skyline just above the "Lower" span which has broken up rocks and debris under it.

Dumbbell A Lower ND 46
CWA LO- 4.2 X .5 ft.
OB- 6.0 X 2.1 ft.
SP- .9 X 1.0 X 7.5 ft.

Bobcat Arch ND 47
FSA LO- 3.9 X 6.2 ft.
OB- 7.0 X 7.0 ft.
SP- 1.9 X 1.1 X 9.5 ft.

Cantilever Arch ND 48
CWA LO- 9.5 X .6 ft.
OB- 11.5 X 3.5 ft.
SP- 6.8 X 4.6 X 18.0 ft.

Evil Eye Arch ND 49
JHA LO- 4.5 X 1.0 ft.
OB- 4.5 X 1.0 ft.
SP- 23.0 X 2.0 X 9.0 ft.

Teatime Arch No ND 50
FSA LO- 7.5 X 5.5 ft.
OB- 7.5 X 5.5 ft.
SP- 20.0 X 18.0 X 41.0 ft.

See Preceding Photo

"Teatime Arch South" is the larger opening on the right side of the photo.

Teatime Arch So ND 51
FSA LO- 10.9 X 11.2 ft
OB- 10.9 X 11.2 ft.
SP- 17.0 X 17.0 X 41.0 ft.

Bypass Arch ND 52
CWA LO- 43.0 X 1.0 ft.
OB- 58.0 X 35.0 ft.
SP- 3.8 X 17.0 X 69.0 ft.

Rectangular Arch ND 53
FSA LO- 7.5 X 5.8 ft.
OB- 7.5 X 5.8 ft.
SP- 17.0 X 60.0 X NA ft.

Canyon Bridge ND 54
NB LO- 10.7 X 4.5 ft.
OB- 10.7 X 4.5 ft.
SP- 2.5 X 3.1 X 24.0 ft.

Redtail Arch ND 55
ECA LO- 1.5 X 8.2 ft.
OB- 1.5 X 8.2 ft.
SP- 7.0 X 7.0 X NA ft.

Turkey Arch ND 56
FSA LO- 5.1 X 4.8 ft.
OB- 5.1 X 4.8 ft.
SP- 3.0 X 7.4 X 12.3 ft.

Lens Arch ND 57
CWA LO- 4.5 X .6 ft.
OB- 4.5 X .6 ft.
SP- 1.8 X 5.5 X 7.0 ft.

Fawn Arch ND 58
ECA LO- 6.5 X 1.0 ft.
OB- 6.5 X 1.0 ft.
SP- 7.0 X 15.0 X NA ft.

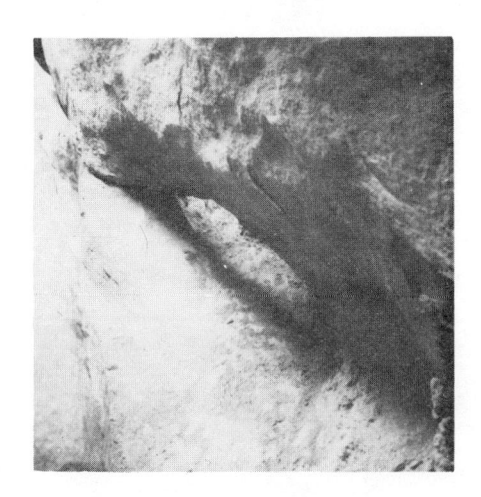

Digger Arch ND 59
CWA LO- 4.8 X .8 ft.
OB- 4.8 X 1.0 ft.
SP- 2.1 X 4.0 X 8.0 ft.

Tension Arch ND 60
CWA LO- 8.2 X 2.4 ft.
OB- 8.2 X 5.2 ft.
SP- .8 X .3 X NA ft.

Oval Arch ND 61
CWA LO- 35.0 X 1.0 ft.
OB- 35.0 X 12.0 ft.
SP- 10.0 X 13.0 X 40.0 ft.

Stale Arch ND 62
CWA LO- 34.0 X 2.0 ft.
OB- 40.0 X 14.0 ft.
SP- 12.0 X 6.0 X 67.0 ft.

Cup Arch ND 63
FSA LO- 9.0 X 6.0 ft.
OB- 9.0 X 6.0 ft.
SP- 7.0 X 12.0 X NA ft.

See Preceding Photo

"Saucer Arch" is the opening on the left. Note that "Cup Arch" on the right resembles an upside-down cup

Saucer Arch   ND 64
FSA LO- 7.5 X 4.0 ft.
OB- 7.5 X 4.0 ft.
SP- 8.0 X 19.0 X NA ft.

Snakehead Arch ND 65
CWA LO- 10.1 X 1.6 ft.
OB- 10.1 X 4.0 ft.
SP- 3.9 X 2.4 X 12.5 ft.

Canine Arch   ND 66
CWA LO- 4.0 X .5 ft.
OB- 4.4 X 1.2 ft.
SP- 1.1 X .9 X 25.0 ft.

Gothic Arch   ND 67
CWA LO- 58.0 X 4.0 ft.
OB- 80.0 X 78.0 ft.
SP- 19.5 X 39.0 X 88.0 ft.

Excavation Arch   ND 68
ECA LO- 5.5 X .8 ft.
OB- 5.5 X .8 ft.
SP- 6.0 X 1.7 X 27.0 ft.

Filagree Arch   ND 69
CWA LO- 9.1 X .7 ft.
OB- 9.1 X 7.2 ft.
SP- 3.3 X 10.5 X 14.3 ft.

Columbine Arch   ND 70
PAA LO- 5.3 X 2.8 ft.
OB- 13.0 X 4.5 ft.
SP- 25.0 X 70.0 X NA ft.

Helmet Arch   ND 71
FSA LO- 7.0 X 9.0 ft.
OB- 7.0 X 9.0 ft.
SP- 12.0 X 8.0 X 22.0 ft.

See Preceding Photo

Helmet Arch is in the lower left-hand corner of the photo. The upper opening is obviously "Top Story Window".

Top Story Window ND 72
FSA LO- 18.0 X 12.5 ft.
OB- 18.0 X 12.5 ft.
SP- 14.0 X 13.0 X 33.0 ft.

Corridor Arch ND 73
ECA LO- 4.1 X .7 ft.
OB- 4.1 X .7 ft.
SP- 12.0 X 11.7 X NA ft.

Boomerang Arch ND 74
CWA LO- 4.0 X .1 ft.
OB- 4.0 X .7 ft.
SP- .3 X .3 X 4.5 ft.

Grey Fox Arch ND 75
CWA LO- 3.2 X 1.4 ft.
OB- 3.2 X 2.3 ft.
SP- 5.0 X 5.0 X 8.0 ft.

Arrow Arch ND 76
FSA LO- 16.0 X 2.0 ft.
OB- 16.0 X 5.3 ft.
SP- 10.6 X 8.6 X 26.0 ft.

Tumbleweed Arch ND 77
FSA LO- 4.2 X 2.5 ft.
OB- 4.5 X 3.0 ft.
SP- 1.8 X 2.0 X 5.5 ft.

Cheatgrass Arch ND 78
SAA LO- 4.3 X 1.5 ft.
OB- 4.3 X 1.8 ft.
SP- 1.8 X 1.2 X 9.0 ft.

Pistol Arch ND 79
CWA LO- 23.0 X 1.5 ft.
OB- 97.0 X 39.0 ft.
SP- 9.0 X 10.0 X 124.0 ft.

Lattice Arch ND 80
ECA LO- 6.5 X 1.1 ft.
OB- 6.5 X 1.1 ft.
SP- 3.8 X 7.3 X 20.5 ft.

Rolled Arch ND 81
CWA LO- 6.0 X .5 ft.
OB- 34.0 X .5 ft.
SP- 3.8 X 1.6 X 45.0 ft.

Hidden Arch ND 82
FSA LO- 35.0 X 26.4 ft.
OB- 41.0 X 26.4 ft.
SP- 26.0 X 22.0 X 61.0 ft.

Pet Arch ND 83
CWA LO- 5.0 X .5 ft.
OB- 7.2 X 4.5 ft.
SP- 10.0 X 21.0 X 21.5 ft.

Rubble Arch NW ND 84
FSA LO- 1.5 X 3.3 ft.
OB- 1.5 X 3.3 ft.
SP- 1.3 X .8 X NA ft.

See Preceding Photo

The larger slanted opening on the left is "Rubble Arch Southeast". The span of "Rubble Arch Northwest" is just barely visible to the right of the larger opening

Rubble Arch SW ND 85
ECA LO- 5.5 X 1.4 ft.
OB- 5.5 X 1.4 ft.
SP- 3.1 X .7 X 5.5 ft.

Destruction Arch ND 86
CWA LO- 3.3 X .8 ft.
OB- 6.2 X 2.4 ft.
SP- 1.4 X .7 X 6.2 ft.

Fantasy Arch ND 87
JHA LO- .5 X 4.0 ft.
OB- .5 X 4.0 ft.
SP- 6.0 X 5.5 X 30.0 ft.

Tongue Arch SD 1
FSA LO- 3.8 X 3.0 ft.
OB- 7.9 X 3.0 ft.
SP- 1.5 X 1.5 X 10.0 ft.

Caterpillar Arch SD 2
ECA LO- 3.5 X .4 ft.
OB- 3.5 X .4 ft.
SP- .7 X 2.0 X 7.0 ft.

Pool Arch SD 3
CWA LO- 7.5 X .4 ft.
OB- 12.0 X 1.3 ft.
SP- 2.9 X .9 X 17.0 ft.

See Preceding Photo

"Skeptical Arch is indicated by the arrow on the right. The left arrow points to "Willow Arch".

Willow Arch SD 4
CWA LO- 18.5 X .8 ft.
OB- 54.0 X 2.5 ft.
SP- 5.7 X 2.5 X 78.0 ft.

Skeptical Arch SD 5
JHA LO- .5 X 5.0 ft.
OB- 1.5 X 15.0 ft.
SP- 1.5 X .4 X 15.0 ft.

Shelf Arch SD 6
CWA LO- 7.5 X .1 ft.
OB- 7.5 X 3.2 ft.
SP- 1.5 X .5 X 13.0 ft.

See Preceding Photo

"Dah Arch" is the larger of the lens-shaped openings on the right hand side.

Anteater Arch SD 7
ECA LO- 3.5 X 1.0 ft.
OB- 3.5 X 1.0 ft.
SP- .4 X .4 X 7.0 ft.

Doo Arch SD 8
ECA LO- 5.0 X .5 ft.
OB- 5.0 X .5 ft.
SP- 1.0 X .5 X 6.0 ft.

Dah Arch SD 9
FSA LO- 5.4 X 2.0 ft.
OB- 5.4 X 2.0 ft.
SP- 12.0 X 12.0 X NA ft.

Shadow Box Arch SD 10
FSA LO- 8.2 X 3.6 ft.
OB- 8.2 X 3.6 ft.
SP- 20.0 X 21.0 X 25.0 ft.

Around Back Arch SD 11
ECA LO- 4.5 X .5 ft.
OB- 17.0 X 3.5 ft.
SP- 5.2 X 3.3 X 17.0 ft.

Two Blocks Arch SD 12
FSA LO- 19.7 X 7.0 ft.
OB- 24.5 X 7.0 ft.
SP- 9.3 X 9.3 X 33.0 ft.

Box Arch SD 13
FSA LO- 31.0 X 14.5 ft
OB- 31.0 X 14.5 ft.
SP- 13.0 X 8.5 X 69.0 ft.

Ringtail A Lower SD 14
FSA LO- 13.3 X 4.8 ft.
OB- 13.3 X 4.8 ft.
SP- 4.5 X 11.6 X 21.0 ft.

Ringtail A Upper SD 15
ECA LO- 3.3 X 1.1 ft.
OB- 3.3 X 1.1 ft.
SP- 1.0 X 2.3 X NA ft.

See Preceding Photo

"Ringtail Arch Upper" is above and to the left of the obvious larger opening of "Ringtail Arch Lower".

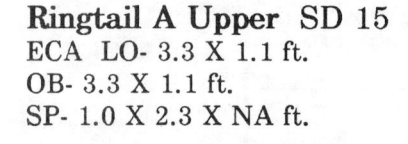

Dead Juniper Arch SD 16
ECA LO- 3.1 X 1.3 ft.
OB- 5.0 X 1.3 ft.
SP- 4.5 X 5.5 X NA ft.

Double O A Upper SD 17
FSA LO- 66.5 X 35.3 ft.
OB- 66.5 X 35.3 ft.
SP- 11.0 X 9.5 X 130.0 ft.

Double O A Lower SD 18
FSA LO- 21.1 X 9.3 ft.
OB- 21.1 X 9.3 ft.
SP- 11.0 X 11.2 X 55.0 ft.

See Preceding Photo

What appears as a dark hole below the left edge of the large arch is "Double O Arch Lower".

Nand Arch Outer SD 19
CWA LO- 164.0 X 2.0 ft.
OB- 205.0 X 56.0 ft.
SP- 11.0 X 20.0 X 250.0 ft.

Nand Arch Inner SD 20
CWA LO- 45.0 X .3 ft.
OB- 170.0 X 57.0 ft.
SP- 2.0 X 20.0 X 185.0 ft.

See Preceding Photo

The "Inner" arch is not obvious on the photo as it is behind and parallel to the "Outer" arch.

Sand Arch Outer SD 21
CWA LO- 19.0 X 3.0 ft.
OB- 87.0 X 78.0 ft.
SP- 6.0 X 29.0 X 104.0 ft.

See Preceding Photo

The "Inner" arch is not obvious on the photo as it is behind and parallel to the "Outer" arch.

Sand Arch Inner SD 22
CWA LO- 68.0 X 3.8 ft.
OB- 78.0 X 83.0 ft.
SP- 7.0 X 34.0 X 85.0 ft.

Contoured Arch SD 23
CWA LO- 17.5 X .5 ft.
OB- 17.5 X 8.8 ft.
SP- 2.3 X 3.2 X 19.0 ft.

Black Arch SD 24
FSA LO- 70.8 X 39.0 ft.
OB- 70.8 X 39.0 ft.
SP- 12.0 X 57.0 X 71.0 ft.

Camel Leg Arch SD 25
SAA LO- 3.4 X 2.0 ft.
OB- 4.3 X 2.0 ft.
SP- .8 X 1.3 X 4.8 ft.

Lazy Arch SD 26
CWA LO- 8.0 X 2.5 ft.
OB- 15.0 X 3.2 ft.
SP- 1.8 X 1.2 X 19.0 ft.

Search Party Ar SD 27
CWA LO- 4.0 X .1 ft.
OB- 6.0 X 1.2 ft.
SP- .9 X 1.3 X 12.0 ft.

Rabbit Trap Arch SD 28
SAA LO- 7.0 X 2.0 ft.
OB- 7.0 X 2.0 ft.
SP- .8 X .6 X 7.0 ft.

Trail Arch SD 29
CWA LO- 7.5 X .3 ft.
OB- 10.0 X 2.0 ft.
SP- 2.5 X 3.0 X 10.0 ft.

Black Cave Outer SD 30
CWA LO- 32.0 X .2 ft.
OB- 76.0 X 22.9 ft.
SP- 14.0 X 12.5 X 88.0 ft.

See Preceding Photo

The "Inner" arch is not obvious on the photo as it is behind and parallel to the "Outer" arch.

Black Cave Inner SD 31
CWA LO- 16.0 X .3 ft.
OB- 70.0 X 30.5 ft.
SP- 2.5 X .9 X 70.0 ft.

Beam Arch SD 32
CWA LO- 4.3 X .3 ft.
OB- 5.3 X .6 ft.
SP- .8 X .7 X 8.4 ft.

Boost Arch SD 33
SAA LO- 6.0 X 5.0 ft.
OB- 6.0 X 5.0 ft.
SP- .7 X 6.3 X 10.0 ft.

Limbo Arch SD 34
CWA LO- 10.0 X .5 ft.
OB- 19.8 X 9.9 ft.
SP- 6.0 X 7.4 X 20.0 ft.

Debris Arch SD 35
FSA LO- 85.0 X 12.5 ft.
OB- 85.0 X 15.0 ft.
SP- 15.0 X 29.0 X 135.0 ft.

Tip Top Arch SD 36
FSA LO- 4.3 X 4.6 ft.
OB- 4.3 X 4.6 ft.
SP- 3.0 X 8.2 X NA ft.

Wedge Arch SD 37
FSA LO- 6.7 X 2.0 ft.
OB- 11.7 X 10.0 ft.
SP- 7.0 X 8.8 X NA ft.

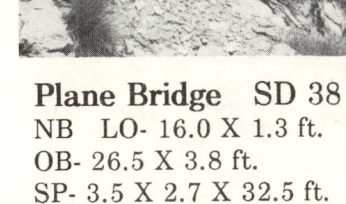

Plane Bridge SD 38
NB LO- 16.0 X 1.3 ft.
OB- 26.5 X 3.8 ft.
SP- 3.5 X 2.7 X 32.5 ft.

Crystal Ar South SD 39
FSA LO- 5.5 X 8.0 ft.
OB- 5.5 X 8.0 ft.
SP- 12.0 X 25.0 X 125.0 ft.

See Preceding Photo

The smaller opening in the upper right corner of the photo is "Crystal Arch North".

Crystal Ar North SD 40
FSA LO- 31.0 X 27.2 ft.
OB- 31.0 X 27.2 ft.
SP- 23.5 X 44.0 X 125.0 ft.

Blocked Arch SD 41
CWA LO- 14.0 X .5 ft.
OB- 20.0 X 17.0 ft.
SP- 9.0 X 20.0 X 32.0 ft.

White Fin Arch SD 42
FSA LO- 22.0 X 5.0 ft.
OB- 22.0 X 5.0 ft.
SP- 7.5 X 3.5 X 35.0 ft.

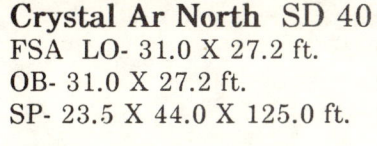

Terminal Arch SD 43
ECA LO- 4.0 X .5 ft.
OB- 5.5 X 1.5 ft.
SP- 4.0 X 4.0 X 8.5 ft.

Lichen Arch SD 44
FSA LO- 5.0 X 2.0 ft.
OB- 5.0 X 2.0 ft.
SP- 3.5 X 5.1 X NA ft.

Fallen Slab Br SD 45
NB LO- 10.0 X .4 ft.
OB- 48.0 X 11.3 ft.
SP- 2.0 X 6.0 X 48.0 ft.

Washboard Arch SD 46
CWA LO- 3.5 X .2 ft.
OB- 6.9 X 5.0 ft.
SP- 1.5 X 4.0 X 7.0 ft.

Stem Arch SD 47
JHA LO- .4 X 5.0 ft.
OB- .4 X 5.0 ft.
SP- .8 X .5 X 6.5 ft.

Exfoliation Arch SD 48
PFA LO- 9.2 X .8 ft.
OB- 9.2 X .8 ft.
SP- 2.1 X .3 X 9.2 ft.

Navajo Arch SD 49
FSA LO- 41.0 X 13.3 ft.
OB- 41.0 X 13.3 ft.
SP- 31.0 X 34.0 X 77.0 ft.

Wall Arch SD 50
FSA LO- 71.0 X 33.5 ft.
OB- 71.0 X 33.5 ft.
SP- 7.0 X 8.0 X 115.0 ft.

Guano Arch SD 51
CWA LO- 25.0 X 1.2 ft.
OB- 29.0 X 8.9 ft.
SP- 6.0 X 8.0 X 45.0 ft.

See Preceding Photo

"Magpie Arch South" is to the left of "Magpie Arch North" which is in the center of the photo near the crest of the rock face.

Magpie Arch North SD 52
CWA LO- 10.0 X .5 ft.
OB- 14.0 X 1.0 ft.
SP- .6 X 1.8 X 19.0 ft.

Magpie Arch South SD 53
CWA LO- 3.3 X .4 ft.
OB- 3.3 X .4 ft.
SP- .5 X .2 X 3.3 ft.

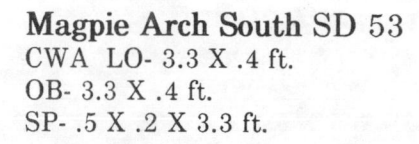

Partition Ar No SD 54
FSA LO- 29.8 X 30.0 ft.
OB- 76.0 X 30.6 ft.
SP- 24.0 X 38.0 X 135.0 ft.

See Preceding Photo

The smaller of the two openings is "Partition Arch South".

Partition Ar So SD 55
FSA LO- 8.5 X 9.1 ft.
OB- 8.5 X 9.1 ft.
SP- 31.0 X 48.0 X 135.0 ft.

Landscape Arch SD 56
FSA LO-306.0 X 88.6 ft.
OB- 306.0 X 88.6 ft.
SP- 15.5 X 16.0 X 434.0 ft.

Coke Oven Arch SD 57
CWA LO- 28.0 X 5.5 ft.
OB- 28.0 X 14.0 ft.
SP- 7.0 X 8.9 X 37.0 ft.

Devils Eye Arch SD 58
CWA LO- 5.0 X .8 ft.
OB- 5.0 X 2.8 ft.
SP- 5.0 X 15.0 X 14.0 ft.

Canopy Arch SD 59
CWA LO- 4.0 X .5 ft.
OB- 4.0 X 3.5 ft.
SP- 3.0 X 10.0 X 5.0 ft.

Tee Arch SD 60
FSA LO- 5.5 X 2.0 ft.
OB- 5.5 X 2.0 ft.
SP- 7.0 X 4.0 X 7.0 ft.

Crossbow Arch SD 61
CWA LO- 11.0 X 1.0 ft.
OB- 11.2 X 3.5 ft.
SP- 6.0 X 15.0 X 14.0 ft.

Ledge Arch SD 62
CWA LO- 73.0 X 1.3 ft.
OB- 73.0 X 13.0 ft.
SP- 2.3 X 4.0 X 89.0 ft.

Perseverance Arch SD 63
CWA LO- 6.5 X 2.0 ft.
OB- 6.5 X 2.0 ft.
SP- 4.0 X 5.0 X 11.5 ft.

Pine Tree Arch SD 64
FSA LO- 45.0 X 44.0 ft.
OB- 45.0 X 44.0 ft.
SP- 23.0 X 35.0 X 120.0 ft.

Devils Jughandle SD 65
JHA LO- 2.0 X 5.0 ft.
OB- 2.0 X 5.0 ft.
SP- 1.0 X 2.0 X 18.0 ft.

Punch Bowl Arch SD 66
FSA LO- 4.5 X 1.1 ft.
OB- 4.5 X 1.1 ft.
SP- 3.5 X 1.2 X 5.5 ft.

See Preceding Photo

"Pan Arch" is shown by the arrow on the right.

Pot Arch SD 67
CWA LO- 10.0 X .2 ft.
OB- 10.0 X 2.0 ft.
SP- 4.0 X 10.0 X 20.0 ft.

Pan Arch SD 68
CWA LO- 11.0 X .2 ft.
OB- 11.0 X 5.5 ft.
SP- 5.5 X 10.0 X 11.0 ft.

Least Arch SD 69
ECA LO- 4.5 X .1 ft.
OB- 4.5 X .1 ft.
SP- .8 X 4.5 X 8.0 ft.

Urn Arch SD 70
PHA LO- 5.1 X 10.2 ft.
OB- 5.1 X 10.2 ft.
SP- .2 X .2 X 23.0 ft.

Rock Catcher Arch SD 71
CWA LO- 5.0 X 1.0 ft.
OB- 21.5 X 16.9 ft.
SP- 2.0 X 3.5 X 29.0 ft.

Tunnel Arch SD 72
FSA LO- 23.5 X 25.8 ft.
OB- 23.5 X 25.8 ft.
SP- 15.0 X 37.0 X 27.0 ft.

See Preceding Photo

"East Tunnel Arch" is above and to the left of "Tunnel Arch". It is actually to the southeast, not due east of the larger opening.

East Tunnel Arch SD 73
PHA LO- 12.0 X 6.9 ft.
OB- 15.9 X 10.2 ft.
SP- 11.0 X 6.2 X 25.0 ft.

Styled Arch SD 74
PAA LO- 18.9 X 8.9 ft.
OB- 63.0 X 12.9 ft.
SP- 16.5 X 29.0 X 109.0 ft.

Arc de Triomphe SD 75
CWA LO- 15.0 X 1.0 ft.
OB- 20.0 X 17.0 ft.
SP- 10.0 X 5.7 X 35.0 ft.

Diamond Arch SD 76
FSA LO- 19.7 X 14.0 ft.
OB- 19.7 X 14.0 ft.
SP- 11.0 X 21.0 X 38.0 ft.

Tapestry Arch SD 77
FSA LO- 46.0 X 13.0 ft.
OB- 50.5 X 30.5 ft.
SP- 14.0 X 14.0 X 68.0 ft.

Ruin Arch SD 78
CWA LO- 59.0 X 1.1 ft.
OB- 71.0 X 12.5 ft.
SP- 25.5 X 17.0 X 115.0 ft.

Skyline Arch SD 79
FSA LO- 71.0 X 33.5 ft.
OB- 71.0 X 33.5 ft.
SP- 24.0 X 13.2 X 90.0 ft.

Goblet Arch SD 80
JHA LO- 1.5 X 4.5 ft.
OB- 1.5 X 4.5 ft.
SP- 3.0 X 2.2 X 6.0 ft.

Rinky Dink Arch SD 81
SAA LO- 3.5 X 1.5 ft.
OB- 4.1 X 1.8 ft.
SP- 1.4 X 2.0 X NA ft.

Dogbone Arch SD 82
CWA LO- 8.8 X 1.0 ft.
OB- 11.5 X 13.0 ft.
SP- 1.2 X 1.5 X 14.0 ft.

Squeezed Jughand SD 83
JHA LO- 10.2 X .6 ft.
OB- 13.0 X .6 ft.
SP- 4.2 X 2.9 X 19.0 ft.

Broken Arch SD 84
FSA LO- 53.0 X 41.0 ft.
OB- 53.0 X 41.0 ft.
SP- 17.0 X 12.0 X 78.0 ft.

Magic Mystery Br SD 85
NB   LO- 62.0 X 12.0 ft.
OB- 62.0 X 48.0 ft.
SP- 11.0 X 8.0 X 95.0 ft.

Raindrop Arch KB 1
CWA LO- 10.6 X 1.7 ft.
OB- 10.6 X 1.7 ft.
SP- 5.5 X 9.0 X 18.0 ft.

Cliff Crest Arch KB 2
PFA LO- 7.9 X .6 ft.
OB- 7.9 X .6 ft.
SP- 2.1 X .3 X 14.0 ft.

Buckle Arch KB 3
FSA LO- 4.0 X 1.2 ft.
OB- 4.0 X 1.2 ft.
SP- .5 X .5 X 4.0 ft.

Five Hundred Br KB 4
NB LO- 6.0 X 2.3 ft.
OB- 6.0 X 2.3 ft.
SP- 4.7 X 3.2 X 9.0 ft.

Turtle Shell Arch KB 5
CWA LO- 4.5 X 1.5 ft.
OB- 4.5 X 1.8 ft.
SP- 5.0 X 2.0 X 19.0 ft.

Thigh in the Sky KB 6
JHA LO- 14.5 X 2.0 ft.
OB- 14.5 X 2.0 ft.
SP- 2.8 X 1.4 X 16.0 ft.

Tower Arch KB 7
FSA LO- 101 X 45 ft.
OB- 101.0 X 45.0 ft.
SP- 28.0 X 46.0 X 145.0 ft.

Cavity Arch KB 8
CWA LO- 6.0 X .6 ft.
OB- 43.0 X 34.0 ft.
SP- 9.0 X 12.0 X 43.0 ft.

Parallel Ar Outer KB 9
CWA LO- 32.0 X 1.0 ft.
OB- 36.0 X 40.0 ft.
SP- 4.0 X 4.5 X 68.0 ft.

See Preceding Photo

The "Inner" arch is behind, lower, and parallel to the "Outer" arch.

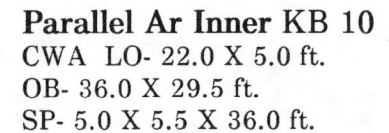

Parallel Ar Inner KB 10
CWA LO- 22.0 X 5.0 ft.
OB- 36.0 X 29.5 ft.
SP- 5.0 X 5.5 X 36.0 ft.

Buffalo Arch KB 11
FSA LO- 3.9 X 2.8 ft.
OB- 3.9 X 2.8 ft.
SP- .5 X 1.2 X 6.9 ft.

Anniversary Ar No KB 12
FSA LO- 16.0 X 11.0 ft.
OB- 16.0 X 11.0 ft.
SP- 16.0 X 40.0 X 23.0 ft.

See Preceding Photo

"Anniversary Arch South" shows in the photo as the closest (left) arch.

Anniversary Ar So KB 13
FSA LO- 7.2 X 6.5 ft.
OB- 14.0 X 7.0 ft.
SP- 15.0 X 8.0 X 19.0 ft.

Recon Bridge KB 14
NB LO- 3.3 X .3 ft.
OB- 4.5 X .7 ft.
SP- 1.6 X .3 X 4.6 ft.

Wine Bottle Arch KB 15
ECA LO- 1.5 X 6.0 ft.
OB- 9.8 X 6.0 ft.
SP- 4.0 X 4.2 X NA ft.

Sand Hill Arch KB 16
CWA LO- 48.0 X 1.5 ft.
OB- 55.0 X 34.0 ft.
SP- 9.0 X 13.0 X 60.0 ft.

Chunk Arch KB 17
CWA LO- 65.0 X 1.0 ft.
OB- 65.0 X 23.0 ft.
SP- 19.0 X 12.0 X 127.0 ft.

Rock in the Hole KB 18
ECA LO- 7.0 X .4 ft.
OB- 9.5 X 3.7 ft.
SP- 13.0 X 12.0 X NA ft.

Clover Canyon Arch FF 1
CWA LO- 31.0 X 1.5 ft.
OB- 88.0 X 30.0 ft.
SP- 13.0 X 26.0 X 88.0 ft.

Sand Dune Arch FF 2
FSA LO- 25.0 X 11.5 ft.
OB- 34.0 X 11.5 ft.
SP- 8.0 X 2.5 X 45.0 ft.

Slit Arch FF 3
ECA LO- 19.0 X 1.3 ft.
OB- 35.0 X 1.3 ft.
SP- 16.0 X 15.0 X 35.00 ft.

Garbage Arch FF 4
ECA LO- 4.4 X 1.0 ft.
OB- 4.4 X 1.5 ft.
SP- 3.0 X 1.5 X NA ft.

Tail Arch FF 5
JHA LO- .5 X 3.4 ft.
OB- .5 X 3.4 ft.
SP- 2.8 X 1.4 X 5.0 ft.

Biscuitroot Arch FF 6
CWA LO- 3.0 X .1 ft.
OB- 3.0 X .5 ft.
SP- .5 X 1.5 X 3.5 ft.

Vulture Arch FF 7
FSA LO- 5.9 X 1.8 ft.
OB- 5.9 X 1.8 ft.
SP- .4 X .1 X 5.9 ft.

Fragile Arch FF 8
JHA LO- 3.5 X .7 ft.
OB- 3.5 X 1.5 ft.
SP- .4 X .3 X 4.5 ft.

Hoof Arch FF 9
CWA LO- 3.3 X .2 ft.
OB- 3.3 X 1.7 ft.
SP- .2 X 3.5 X 6.0 ft.

Swept Arch   FF 10
JHA LO- 13.0 X 1.2 ft.
OB- 13.0 X 1.2 ft.
SP- 4.2 X 1.5 X 33.0 ft.

Pagoda Arch   FF 11
FSA LO- 7.5 X 1.9 ft.
OB- 7.5 X 1.9 ft.
SP- 7.5 X 3.1 X NA ft.

Mukluk Arch   FF 12
FSA LO- 3.9 X 3.7 ft.
OB- 3.9 X 3.7 ft.
SP- 3.0 X 2.9 X NA ft.

Roadside Arch   FF 13
CWA LO- 48.0 X 1.0 ft.
OB- 64.0 X 44.0 ft.
SP- 29.0 X 58.0 X 96.0 ft.

Monocle Arch   FF 14
FSA LO- 4.4 X 1.4 ft.
OB- 4.4 X 1.4 ft.
SP- .9 X 3.0 X 7.0 ft.

Mini Spectacles N FF 15
FSA LO- 3.2 X 1.5 ft.
OB- 3.2 X 1.5 ft.
SP- 1.1 X 3.8 X NA ft.

See Preceding Photo

"Mini Spectacles Arch South" shows in the photo as the opening on the left.

Mini Spectacles S FF 16
FSA LO- 4.5 X 1.1 ft.
OB- 4.5 X 1.1 ft.
SP- 1.4 X 3.1 X NA ft.

Crocodile Arch   FF 17
CWA LO- 8.8 X .3 ft.
OB- 12.5 X 1.5 ft.
SP- 2.2 X 1.5 X 17.0 ft.

Strap Arch   FF 18
CWA LO- 4.0 X .1 ft.
OB- 6.5 X .5 ft.
SP- .5 X .2 X 7.8 ft.

Elephant Chin Ar FF 19
FSA LO- 13.0 X 8.0 ft.
OB- 13.0 X 8.0 ft.
SP- 9.0 X 35.0 X 20.0 ft.

Reptile Arch   FF 20
ECA LO- 4.5 X .5 ft.
OB- 4.5 X .5 ft.
SP- 3.7 X 2.7 X 9.0 ft.

Secretive Arch FF 21
ECA LO- 3.3 X .3 ft.
OB- 3.7 X .4 ft.
SP- 1.1 X .4 X 5.5 ft.

Webbing Arch   FF 22
CWA LO- 15.0 X .5 ft.
OB- 15.0 X 5.0 ft.
SP- 7.0 X 27.0 X 18.0 ft.

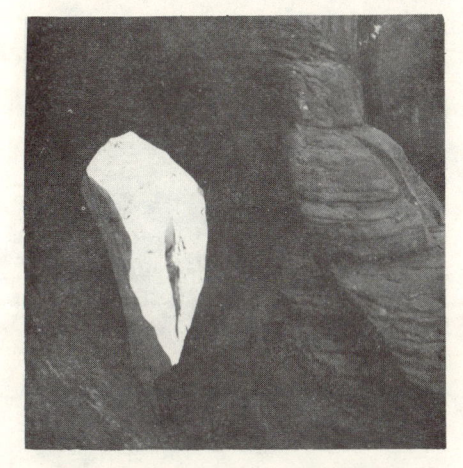

Teardrop Arch   FF 23
FSA LO- 17.0 X 3.2 ft.
OB- 17.0 X 21.0 ft.
SP- 3.2 X 6.0 X 24.0 ft.

Queue Jughandle FF 24
JHA LO- 1.0 X 3.0 ft.
OB- 1.0 X 3.0 ft.
SP- 1.6 X 1.5 X NA ft.

Wine Glass Arch FF 25
CWA LO- 8.0 X .8 ft.
OB- 27.0 X 16.0 ft.
SP- 6.0 X 6.4 X 34.0 ft.

Cliff Arch   FF 26
CWA LO- 27.5 X 3.5 ft.
OB- 38.0 X 12.0 ft.
SP- 15.0 X 11.0 X 39.0 ft.

Surprise Arch FF 27
FSA LO- 63.0 X 11.0 ft.
OB- 63.0 X 53.0 ft.
SP- 5.3 X 5.0 X 87.0 ft.

Unseen Arch FF 28
FSA LO- 5.0 X 6.0 ft.
OB- 5.0 X 6.0 ft.
SP- 5.0 X 4.5 X 14.0 ft.

Hole in Fin FF 29
FSA LO- 13.0 X 9.0 ft.
OB- 13.0 X 16.0 ft.
SP- 8.0 X 27.0 X 15.0 ft.

Dual Arch NE FF 30
ECA LO- 4.4 X 1.8 ft.
OB- 2.8 X 5.3 ft.
SP- 4.5 X 11.0 X 8.0 ft.

See Preceding Photo

"DualArchSouthwest" shows in the photo as the opening on the left.

Dual Arch SW FF 31
ECA LO- 4.0 X 1.7 ft.
OB- 4.0 X 4.5 ft.
SP- 4.5 X 11.0 X 8.0 ft.

Apostrophe Arch FF 32
FSA LO- 3.9 X 6.0 ft.
OB- 3.9 X 6.0 ft.
SP- 2.9 X 6.0 X 7.0 ft.

Dream Arch FF 33
CWA LO- 14.0 X 2.5 ft.
OB- 14.0 X 16.0 ft.
SP- 3.5 X 8.0 X 25.0 ft.

Dragon Arch FF 34
CWA LO- 32.5 X .3 ft.
OB- 42.0 X 24.7 ft.
SP- 4.0 X 8.7 X 55.0 ft.

Lightning Bolt A FF 35
JHA LO- 1.5 X 20.0 ft.
OB- 1.5 X 40.0 ft.
SP- 5.0 X 2.0 X 51.0 ft.

E Arch FF 36
FSA LO- 3.1 X 5.0 ft.
OB- 3.1 X 5.0 ft.
SP- 4.0 X 10.0 X 7.0 ft.

Flatiron Arch FF 37
FSA LO- 14.0 X 4.5 ft.
OB- 14.0 X 5.5 ft.
SP- 8.0 X 7.0 X 19.0 ft.

Louver Arch FF 38
FSA LO- 3.0 X 11.0 ft.
OB- 3.0 X 11.0 ft.
SP- 5.0 X 13.5 X NA ft.

Kissing Turtles FF 39
FSA LO- 6.1 X 4.5 ft.
OB- 7.3 X 5.2 ft.
SP- 3.5 X 4.5 X 11.0 ft.

See Preceding Photo

"Twin Arch North" shows in the photo as the opening on the right.

Twin Arch South FF 40
FSA LO- 47.0 X 30.0 ft.
OB- 47.0 X 30.0 ft.
SP- 20.0 X 25.0 X 150.0 ft.

Twin Arch North FF 41
FSA LO- 27.8 X 27.0 ft
OB- 27.8 X 27.0 ft.
SP- 27.0 X 28.0 X 35.0 ft.

Sliver Arch FF 42
CWA LO- 6.0 X .2 ft.
OB- 6.0 X 14.5 ft.
SP- 1.1 X 3.5 X 8.3 ft.

Cloister Arch FF 43
CWA LO- 10.1 X 1.0 ft.
OB- 10.1 X 14.5 ft.
SP- 3.5 X 26.5 X 18.0 ft.

Crawl Thru Arch FF 44
ECA LO- 5.9 X 1.4 ft.
OB- 5.9 X 1.4 ft.
SP- 7.5 X 12.8 X NA ft.

Walk Thru Bridge FF 45
NB LO- 8.5 X 6.2 ft.
OB- 10.2 X 8.0 ft.
SP- 2.6 X 2.5 X 13.4 ft.

Inner Sanctum Br   FF 46
NB   LO- 11.5 X 14.0 ft.
OB- 11.5 X 20.0 ft.
SP- 7.8 X 5.0 X 30.0 ft.

Eiffel Tower Br   FF 47
NB   LO- 3.4 X 3.0 ft.
OB- 3.4 X 3.1 ft.
SP- 6.5 X 28.5 X 5.0 ft.

Whipped Cream Ar   FF 48
ECA   LO- 3.1 X .3 ft.
OB- 3.1 X .3 ft.
SP- 1.5 X 3.0 X NA ft.

Landmark Arch   FF 49
FSA   LO- 3.5 X 2.0 ft.
OB- 4.0 X 5.3 ft.
SP- 1.9 X .9 X 8.0 ft.

Talus Arch   FF 50
CWA   LO- 5.1 X .8 ft.
OB- 5.1 X 1.5 ft.
SP- 2.0 X 1.9 X 7.0 ft.

Bench Arch   FF 51
PHA   LO- 31.0 X 19.0 ft.
OB- 36.0 X 33.3 ft.
SP- 17.5 X 24.0 X 62.0 ft.

Swanky Arch SW 1
FSA LO- 19.5 X 5.0 ft.
OB- 19.5 X 5.0 ft.
SP- 18.0 X 25.0 X 48.0 ft.

Salt Wash Arch SW 2
PHA LO- 5.5 X 4.5 ft.
OB- 80.0 X 34.0 ft.
SP- 10.8 X 3.0 X 104.0 ft.

One Legged Arch SW 3
JHA LO- 3.0 X .8 ft.
OB- 3.2 X 2.4 ft.
SP- .4 X .6 X 4.6 ft.

Boot Arch SW 4
FSA LO- 2.0 X 5.0 ft.
OB- 4.5 X 5.0 ft.
SP- 2.2 X .8 X 6.5 ft.

Troubled Water Br SW 5
NB LO- 13.0 X 2.0 ft.
OB- 21.0 X 2.0 ft.
SP- 2.9 X 1.2 X 23.0 ft.

Morrison Bridge SW 6
NB LO- 3.8 X 1.3 ft.
OB- 3.8 X 3.0 ft.
SP- 51.0 X 5.2 X NA ft.

Brushy Basin Br SW 7
NB LO- 6.5 X 3.2 ft.
OB- 7.0 X 3.4 ft.
SP- 10.0 X 5.5 X NA ft.

Blue Arch SW 8
NB LO- 6.2 X 5.0 ft.
OB- 6.2 X 5.0 ft.
SP- 2.3 X 1.8 X NA ft.

Wolfe Ranch Arch SW 9
CWA LO- 10.5 X .5 ft.
OB- 10.5 X 7.0 ft.
SP- 4.5 X 5.5 X NA ft.

Cobblestone Br SW 10
NB LO- 11.0 X 2.0 ft.
OB- 11.0 X 2.0 ft.
SP- 5.0 X 1.3 X 30.0 ft.

Ivy Arch SW 11
CWA LO- 28.0 X 1.0 ft.
OB- 31.0 X 10.0 ft.
SP- 1.5 X 9.0 X 32.0 ft.

Wolfe Bluffs Arch SW 12
CWA LO- 141.0 X .5 ft.
OB- 190.0 X 28.5 ft.
SP- 31.0 X 33.4 X 210.0 ft.

Frame Arch SW 13
FSA LO- 14.5 X 12.5 ft.
OB- 14.5 X 12.5 ft.
SP- 13.0 X 14.0 X 18.0 ft.

Delicate Arch SW 14
FSA LO- 32.0 X 46.0 ft.
OB- 32.0 X 46.0 ft.
SP- 14.2 X 5.8 X NA ft.

Echo Arch SW 15
FSA LO- 16.5 X 13.2 ft.
OB- 43.0 X 26.0 ft.
SP- 20.0 X 14.0 X 62.0 ft.

Tapered Arch SW 16
PHA LO- 4.1 X 2.3 ft.
OB- 4.1 X 2.3 ft.
SP- 3.5 X 3.6 X 15.0 ft.

Cliff Top Arch SW 17
FSA LO- 6.0 X 2.8 ft.
OB- 6.0 X 2.8 ft.
SP- 7.0 X 3.1 X 8.0 ft.

Winter Camp Arch SW 18
SAA LO- 3.5 X 2.4 ft.
OB- 3.5 X 2.4 ft.
SP- .3 X .5 X 5.2 ft.

Donut Arch   SW 19
CWA LO- 3.1 X 1.4 ft.
OB- 4.9 X 6.8 ft.
SP- 4.0 X 1.4 X 6.0 ft.

Mirror Arch   SW 20
SAA LO- 5.5 X 4.0 ft.
OB- 5.5 X 4.0 ft.
SP- 2.1 X 8.0 X NA ft.

Solo Arch   SW 21
JHA LO-1.5 X 3.0 ft.
OB-4.0 X 3.0 ft.
SP-1.0 X 1.0 X 6.0 ft.

Diving Board Arch SW 22
CWA LO- 3.5 X .7 ft.
OB- 77.0 X 5.0 ft.
SP- 5.0 X 4.0 X 135.0 ft.

Goosehead Arch   SW 23
CWA LO- 7.5 X 1.0 ft.
OB- 7.5 X 21.0 ft.
SP- 7.0 X 10.7 X 37.5 ft.

Rim Arch   SW 24
CWA LO- 36.0 X .5 ft.
OB- 36.0 X 2.0 ft.
SP- 3.5 X 1.1 X 45.0 ft.

Illusion Arch HP 19
FSA LO- 2.0 X 8.0 ft.
OB- 2.0 X 8.0 ft.
SP- 6.0 X 4.5 X 11.0 ft.

Microphone Arch HP 20
FSA LO- 4.5 X 4.5 ft.
OB- 4.5 X 4.5 ft.
SP- 2.5 X 2.0 X 6.0 ft.

Top of the Slope A HP 1
CWA LO- 8.0 X .2 ft.
OB- 11.0 X 6.0 ft.
SP- 4.8 X 7.3 X 25.0 ft.

Hidden Canyon Arch HP 2
PAA LO- 7.5 X 2.5 ft.
OB- 20.0 X 3.2 ft.
SP- 39.0 X 22.0 X 75.0 ft.

Leaping Arch   HP 3
FSA LO- 47.0 X 50.0 ft.
OB- 68.0 X 52.0 ft.
SP- 7.0 X 7.0 X 100.0 ft.

Flying Buttress Ar HP 4
JHA LO- 21.0 X 2.0 ft.
OB- 21.0 X 24.0 ft.
SP- 11.0 X 7.0 X 35.0 ft.

Slot Arch   HP 5
ECA LO- 5.5 X .5 ft.
OB- 19.0 X 1.0 ft.
SP- 5.8 X 3.5 X 22.5 ft.

See Preceding Photo

"Slat Arch" is in the lower-central part of the photo, while "Slot Arch" is above and to the right of "Slat Arch".

Slat Arch   HP 6
ECA LO- 6.0 X 1.0 ft.
OB- 6.0 X 1.5 ft.
SP- 4.7 X 3.7 X 16.0 ft.

Attic Arch   HP 7
FSA LO- 5.0 X 2.5 ft.
OB- 7.0 X 6.0 ft.
SP- 6.0 X 10.0 X NA ft.

Eye of the Whale HP 8
FSA LO- 36.0 X 20.0 ft.
OB- 63.0 X 20.0 ft.
SP- 43.0 X 29.0 X 89.0 ft.

Lost and Found Br HP 9
NB LO- 14.6 X 2.5 ft.
OB- 14.6 X 2.5 ft.
SP- 1.8 X .5 X 16.0 ft.

Reflex Arch   HP 10
CWA LO- 15.0 X .2 ft.
OB- 15.0 X 2.2 ft.
SP- 4.2 X .9 X 28.0 ft.

Legbone Arch   HP 11
JHA LO- .2 X 3.2 ft.
OB- .2 X 3.2 ft.
SP- 2.0 X .2 X 5.8 ft.

Figure Arch   HP 12
CWA LO- 8.0 X .5 ft.
OB- 8.4 X 15.0 ft.
SP- 1.0 X 1.5 X 11.5 ft.

Sit Down Arch   HP 13
CWA LO- 12.0 X .3 ft.
OB- 15.0 X 1.5 ft.
SP- 2.9 X 1.8 X NA ft.

Falcon Arch   HP 14
ECA LO- 3.7 X .8 ft.
OB- 3.7 X .8 ft.
SP- 1.0 X 1.0 X NA ft.

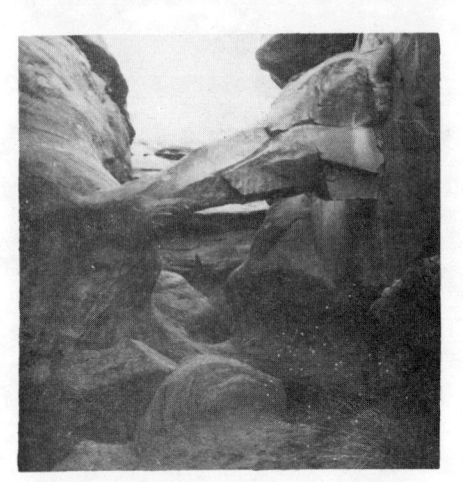

Concealed Bridge   HP 15
NB LO- 9.5 X 10.0 ft.
OB- 14.0 X 12.2 ft.
SP- 2.2 X 1.9 X 21.0 ft.

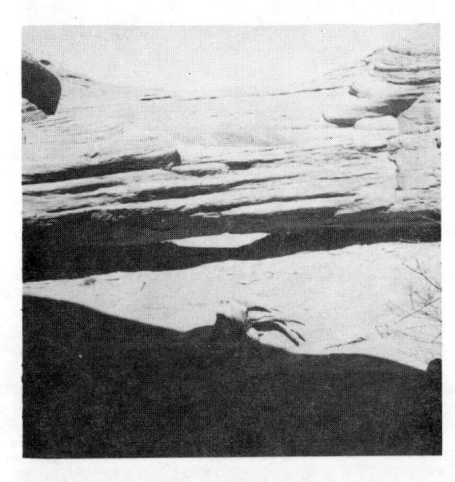

Dam Arch   HP 16
FSA LO- 8.0 X .9 ft.
OB- 8.0 X .9 ft.
SP- 5.5 X 3.2 X NA ft.

Slanted Eye Arch   HP 17
PFA LO- 15.0 X .7 ft.
OB- 31.0 X 14.0 ft.
SP- 4.0 X 1.4 X NA ft.

Willow Springs Br   HP 18
NB LO- 8.0 X 1.2 ft.
OB- 11.5 X 1.2 ft.
SP- 3.4 X .8 X NA ft.

See Saw Arch PB 1
SAA LO- 3.9 X .9 ft.
OB- 3.9 X .9 ft.
SP- 1.7 X .6 X 7.0 ft.

Horn of Plenty Ar PB 2
PAA LO- 5.2 X 1.3 ft.
OB- 9.0 X 2.5 ft.
SP- 15 X 17 X 14 ft.

E T Arch PB 3
JHA LO- .6 X 4.5 ft.
OB- .6 X 4.5 ft.
SP- 3.1 X .9 X 7.0 ft.

Ball Arch PB 4
CWA LO- 3.7 X 1.4 ft.
OB- 3.7 X 1.9 ft.
SP- .8 X 1.5 X 4.5 ft.

Perforated Pillar PB 5
SAA LO- 3.6 X 3.6 ft.
OB- 3.6 X 3.6 ft.
SP- 2.5 X .5 X 8.0 ft.

Piano Arch PB 6
SAA LO- 3.0 X 2.0 ft.
OB- 6.0 X 2.0 ft.
SP- 1.0 X .4 X NA ft.

Polypillar Arch N PB 7
SAA LO- 4.0 X .8 ft.
OB- 4.1 X 1.1 ft.
SP- 16.0 X 1.0 X 16.0 ft.

See Preceding Photo

The opening on the left side of the photo is "Polypillar Arch South".

Polypillar Arch S PB 8
SAA LO- 3.5 X .8 ft.
OB- 4.0 X 1.1 ft.
SP- 16.0 X 1.0 X 16.0 ft.

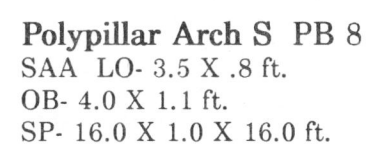

Big Top Arch PB 9
ECA LO- 4.5 X 1.1 ft.
OB- 4.5 X 1.1 ft.
SP- 3.5 X 1.4 X 6.0 ft.

See Preceding Photo

"Blackbrush Arch" is the small dark arch above and to the left of "Spalling Arch", which is located in the center of the photo.

Blackbrush Arch   PB 10
CWA LO- 4.5 X 1.0 ft.
OB- 4.5 X 1.9 ft.
SP- 6.0 X 1.0 X NA ft.

Spalling Arch   PB 11
CWA LO- 13.5 X 2.5 ft.
OB- 15.0 X 4.0 ft.
SP- 5.0 X 9.0 X 17.0 ft.

Stilt Arch   PB 12
CWA LO- 4.0 X .3 ft.
OB- 7.0 X 2.0 ft.
SP- 2.0 X 1.5 X 7.0 ft.

Potato Arch   PB 13
CWA LO- 3.5 X .4 ft.
OB- 5.0 X 2.5 ft.
SP- 3.0 X 4.5 X 9.0 ft.

Panorama Bluffs A PB 14
PAA LO- 4.9 X 1.3 ft.
OB- 8.7 X 6.0 ft.
SP- 5.5 X 14.7 X 10.5 ft.

Visor Arch   PB 15
CWA LO- 3.2 X .1 ft.
OB- 3.2 X 2.2 ft.
SP- 5.0 X 5.5 X 4.0 ft.

Neglected Arch   PB 16
CWA LO- 10.5 X 1.3 ft.
OB- 10.5 X 4.5 ft.
SP- .8 X 1.7 X 14.0 ft.

Clam Shell Arch   PB 17
SAA LO- 3.1 X .4 ft.
OB- 3.1 X .4 ft.
SP- 2.0 X 2.5 X NA ft.

Slope Arch   PB 18
CWA LO- 3.6 X 1.2 ft.
OB- 19.8 X 4.7 ft.
SP- 7.0 X 2.0 X 19.8 ft.

PANORAMA BLUFFS
⬅ Section

WINDOWS Section
⬇

Flame Arch   PB 19
FSA LO- 7.5 X 14.2 ft.
OB- 7.5 X 14.2 ft.
SP- 19.0 X 9.5 X 15.0 ft.

Tuba Arch   PB 20
SAA LO- 3.3 X .9 ft.
OB- 3.3 X .9 ft.
SP- 1.5 X .4 X 5.5 ft.

See Preceding Photo

The narrow slit above the main arch separates "Pot Hole Arch Upper" from "Pot Hole Arch Lower".

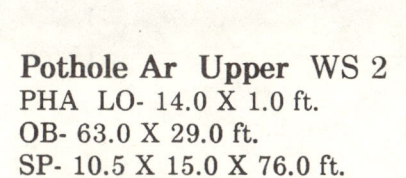

Pothole Ar Lower   WS 1
PHA LO- 37.0 X 20.0 ft.
OB- 67.0 X 24.0 ft.
SP- 4.5 X 1.9 X 76.0 ft.

Pothole Ar Upper   WS 2
PHA LO- 14.0 X 1.0 ft.
OB- 63.0 X 29.0 ft.
SP- 10.5 X 15.0 X 76.0 ft.

Cactus Arch   WS 3
PFA LO- 10.0 X .3 ft.
OB- 10.0 X .3 ft.
SP 7.5 X .5 X 35.0 ft.

Serpentine Arch   WS 4
FSA LO- 16.0 X 28.0 ft.
OB- 16.0 X 28.0 ft.
SP- 6.0 X 21.0 X NA ft.

Ghost Arch   WS 5
CWA LO- 9.0 X 1.3 ft.
OB- 32.0 X 64.0 ft.
SP- 6.4 X 7.0 X 36.0 ft.

Bow Tie Arch   WS 6
CWA LO- 4.0 X 1.0 ft.
OB- 13.6 X 14.0 ft.
SP 2.0 X 6.4 X 20.0 ft.

Porcupine Arch WS 7
CWA LO- 4.0 X 1.0 ft.
OB- 8.0 X 1.5 ft.
SP- 2.4 X .4 X 8.0 ft.

Sage Arch WS 8
FSA LO- 4.8 X 3.0 ft.
OB- 4.8 X 3.0 ft.
SP- 3.5 X 4.0 X NA ft.

Cove Arch WS 9
FSA LO- 50.0 X 33.5 ft.
OB- 50.0 X 38.0 ft.
SP- 27.0 X 158.0 X 65.0 ft.

Triangle Arch WS 10
FSA LO- 9.0 X 8.0 ft.
OB- 9.0 X 8.0 ft.
SP- 7.0 X 2.0 X NA ft.

Eagle Head Arch WS 11
PHA LO- 17.0 X 24.0 ft.
OB- 17.0 X 24.0 ft.
SP- 13.0 X 5.0 X 29.0 ft.

Ribbon Arch WS 12
FSA LO- 43.8 X 23.5 ft.
OB- 43.8 X 28.0 ft.
SP- 3.0 X .7 X 59.0 ft.

Alcove Arch WS 13
CWA LO- 16.0 X 1.0 ft.
OB- 92.0 X 51.0 ft.
SP- 20.0 X 11.0 X 106.0 ft.

Trough Arch WS 14
CWA LO- 5.0 X 3.0 ft.
OB- 6.5 X 9.0 ft.
SP- 5.0 X 3.5 X 11.0 ft.

Double Arch West WS 15
FSA LO- 61.0 X 86.0 ft.
OB- 67.0 X 86.0 ft.
SP- 34.0 X 37.0 X 95.0 ft.

See Preceding Photo

The obvious arch in the center of the photo is "Double Arch South". "Double Arch West" is through and to the left of "Double Arch South".

See WS 15 Photo

The arrow pointing to the dark slit in the span of "Double Arch South" shows "Narrow Arch".

Double Arch So   WS 16
FSA LO- 144 X 112 ft.
OB- 144.0 X 112.0 ft.
SP- 26.0 X 28.0 X 190 ft.

Narrow Arch   WS 17
ECA LO- 8.0 X 1.0 ft.
OB- 8.0 X 1.0 ft.
SP- 26.0 X 16.0 X 24.0 ft.

Jicama Arch   WS 18
JHA LO- 2.0 X 10.0 ft.
OB- 2.0 X 10.0 ft.
SP- 5.6 X 4.5 X 34.0 ft.

Christmas Tree Ar WS 19
FSA LO- 21.0 X 28.0 ft.
OB- 21.0 X 28.0 ft.
SP- 11.0 X 13.0 X 36.0 ft.

Raven Arch   WS 20
ECA LO- 7.0 X 2.5 ft.
OB- 7.0 X 2.5 ft.
SP- 7.0 X 26.0 X NA ft.

Parade of Eleph N WS 21
FSA LO- 17.0 X 21.0 ft.
OB- 17.0 X 21.0 ft.
SP- 22.0 X 48.0 X 25.0 ft.

Parade of Eleph S WS 22
CWA LO- 68.0 X 10.0 ft.
OB- 68.0 X 90.0 ft.
SP- 24.0 X 38.0 X 122.0 ft.

Mule Deer Arch   WS 23
ECA LO- 4.8 X .6 ft.
OB- 4.8 X .6 ft.
SP- 3.0 X 6.3 X NA ft.

Drumstick Arch   WS 24
CWA LO- 8.6 X .1 ft.
OB- 37.5 X 12.0 ft.
SP- 2.6 X 3.0 X 43.0 ft.

Little Duck Win WS 25
FSA LO- 8.0 X 3.5 ft.
OB- 8.0 X 3.5 ft.
SP- 6.0 X 8.5 X 12.0 ft.

Thanksgiving Br WS 26
NB LO- 5.2 X .7 ft.
OB- 6.2 X 2.1 ft.
SP- 1.3 X .5 X 11.0 ft.

Gimpy Arch WS 27
PFA LO- 5.0 X .1 ft.
OB- 5.0 X .1 ft.
SP- 4.5 X .7 X 16.0 ft.

Scab Arch WS 28
PFA LO- 4.0 X .3 ft.
OB- 5.3 X .3 ft.
SP- .9 X .2 X 8.0 ft.

Seagull Arch WS 29
FSA LO- 22.7 X 18.2 ft.
OB- 22.7 X 18.2 ft.
SP- 30.0 X 63.0 X NA ft.

See Preceding Photo

"Biceps Arch" is the large arch in the center of the photo. "Seagull Arch" is the smaller opening below and to the left of "Biceps Arch".

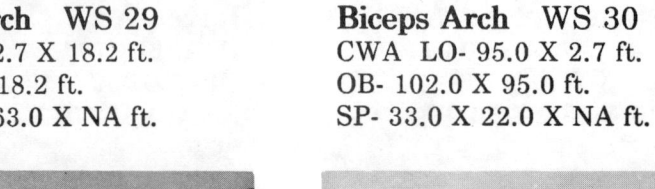

Biceps Arch WS 30
CWA LO- 95.0 X 2.7 ft.
OB- 102.0 X 95.0 ft.
SP- 33.0 X 22.0 X NA ft.

North Window WS 31
FSA LO- 90.0 X 48.0 ft.
OB- 90.0 X 48.0 ft.
SP- 26.0 X 49.0 X 113.0 ft.

South Window WS 32
FSA LO- 115 X 56.0 ft.
OB- 115.0 X 56.0 ft.
SP- 32.0 X 37.0 X 145.0 ft.

Turret Arch North WS 33
FSA LO- 35.0 X 65.0 ft.
OB- 35.0 X 65.0 ft.
SP- 16.0 X 19.0 X 35.0 ft.

See Preceding Photo

The smaller arch to the left in the photo is "Turret Arch South".

Turret Arch South WS 34
FSA LO- 10.5 X 12.0 ft.
OB- 10.5 X 12.0 ft.
SP- 18.0 X 38.0 X NA ft.

Sunlight Arch WS 35
ECA LO- .3 X 3.5 ft.
OB- .3 X 3.5 ft.
SP- 7.0 X 2.0 X 9.0 ft.

Bighorn Arch WS 36
FSA LO- 9.0 X 8.0 ft.
OB- 9.0 X 8.0 ft.
SP- 4.0 X 43.0 X NA ft.

See Preceding Photo

The two spans of these arches can be seen in the photo below the arrow. "Duplex Arch Lower" is below, but in line with "Duplex Arch Upper".

Dry Falls Arch WS 37
CWA LO- 3.1 X .2 ft.
OB- 3.1 X .7 ft.
SP- .8 X .3 X 8.0 ft.

Duplex Arch Upper WS 38
CWA LO- 5.5 X .3 ft.
OB- 5.5 X .6 ft.
SP- .8 X .4 X 9.0 ft.

Duplex Arch Lower WS 39
CWA LO- 5.5 X .5 ft.
OB- 6.0 X .5 ft.
SP- .6 X .2 X 9.0 ft.

Sunglass Arch WS 40
SAA LO- 4.0 X 1.3 ft.
OB- 4.6 X 1.4 ft.
SP- .7 X .7 X 4.6 ft.

Reverend Arch WS 41
JHA LO- .9 X 4.9 ft.
OB- .9 X 4.9 ft.
SP- 1.2 X .3 X 7.0 ft.

Sink Arch WS 42
FSA LO- 3.1 X .8 ft.
OB- 3.1 X 1.6 ft.
SP- 3.5 X 1.4 X 7.0 ft.

Ephedra Arch GW 1
CWA LO- 4.0 X 1.0 ft.
OB- 8.0 X 9.0 ft.
SP- 3.6 X .8 X 9.0 ft.

Little Pothole Ar GW 2
PHA LO- 3.5 X 3.6 ft.
OB- 5.5 X 4.5 ft.
SP- 4.0 X 5.8 X 10.0 ft.

Barbed Arch GW 3
FSA LO- 3.5 X 3.6 ft.
OB- 3.5 X 3.6 ft.
SP- 3.0 X 3.0 X 18.0 ft.

Arch of Motion GW 4
FSA LO- 24.5 X 10.0 ft.
OB- 24.5 X 10.0 ft.
SP- 9.5 X 11.5 X 42.0 ft.

Regained Arch GW 5
CWA LO- 8.0 X 1.5 ft.
OB- 8.5 X 1.5 ft.
SP- 2.6 X 3.1 X 8.5 ft.

Bean Pot Arch GW 6
PHA LO- 20.0 X 18.0 ft.
OB- 26.0 X 29.0 ft.
SP- 14.0 X 28.0 X 26.0 ft.

Serviceberry Arch GW 7
PFA LO- 7.0 X .2 ft.
OB- 7.0 X .2 ft.
SP- 3.1 X .3 X 7.8 ft.

Fishtail Arch GW 8
ECA LO- 10.3 X .4 ft.
OB- 10.3 X .4 ft.
SP- 2.5 X .7 X 12.0 ft.

Deep Arch GW 9
ECA LO- 5.5 X 1.8 ft.
OB- 9.5 X 2.0 ft.
SP- 17.0 X 5.5 X 16.0 ft.

Plank Arch GW 10
CWA LO- 3.1 X .3 ft.
OB- 5.5 X 1.0 ft.
SP- 1.2 X .3 X 7.0 ft.

Artistic Arch GW 11
FSA LO- 5.1 X 1.8 ft.
OB- 5.1 X 1.8 ft.
SP- 2.3 X 1.0 X 10.0 ft.

Pinched Jughandle GW 12
JHA LO- .8 X 8.3 ft.
OB- .8 X 22.4 ft.
SP- 2.7 X .8 X 35.0 ft.

Bar Room Door Ar GW 13
CWA LO- 22.6 X 3.0 ft.
OB- 50.0 X 35.0 ft.
SP- 3.5 X 22.5 X 51.0 ft.

Laughing Coyote A GW 14
CWA LO- 20.0 X .8 ft.
OB- 55.0 X 27.0 ft.
SP- 6.0 X 26.0 X 73.0 ft.

Birds Eye Arch GW 15
SAA LO- 4.0 X 1.9 ft.
OB- 4.0 X 1.9 ft.
SP- 2.3 X 2.2 X 5.2 ft.

Ugly Arch GW 16
CWA LO- 27.0 X 1.0 ft.
OB- 28.0 X 36.0 ft.
SP- 10.0 X 79.0 X 60.0 ft.

Buttonhook Arch GW 17
CWA LO- 10.1 X 2.6 ft.
OB- 10.1 X 50.0 ft.
SP- 15.5 X 9.4 X 19.0 ft.

Little Gothic Ar GW 18
CWA LO- 53.0 X 1.0 ft.
OB- 72.0 X 110.0 ft.
SP- 8.0 X 20.0 X 116.0 ft.

Clear View Arch GW 19
FSA LO- 7.5 X 7.5 ft.
OB- 7.5 X 7.5 ft.
SP- 2.9 X 3.0 X 10.0 ft.

Owl Eye Arch GW 20
SAA LO- 6.5 X 4.1 ft.
OB- 6.5 X 4.1 ft.
SP- 3.5 X 2.2 X 10.0 ft.

Pillar Arch GW 21
SAA LO-3.1 X 5.2 ft.
OB- 3.1 X 5.2 ft.
SP- 1.6 X 3.5 X 8.0 ft.

Hoop Arch GW 22
SAA LO- 1.6 X 3.2 ft.
OB- 1.6 X 3.2 ft.
SP- .6 X 3.0 X 4.0 ft.

Spring Arch GW 23
CWA LO- 11.0 X .4 ft.
OB- 23.0 X 2.5 ft.
SP- 1.2 X 1.7 X 32.0 ft.

Subtle Arch GW 24
CWA LO- 4.9 X .2 ft.
OB- 4.9 X .3 ft.
SP- .8 X .3 X 6.1 ft.

Three Hundred Ar GW 25
CWA LO- 19.0 X 5.5 ft.
OB- 46.0 X 5.5 ft.
SP- 9.0 X 2.0 X 64.0 ft.

Burnt Ceiling Ar GW 26
JHA LO- 4.4 X .9 ft.
OB- 4.4 X .9 ft.
SP- 2.8 X 1.1 X 5.0 ft.

Poison Ivy Arch UC 1
CWA LO- 49.0 X 3.0 ft.
OB- 145.0 X 53.0 ft.
SP- 4.0 X 42.0 X 145.0 ft.

Confluence Arch UC 2
CWA LO- 20.0 X .3 ft.
OB- 99.0 X 48.0 ft.
SP- 12.0 X 36.0 X 109.0 ft.

Nutcracker Arch UC 3
JHA LO- 2.0 X 8.0 ft.
OB- 8.0 X 8.0 ft.
SP- 7.0 X 12.6 X 22.0 ft.

Quicksand Arch UC 4
JHA LO- .2 X 4.0 ft.
OB- 3.5 X 5.0 ft.
SP- 3.9 X 1.2 X 6.0 ft.

Steep Slope Arch UC 5
CWA LO- 17.0 X .2 ft.
OB- 57.0 X 44.0 ft.
SP- 3.0 X 3.0 X 70.0 ft.

Bend Arch UC 6
CWA LO- 4.3 X .3 ft.
OB- 20.0 X 12.0 ft.
SP- 3.7 X 3.3 X 30.0 ft.

The Tunnel UC 7
NT LO- 5.2 X 4.0 ft.
OB- 6.0 X 7.0 ft.
SP- 53.0 X 12.0 X NA ft.

Running Coyote Ar UC 8
CWA LO- 11.0 X .7 ft.
OB- 16.5 X 4.0 ft.
SP- 6.0 X 7.0 X 29.0 ft.

Dead End Arch UC 9
FSA LO- 8.5 X 2.4 ft.
OB- 8.5 X 2.4 ft.
SP- 3.5 X 2.5 X 10.0 ft.

See Preceding Photo

"Trail End Arch" is shown in the photo as the narrow opening on the right. "Dead End Arch" is the light-filled arch on the left.

Trail End Arch   UC 10
ECA LO- 3.3 X .4 ft.
OB- 3.3 X .4 ft.
SP- 3.5 X 7.0 X NA ft.

Cliffside Strip A UC 11
CWA LO- 12.0 X .4 ft.
OB- 205.0 X 31.0 ft.
SP- 11.0 X 11.0 X 205.0 ft.

Deception Arch   UC 12
PHA LO- 8.5 X 4.5 ft.
OB- 15.0 X 5.0 ft.
SP- 1.6 X .8 X 28.0 ft.

Bar Arch   UC 13
CWA LO- 9.5 X .8 ft.
OB- 9.5 X 5.0 ft.
SP- 2.0 X .8 X NA ft.

Sunshine Arch   UC 14
CWA LO- 13.0 X 5.0 ft.
OB- 27.0 X 10.0 ft.
SP- 10.0 X 43.0 X 40.0 ft.

West Boundary Ar UC 15
FSA LO- 52.0 X 6.0 ft.
OB- 52.0 X 34.0 ft.
SP- 5.0 X 7.5 X 79.0 ft.

Boundary Tw Outer UC 16
CWA LO- 13.0 X .6 ft.
OB- 14.0 X 4.0 ft.
SP- .9 X 1.4 X 20.5 ft.

See Preceding Photo

"Boundary Twins Inner" arch appears in the photo as part of the span which is visible in the center of the photo. There are actually two parallel spans.

Boundary Tw Inner UC 17
CWA LO- 9.0 X 1.0 ft.
OB- 11.0 X 3.0 ft.
SP- .6 X 1.0 X 20.5 ft.

Yucca Arch   UC 18
CWA LO- 5.2 X .1 ft.
OB- 16.5 X 6.2 ft.
SP- 2.1 X 1.2 X 18.0 ft.

Ring Arch   UC 19
PHA LO- 45.0 X 39.0 ft
OB- 56.0 X 39.0 ft.
SP- 4.9 X 4.6 X 61.0 ft.

Stale Cracker Ar UC 20
CWA LO- 7.2 X 1.8 ft.
OB- 8.5 X 2.1 ft.
SP- 1.4 X .7 X NA ft.

Brand A Arch   UC 21
CWA LO- 33.0 X 1.2 ft.
OB- 52.5 X 13.0 ft.
SP- 4.5 X 6.0 X 53.0 ft.

Pretzel Arch LC 1
PFA LO- 4.5 X .2 ft.
OB- 5.5 X .2 ft.
SP- 1.2 X .1 X 7.0 ft.

Target Arch LC 2
CWA LO- 15.0 X 1.0 ft.
OB- 23.0 X 14.0 ft.
SP- 9.0 X 11.0 X 36.0 ft.

Wildflower Arch LC 3
CWA LO- 6.0 X .2 ft.
OB- 33.0 X 11.8 ft.
SP- 4.8 X 2.5 X 44.0 ft.

See Preceding Photo

"Whale Arch North" is an elongated opening in the bedding plane to the right of the larger "Whale Arch South".

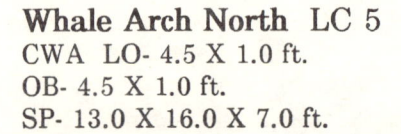

Whale Arch South LC 4
CWA LO- 12.0 X 1.5 ft.
OB- 12.0 X 8.0 ft.
SP- 13.0 X 14.0 X 15.0 ft.

Whale Arch North LC 5
CWA LO- 4.5 X 1.0 ft.
OB- 4.5 X 1.0 ft.
SP- 13.0 X 16.0 X 7.0 ft.

Slipper Arch LC 6
ECA LO- 5.5 X 1.5 ft.
OB- 5.5 X 1.5 ft.
SP- 2.5 X 8.5 X NA ft.

Hummingbird Arch LC 7
CWA LO- 4.1 X .5 ft.
OB- 160.0 X 13.0 ft.
SP- 5.0 X 7.0 X 160.0 ft.

Streaked Arch LC 8
CWA LO- 41.0 X 1.0 ft.
OB- 65.0 X 67.0 ft.
SP- 6.2 X 18.0 X 82.0 ft.

Cathedral Arch LC 9
CWA LO- 5.2 X 1.0 ft.
OB- 44.0 X 19.0 ft.
SP- 5.0 X 5.0 X 57.0 ft.

Dictionary Arch LC 10
ECA LO- 4.9 X 1.2 ft.
OB- 4.9 X 1.2 ft.
SP- 3.0 X 2.6 X NA ft.

Bigfoot Arch LC 11
CWA LO- 12.0 X 1.5 ft.
OB- 14.3 X 7.0 ft.
SP- 6.8 X 2.0 X 14.3 ft.

Boulder Arch LC 12
FSA LO- 12.0 X 3.0 ft.
OB- 33.0 X 31.0 ft.
SP- 23.0 X 31.0 X 42.0 ft.

Buckthorn Arch LC 13
CWA LO- 9.0 X .3 ft.
OB- 32.0 X 12.0 ft.
SP- 3.5 X 4.2 X 45.0 ft.

Tandem Arch South LC 14
SAA LO- 5.0 X 5.5 ft.
OB- 5.0 X 5.5 ft.
SP- 6.0 X 4.5 X 11.0 ft.

See Preceding Photo

"Tandem Arch North" is to the left of "Tandem Arch South" in the center of the photo.

Tandem Arch North LC 15
SAA LO- 3.0 X 13.0 ft.
OB- 3.0 X 13.0 ft.
SP- 9.4 X 9.0 X 24.0 ft.

Half Moon Arch LC 16
CWA LO- 4.0 X .5 ft.
OB- 26.0 X 21.0 ft.
SP- 8.0 X 15.0 X 28.0 ft.

Lizard Arch LC 17
SAA LO- 4.2 X 4.1 ft.
OB- 4.2 X 4.1 ft.
SP- 1.9 X .9 X 10.0 ft.

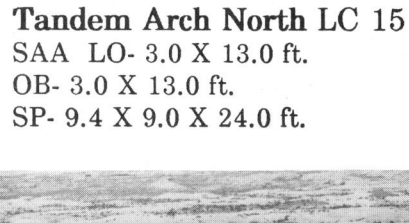

Tea Kettle Arch LC 18
CWA LO- 39.0 X .8 ft.
OB- 52.0 X 65.0 ft.
SP- 8.0 X 16.0 X NA ft.

Moss Arch   LC 19
SAA LO- 3.5 X 2.0 ft.
OB- 5.0 X 4.5 ft.
SP- 1.4 X 2.0 X 6.0 ft.

Tyrannosaurus Ar   LC 20
ECA LO- 6.0 X 1.2 ft.
OB- 7.0 X 3.0 ft.
SP- 2.0 X 2.4 X 14.0 ft.

Backside A Inner   LC 21
CWA LO- 9.4 X .4 ft.
OB- 9.4 X 4.1 ft.
SP- 1.4 X 1.1 X 12.0 ft.

See Preceding Photo

"Backside Arch Outer" is an arch that is attached to the main span of "Backside Arch Inner". It is on the left side of the main span.

See Preceding Photo

"Backside Arch Upper" is an arch that is above the main span of "Backside Arch Inner". It is not readily visible in the photo.

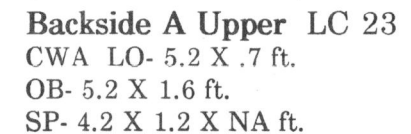

Backside A Outer   LC 22
CWA LO- 7.8 X 1.0 ft.
OB- 15.8 X 5.0 ft.
FP- .8 X 2.7 X 19.5 ft.

Backside A Upper   LC 23
CWA LO- 5.2 X .7 ft.
OB- 5.2 X 1.6 ft.
SP- 4.2 X 1.2 X NA ft.

Squawbush Arch   LC 24
JHA LO- .2 X 4.5 ft.
OB- 3.0 X 4.5 ft.
SP- 1.5 X .1 X 7.8 ft.

Trap Door Arch   LC 25
PAA LO- 1.6 X 4.0 ft.
OB- 17.5 X 6.0 ft.
SP- 4.0 X 1.5 X 17.5 ft.

Balcony Arch   LC 26
PAA LO- 3.7 X .3 ft.
OB- 5.0 X 2.2 ft.
SP- 3.0 X 4.0 X 7.0 ft.

Spindle Arch   LC 27
CWA LO- 3.5 X .3 ft.
OB- 4.2 X 1.4 ft.
SP- .3 X .1 X 5.0 ft.

Gauge Arch   LC 28
CWA LO- 11.0 X 2.0 ft.
OB- 11.0 X 3.5 ft.
SP- 8.8 X 2.2 X 13.0 ft.

Rupture Arch   LC 29
CWA LO- 4.9 X 1.5 ft.
OB- 9.0 X 3.0 ft.
SP- .2 X .7 X 10.0 ft.

Dove Feather Arch LC 30
CWA LO- 18.0 X .8 ft.
OB- 190.0 X 44.0 ft.
SP- 38.0 X 30.0 X 262.0 ft.

Babel Arch SA 1
FSA LO- 3.8 X 1.5 ft.
OB- 3.8 X 1.5 ft.
SP- 5.0 X 16.5 X NA ft.

Cliffhanger Arch SA 2
CWA LO- 4.8 X .2 ft.
OB- 6.1 X 3.2 ft.
SP- .8 X .4 X 7.0 ft.

Dog Head Arch SA 3
SAA LO- 5.0 X 2.5 ft.
OB- 5.0 X 2.5 ft.
SP- 2.5 X 2.5 X 7.0 ft.

Shoe Arch SA 4
ECA LO- 7.6 X 2.0 ft.
OB- 7.6 X 2.0 ft.
SP- 7.5 X 16.5 X NA ft.

Baby Arch SA 5
FSA LO- 24.5 X 14.5 ft.
OB- 42.0 X 16.0 ft.
SP- 22.5 X 205.0 X 61.0 ft.

Gossips Arch SA 6
CWA LO- 15.0 X .6 ft.
OB- 36.0 X 7.0 ft.
SP- 6.0 X 8.5 X 47.0 ft.

Four Hundred Arch SA 7
FSA LO- 2.5 X 4.5 ft.
OB- 2.5 X 4.5 ft.
SP- 3.9 X 6.5 X 13.0 ft.

Flat Arch SA 8
PFA LO- 7.0 X .1 ft.
OB- 7.0 X .2 ft.
SP- 1.9 X .3 X NA ft.

Slant Arch Upper SA 9
FSA LO- 5.0 X 2.2 ft.
OB- 5.0 X 2.2 ft.
SP- 9.0 X 2.5 X 14.0 ft.

See Preceding Photo

"Slant Arch Lower" is the smaller arch below "Slant Arch Upper".

Slant Arch Lower SA 10
FSA LO- 3.3 X 1.5 ft.
OB- 3.3 X 1.5 ft.
SP- 2.2 X .3 X 5.0 ft.

Badger Arch   SA 11
FSA LO- 4.0 X 2.7 ft.
OB- 4.0 X 2.7 ft.
SP- 22.0 X 7.0 X NA ft.

Pinyon Jay Arch   SA 12
ECA LO- .9 X 3.4 ft.
OB- .9 X 3.4 ft.
SP- 3.3 X 5.5 X NA ft.

Skate Key Arch   SA 13
FSA LO- 3.7 X 3.5 ft.
OB- 3.7 X 3.5 ft.
SP- 3.5 X 1.2 X NA ft.

Mandolin Arch   SA 14
CWA LO- 9.0 X 5.0 ft.
OB- 22.0 X 38.0 ft.
SP- 8.0 X 78.0 X NA ft.

Park Avenue Arch SA 15
CWA LO- 7.0 X .5 ft.
OB- 70.0 X 62.0 ft.
SP- 8.0 X 8.5 X 73.0 ft.

Snout Arch   SA 16
PFA LO- 5.5 X .3 ft.
OB- 5.5 X .3 ft.
SP- .8 X .2 X 5.8 ft.

Squirrel Arch   SA 17
CWA LO- 7.0 X .1 ft.
OB- 9.5 X 2.3 ft.
SP- .8 X 1.5 X 9.5 ft.

Wrinkled Arch   SA 18
CWA LO- 11.0 X .3 ft.
OB- 19.5 X 2.5 ft.
SP- 3.5 X 1.2 X NA ft.

See Preceding Photo

"Above the Alcove Arch North" is shown in the photo as the smaller opening to the right of "Above the Alcove Arch South".

Above the Alcove S SA 19
FSA LO- 5.5 X 11.0 ft.
OB- 21.0 X 19.0 ft.
SP- 35.0 X 38.0 X NA ft.

Above the Alcove N SA 20
FSA LO- 2.0 X 5.0 ft.
OB- 21.0 X 19.0 ft.
SP- 35.0 X 38.0 X NA ft.

Jack Rabbit Arch SA 21
JHA LO- 1.0 X 3.6 ft.
OB- 1.0 X 3.6 ft.
SP- .3 X .3 X 5.0 ft.

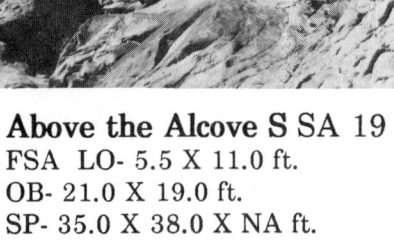

Juniper Arch   SA 22
FSA LO- 3.1 X 3.7 ft.
OB- 3.1 X 3.7 ft.
SP- .5 X 1.5 X NA ft.

Edge Arch   SA 23
NB LO- 12.5 X 1.7 ft.
OB- 12.5 X 1.7 ft.
SP- 7.5 X .8 X 17.0 ft.

Split Bottom Arch SA 24
CWA LO- 32.0 X .3 ft.
OB- 79.0 X 27.0 ft.
SP- 3.5 X 8.3 X 79.0 ft.

Mahogany Arch   SA 25
CWA LO- 6.0 X .2 ft.
OB- 10.0 X 3.7 ft.
SP- 2.0 X 2.3 X 16.0 ft.

Porthole Cave Ar SA 26
SAA LO- 5.0 X 8.0 ft.
OB- 17.5 X 12.0 ft.
SP- 6.0 X 6.5 X NA ft.

Split Top Arch   SA 27
CWA LO- 19.0 X 1.5 ft.
OB- 45.0 X 26.0 ft.
SP- 9.0 X 6.0 X 58.0 ft.

Two Hundred Arch SA 28
FSA LO- 6.5 X 5.0 ft.
OB- 6.5 X 5.0 ft.
SP- 4.6 X 3.5 X 14.0 ft.

Demon Arch   SA 29
FSA LO- 6.8 X 2.5 ft.
OB- 6.8 X 3.0 ft.
SP- 5.5 X 9.0 X 10.0 ft.

Ute Bridge   SA 30
NB LO- 9.0 X 1.8 ft.
OB- 13.5 X 6.0 ft.
SP- 3.8 X 1.7 X 17.0 ft.

See Preceding Photo

The arrow on the right points to "Leech Arch". It clings to the side of the span of "Visitor Center Arch"

Tepee Arch   SA 31
FSA LO- 3.0 X 3.7 ft.
OB- 4.1 X 4.8 ft.
SP- 6.0 X 1.8 X NA ft.

Visitor Center Ar SA 32
CWA LO- 4.0 X 1.0 ft.
OB- 21.5 X 30.5 ft.
SP- 10.5 X 16.0 X 57.0 ft.

Leech Arch   SA 33
CWA LO- 3.5 X .5 ft.
OB- 5.0 X 21.0 ft.
SP- .4 X .4 X 12.0 ft.

Penguin Arch   SA 34
CWA LO- 7.0 X .1 ft.
OB- 51.0 X 11.0 ft.
SP- 3.7 X 2.5 X 58.0 ft.

Graceful Arch   SA 35
CWA LO- 9.5 X .1 ft.
OB- 17.0 X 1.9 ft.
SP- 1.1 X .7 X 25.0 ft.

Capped Arch   SA 36
FSA LO- 4.5 X 1.4 ft.
OB- 8.0 X 1.5 ft.
SP- 7.5 X 4.0 X NA ft.

Cave Arch   SA 37
CWA LO- 8.0 X .3 ft.
OB- 8.0 X 2.5 ft.
SP- 12.0 X 3.8 X 21.0 ft.

Kids Arch West   SA 38
CWA LO- 17.5 X .3 ft.
OB- 30.0 X 3.0 ft.
SP- 4.6 X .6 X 30.0 ft.

Kids Arch East   SA 39
CWA LO- 3.8 X .7 ft.
OB- 6.0 X .8 ft.
SP- 15.0 X 4.5 X NA ft.

See Preceding Photo

The arrow on the photo points to "Kids Arch East". "Kids Arch West" appears as a narrow slit of light on the left side of the photo.

Joggers Arch   SA 40
JHA LO- 2.8 X 4.8 ft.
OB- 3.5 X 5.5 ft.
SP- 1.1 X .7 X 7.0 ft.

Water Tank Arch   SA 41
CWA LO- 31.0 X 12.0 ft.
OB- 32.0 X 31.0 ft.
SP- 5.5 X 11.0 X 39.0 ft.

Crossbed Arch   SA 42
SAA LO- 6.4 X 1.0 ft.
OB- 6.4 X 1.0 ft.
SP- .9 X .7 X NA ft.

Shotgun Arch   SA 43
ECA LO- 4.2 X .7 ft.
OB- 7.0 X 1.0 ft.
SP- 1.5 X .7 X 12.0 ft.

Gap Arch   SA 44
FSA LO- 3.5 X 5.0 ft.
OB- 3.5 X 5.0 ft.
SP- 4.0 X 1.4 X 3.5 ft.

Regap Arch   SA 45
ECA LO- 5.0 X 1.3 ft.
OB- 5.0 X 1.3 ft.
SP- 3.9 X 3.0 X NA ft.

Bull Arch   SA 46
JHA LO- 4.4 X 1.0 ft.
OB- 4.4 X 14.0 ft.
SP- 3.8 X 3.0 X 6.5 ft.

Airfoil Ar Upper SA 47
ECA LO- 3.1 X .2 ft.
OB- 3.1 X .2 ft.
SP- .2 X 1.6 X 5.0 ft.

Airfoil Ar Lower SA 48
ECA LO- 5.6 X .8 ft.
OB- 5.6 X 1.5 ft.
SP- 1.2 X 1.0 X NA ft.

See Preceding Photo

"Airfoil Arch Lower" is shown on the photo as the larger elongated opening near the bottom of the photograph.

Cottontail Arch   SA 49
CWA LO- 3.2 X 2.0 ft.
OB- 15.5 X 4.0 ft.
SP- 6.0 X 6.0 X 15.5 ft.

Pedestal Arch   SA 50
SAA LO- 3.4 X 1.2 ft.
OB- 3.4 X 1.2 ft.
SP- .3 X .4 X NA ft.

Y Arch   SA 51
JHA LO- .5 X 11.0 ft.
OB- .5 X 11.0 ft.
SP- 4.6 X .7 X 20.0 ft.

Can Opener Arch SA 52
PFA LO- 7.0 X .4 ft.
OB- 7.0 X .4 ft.
SP- 1.4 X .2 X 8.0 ft.

Deer Mouse Arch SA 53
FSA LO- 7.0 X 7.3 ft.
OB- 7.0 X 7.3 ft.
SP- .6 X .4 X NA ft.

Spatula Arch   SA 54
CWA LO- 7.5 X .2 ft.
OB- 8.5 X 1.5 ft.
SP- .3 X 1.0 X 12.0 ft.

Thunder Arch   SA 55
CWA LO- 9.0 X 1.0 ft.
OB- 9.0 X 1.0 ft.
SP- 2.7 X 3.0 X 15.0 ft.

CHAPTER 8
STATISTICAL SUMMARY

Many arch characteristics have not been fully described in the previous chapters because of the repetitive nature of such information. For this reason, two major tables were produced which include the statistics that are important on each arch. The first list (Table 1) is arranged alphabetically and includes information on location (latitude & longitude and map location), who reported and named each arch, the year reported and named and the derivation of the name. Also included are geographic site and geologic formation of each arch, and exposure and compass orientation of the span. The second list (Table 2) is arranged by size of arch and is ranked from the largest to the smallest arch. Included in this list are all the dimensions and how each was measured.

Both lists include name, identification number and type of each arch. With this information it is possible to go back and forth between the tables and the photographs in chapter 7 to find almost any type of data on any arch. Because there are so many abbreviations in the tables, an extensive explanatory key is shown for each list.

It should be noted that since the field work ended in 1986, several more arches have been reported that are not included in the lists. Some are listed in the appendix, but no statistical information is included. All of the arches found in the Park since 1986 will be described in a forthcoming supplement to this book.

Table 2

KEY TO ALPHABETICAL LIST

AREA:

EP = Eagle Park
SD = South Devils Garden
FF = Fiery Furnace
HP = Herdina Park
GW = Great Wall
LC = Lower Courthouse Wash

ND = North Devils Garden
KB = Klondike Bluffs
SW = Salt Wash
CA = Central Area
UC = Upper Courthouse Wash
SA = Southwestern Area

SEC: (Sections within areas)

Eagle Park

NWF= Northwest Fins
SVE = Salt Valley Slope

SEF = Southeast Fins

North Devils Garden

YCW= Yellow Cat Wash
ALG = Aladdins Lamp Gulch
GoC = Gothic Canyon
DON = Double O Canyon-N.Side

IHG = Indian Head Canyon
BrC = Bridge Canyon
DkA = Dark Angel
SVN = Salt Valley Slope

South Devils Garden

DOS = Double-O Canyon-S.Side
Cst = Crystal
UTr = Upper Trail
Cmg = Campground

FiC = Fin Canyon
LFC = Lower Fin Canyon Wash
LdT = Landscape Trail
SVS = Salt Valley Slope

Klondike Bluffs

Twr = Tower

Esc = Escarpments

SoK = South

Fiery Furnace
Upr = Upper
Lwr = Lower

Salt Wash
UpW = Upper Wash
Del = Delicate
2JB = Two-Juniper Butte
WCW = Winter Camp Wash

Herdina Park
RrO = Rocky Outcrop
WiF = Willow Flats

Central Area
PB = Panorama Bluffs
WS = Windows Section

Great Wall
BlR = Balanced Rock
PtD = Petrified Dunes
GrW = Great Wall
SiC = Side Canyons of Lower Courthouse Wash

Upper Courthouse Wash
NoU = North
SoU = South

Lower Courthouse Wash
NoL = North
SoL = South

Southwestern Area
CtT = Courthouse Towers
CtF = Courthouse Flats
RBM = Rough and Broken Mesa
SBo = Southern Border

TYPE:

FSA = Free Standing Arch
PHA = Pot Hole Arch
PFA = Platform Arch
NB = Natural Bridge
PAA = Perforated Alcove Arch
CWA = Cliff Wall Arch
JHA = Jug Handle Arch
ECA = Expanded Crevice Arch
SAA = Spanned Alcove Arch
NT = Natural Tunnel

RB or NB: (Reported by or Named by)

1- National Park Service
2- Harry Reed, ANM
3- NPS Exp34, Beckwith
4- NPS Exp.36, Vandiver
5- Hank Schmidt, ANM
6- NPS Exp38, Gould
7- Map
8- Lewis McKinney, ANM
9- Brochure
10- Bates Wilson, ANM
11- Lloyd Pierson, ANM
12- Ed Abbey, ANM
13- USGS map
14- Slim Mabery, ANM
15- Bob Ferris, ANM
16- Vione Kallis, visitor
17- Doug Travers, arch-hunter
18- Dale Stevens, professor
19- Jerry Epperson, ANP
20- Kay Forsythe, ANP
21- Robert Vreeland, arch-h
22- Jim Stiles, ANP
23- Reuben Scolnik, arch-h
24- Ed McCarrick, researcher
25- Mike Meyer, ANP
26- Jim Capps, ANP
27- Jerry Goldstein, ANP
28- Liz Bellantoni, ANP
29- Nick Terzakis, visitor
30- Mike Salamacha, ANP
31- Ed Biery, ANP
32- George Anderson, visitor

33- Joan Swanson, ANP
34- Damian Fagan, ANP
35- Mike Hill, ANP
36- Alice Drogin, ANP
37- Kim Tennyson, ANP
38- Anne Sibley, ANP
39- Steve Swanke, ANP
40- Carl Horton, climber
41- Vicki Wolfe, ANP
42- Jim Heywood, ANP
43- Gordon Jensen, visitor
44- Dick Wunder, visitor
45- Kelly Nielsen, cartog.
46- Chris Robbins, ANP
51- Stevens/McCarrick
52- 51 & Scolnik
53- 51 & Salamacha
54- 51 & Horton
55- 51 & Drogin
56- 52 & Travers
57- 52 & Horton
58- Stevens/Salamacha
59- 58 & Travers
60- 58 & Wolfe
61- Stevens/Stiles
62- Stevens/Scolnik
63- Stevens/Horton
64- Stevens/Drogin
65- Stevens/Cowley
66- McCarrick/Scolnik
67- 66 & Travers
68- 66 & Swanson
69- 66 & Bellantoni
70- 67/Stiles/Swanson
71- McCarrick/Salamacha
72- McCarrick/Stiles
73- 72 & Salamacha
74- McCarrick/Travers
75- McCarr/Fagan/Drogin
76- Salamacha/Stiles
77- 76 & Scolnik
78- Stiles/Sibley
79- Wilson/Mabery
80- Mabery/Ferris
81- Wilson/Pierson
82- 66 & Forsythe
83- Scolnik/Forsythe
84- 66 & Drogin
85- Epperson/Meyer
86- McCarrick/Drogin
87- McCarrick/Fagan
88- Salamacha/Tennyson/Fagan
89- 51 & Nielsen
90- 89 & Horton
91- Stevens/Nielsen
ANM = Arches National Monument
ANP = Arches National Park

YR: Year reported or named, all in 20th century, thus "84" means 1984.

DER: (Derivation of name)

Obj = resembles object
Sit = site or location
Evt = named for event
Vic = something in vicinity
AnP = animal or plant in area
Fet = nearby feature
Chr = characteristic of arch
Oth = other
Unk = unknown

GEOG: (Geographic site)

FlO = flat open area
Sum = summit of rock mass or hill
ObF = obscured by fins
SiH = side of hill
SiC = side of steep cliff
CBt = canyon bottom

GEOL: (Geologic Formation)

BB = Morrsn: Brushy Basin
SW = Morrsn: Salt Wash
TI = Morrsn: Tidwell
MT = Entrada: Moab Tongue
SR = Entrada: Slickrock
DB = Entrada: Dewey Bridge
NA = Navajo   KA = Kayenta
WI = Wingate

125

SD = Slickrock/Dewey Bridge   SM = Slickrock/Moab Tongue

LAT: minutes to two decimal points north of 38 degrees North Latitude

LONG: minutes to two decimal points west of 109 degrees West Longitude

MAP LOCATION:

On each of the twelve large scale maps (1:24,00) there is a letter of the alphabet that denotes a point that can be used to find an arch by measuring the stated distance from this point in the specified direction. The three columns listed under "Map Location" indicate where to measure from **"M"**, the distance to measure **"DIS"** in miles and tenths of a mile, and the direction to measure **"DIR"** using the 16 points of the compass.

- A = Eagle Park on the Salt Valley Road at the Park boundary
- B = Dark Angel in North Devils Garden
- C = Trailhead to Landscape Arch parking area in South Devils Garden
- D = Klondike Bluffs Trailhead to Tower Arch
- E = Fiery Furnace Trailhead Parking
- F = Wolfe Ranch Trailhead Parking to Delicate Arch for the Salt Wash Area
- G = Old road near Herdina Park Wash for Herdina Park
- H = Panorama Point Parking area for the Panorama Bluffs
- I = Double Arch Trailhead Parking in the Windows Section
- J = Roadside Parking northeast of Bean Pot Arch east of The Great Wall
- K = Courthouse Wash Bridge Parking area for Upper Courthouse Wash
- L = Highway 191 Bridge near the mouth of Courthouse Wash for the Lower Courthouse Wash
- M = Arches National Park Visitors Center for the Southwestern Area

EXP: Major exposure of each arch using the eight points of the compass

CMP: Compass orientation of the span, corrected for magnetic declination, range is 0 to 179 degrees: 0 = north/south, 90 degrees = east/west, etc.

ALPHABETICAL LISTING OF ARCHES.

NAME	AREA	SEC	NO	TYPE	RANK	RB	YR	NB	YR	DER	GEOG	GEOL	°LAT	°LONG	MAP LOC MP	MAP LOC DIS	MAP LOC DIR	EXP	CMP
ABOVE THE ALCOVE ARCH NO.	SA	SBo	20	FSA	349	18	85	51	85	Fet	SiC	SR	37.29	37.19	M	.4	N	NE	140
ABOVE THE ALCOVE ARCH SO.	SA	SBo	19	FSA	168	31	81	31	81	Fet	SiC	SR	37.29	37.19	M	.4	N	NE	140
AIRFOIL ARCH LOWER	SA	SBo	48	ECA	313	18	84	18	84	Obj	SiH	NA	36.85	36.27	M	.8	E	W	10
AIRFOIL ARCH UPPER	SA	SBo	47	ECA	519	18	84	18	84	Obj	SiH	NA	36.85	36.27	M	.8	E	W	10
ALADDINS BRIDGE	ND	ALG	35	NB	312	51	84	51	84	Fet	CBt	SR	48.75	37.69	B	.8	N	E	135
ALADDINS LAMP	ND	ALG	36	FSA	138	23	78	23	78	Obj	SiC	SR	48.75	37.66	B	.8	N	SW	140
ALCOVE ARCH	CA	WS	13	CWA	120	5	41	24	76	Sit	SiC	SR	41.65	32.20	I	.4	N	N	138
ALL THE WAY ARCH	EP	NWF	14	CWA	104	22	79	22	83	Oth	SiC	SR	50.15	41.32	A	1.4	N	NW	29
ANNIVERSARY ARCH NORTH	KB	Twr	12	FSA	115	14	62	16	62	Oth	ObF	SR	46.50	40.80	D	1.2	SSW	W	0
ANNIVERSARY ARCH SOUTH	KB	Twr	13	FSA	265	14	62	16	62	Oth	ObF	SR	46.50	40.80	D	1.2	SSW	W	0
ANTEATER ARCH	SD	FiC	7	ECA	472	53	84	18	84	Obj	SiH	SR	48.23	36.75	C	1.7	NNW	N	145
APOSTROPHE ARCH	FF	Lwr	32	FSA	296	23	79	24	81	Obj	CBt	SR	44.74	33.78	E	.2	NE	NE	155
ARC DE TRIOMPHE	SD	Cmg	75	CWA	126	23	77	23	77	Obj	SiC	SR	46.90	35.10	C	.5	E	NE	20
ARCH OF MOTION	GW	GrW	4	FSA	80	18	73	23	77	Oth	Sum	SD	41.24	35.00	J	.4	N	E	0
AROUND BACK ARCH	SD	DOS	11	ECA	393	44	85	44	85	Sit	Sum	SR	48.03	71.40	C	1.8	NW	NE	145
ARROW ARCH	ND	GoC	76	FSA	118	17	80	17	80	Obj	Sum	SR	48.40	37.22	B	.5	NE	SW	145
ARTISTIC ARCH	GW	PtD	11	FSA	341	23	84	18	84	Obj	SiH	NA	40.81	34.58	J	.4	ESE	SW	153
ATTIC ARCH	HP	RrO	7	FSA	346	17	85	17	85	Sit	Sum	SR	42.72	36.56	G	1.0	NNW	W	170
BABEL ARCH	SA	CtT	1	FSA	450	22	84	24	85	Fet	SiC	SD	38.58	35.93	M	2.2	NNE	N	80
BABY ARCH	SA	CtT	5	FSA	79	1	52	1	70	Oth	SiC	SR	38.26	36.37	M	1.6	NNE	E	5
BACKSIDE ARCH INNER	LC	SoL	21	CWA	204	66	82	23	82	Obj	SiH	KA	36.92	34.53	L	.7	NNE	NW	60
BACKSIDE ARCH OUTER	LC	SoL	22	CWA	249	66	82	23	82	Obj	SiH	KA	36.92	34.53	L	.7	NNE	NW	60
BACKSIDE ARCH UPPER	LC	SoL	23	CWA	337	51	84	51	84	Obj	SiH	KA	36.92	32.53	L	.7	NNE	NW	60
BADGER ARCH	SA	RBM	11	FSA	418	66	83	51	84	AnP	ObF	SM	37.83	36.83	M	1.0	NNE	SW	125
BALCONY ARCH	LC	SoL	26	PAA	460	51	84	51	84	Obj	SiH	KA	36.93	34.52	L	.7	NNE	N	90
BALL ARCH	CA	PB	4	CWA	458	66	83	66	83	Obj	Sum	WI	43.28	32.21	H	.8	E	NE	145
BAR ARCH	UC	SoU	13	CWA	201	23	83	23	83	Obj	Sum	SR	38.86	37.83	K	1.7	W	NW	40

127

NAME	AREA	SEC	NO	TYPE	RANK	RB	YR	NB	YR	DER	GEOG	GEOL	°LAT	°LONG	MAP LOC MP DIS DIR	EXP	CMP
BAR ROOM DOOR ARCH	GW	GrW	13	CWA	86	23	77	23	77	Obj	SiC	SR	40.45	35.56	J .8 SW	SW	45
BARBED ARCH	GW	GrW	3	FSA	463	22	83	22	83	Obj	Sum	SD	41.61	34.71	J .9 NNE	NW	60
BEAM ARCH	SD	UTr	32	CWA	408	36	83	18	84	Obj	Sum	SR	47.83	36.87	C 1.5 NW	NE	126
BEAN POT ARCH	GW	GrW	6	PHA	93	5	40	20	76	Obj	SiC	SR	40.88	35.35	J .3 W	E	0
BELLY ARCH	EP	NWF	6	ECA	167	45	85	24	86	Obj	SiC	SR	50.53	42.07	A 2.1 NNW	NW	22
BENCH ARCH	FF	Lwr	51	PHA	61	10	61	81	61	Sit	SiC	SR	44.53	33.36	E .5 E	W	130
BEND ARCH	UC	NoU	6	CWA	406	23	78	24	79	Sit	SiC	SR	39.20	36.94	K 1.9 W	N	120
BICEPS ARCH	CA	WS	30	CWA	7	1	69	23	77	Obj	Sum	SR	41.22	31.95	I .3 ESE	SW	150
BIG BUCK ARCH	EP	NWF	12	CWA	106	22	79	22	79	Vic	SiC	SR	50.22	41.54	A 1.6 NNW	N	80
BIG EYE ARCH	ND	DkA	23	FSA	59	18	73	23	77	Obj	SiC	SR	48.70	38.10	B .8 NW	SW	134
BIG TOP ARCH	CA	PB	9	ECA	384	66	85	66	85	Obj	SiH	WI	43.37	31.89	H 1.2 ENE	NE	135
BIGFOOT ARCH	LC	SoL	11	CWA	160	66	82	24	82	Obj	SiC	NA	37.41	34.63	L 1.2 N	SW	158
BIGHORN ARCH	CA	WS	36	FSA	209	23	85	51	86	AnP	Sum	SR	41.82	31.41	I .9 SE	SW	135
BIRDS EYE ARCH	GW	GrW	15	SAA	419	23	77	23	77	Obj	FlO	SR	40.19	35.68	J 1.0 SSW	SW	135
BISCUITROOT ARCH	FF	Upr	6	CWA	527	66	85	24	86	AnP	SiH	NA	45.54	35.16	E 1.6 NW	SW	140
BLACK ARCH	SD	FiC	24	FSA	14	10	61	10	61	Obj	SiC	SR	47.96	36.63	C 1.4 NW	SW	121
BLACK CAVE ARCH INNER	SD	UTr	31	CWA	122	23	77	23	77	Chr	ObF	SR	47.84	36.90	C 1.5 NW	NE	116
BLACK CAVE ARCH OUTER	SD	UTr	30	CWA	58	23	77	23	77	Chr	ObF	SR	47.84	36.90	C 1.5 NW	NE	116
BLACKBRUSH ARCH	CA	PB	10	CWA	387	52	85	24	85	AnP	SiH	WI	43.30	31.89	H 1.2 E	N	100
BLOCKED ARCH	SD	Cst	41	CWA	142	10	69	23	78	Chr	SiC	SR	47.70	36.00	C .9 NNW	SW	107
BLUE ARCH	SW	2JB	8	NB	291	20	77	20	77	Chr	CBt	BB	44.25	31.88	F .6 W	SE	50
BOBCAT ARCH	ND	BrC	47	FSA	292	51	84	51	84	AnP	SiC	SR	48.68	37.42	B .7 NNE	SW	137
BOOMERANG ARCH	ND	GoC	74	CWA	441	51	84	51	84	Obj	ObF	SR	48.38	37.22	B .5 NE	NE	118
BOOST ARCH	SD	FiC	33	SAA	294	37	83	30	83	Evt	ObF	SR	47.79	36.40	C 1.3 NW	NE	126
BOOT ARCH	SW	2JB	4	FSA	351	24	81	24	81	Obj	Sum	SW	44.13	32.55	F 1.2 W	SE	47
BOULDER ARCH	LC	SoL	12	FSA	159	22	79	23	81	Chr	SiC	NA	37.41	34.47	L 1.3 NNE	SW	130
BOUNDARY TWINS INNER	UC	SoU	17	CWA	216	31	81	31	81	Sit	SiH	SR	38.18	38.10	K 2.1 WSW	SW	140
BOUNDARY TWINS OUTER	UC	SoU	16	CWA	152	31	81	31	81	Sit	SiH	SR	38.18	38.10	K 2.1 WSW	SW	140

NAME	AREA	SEC	NO	TYPE	RANK	RB	YR	NB	YR	DER	GEOG	GEOL	°LAT	°LONG	MP	MAP LOC DIS	DIR	EXP	CMP
BOW JUGHANDLE	ND	ALG	29	JHA	162	17	82	67	83	Obj	SiC	SR	48.82	37.70	B	.9	N	NE	120
BOW TIE ARCH	CA	WS	6	CWA	425	18	84	18	84	Obj	SiC	SD	41.90	32.38	I	.7	N	NW	50
BOX ARCH	SD	FiC	13	FSA	62	10	70	17	70	Obj	ObF	SR	48.08	36.84	C	1.8	NW	NE	106
BRAND A ARCH	UC	SoU	21	CWA	53	23	77	23	77	Vic	SiC	SR	38.86	36.82	K	.8	W	E	155
BROKEN ARCH	SD	Cmg	84	FSA	25	1	66	1	66	Chr	SiC	SR	46.23	34.80	C	1.2	SE	SW	124
BRUSHY BASIN BRIDGE	SW	2JB	7	NB	282	24	82	24	82	Chr	CBt	BB	44.25	31.88	F	.6	W	W	0
BUCKLE ARCH	KB	Esc	3	FSA	423	63	84	18	84	Obj	Sum	SR	47.79	41.24	D	.8	WNW	NE	40
BUCKTHORN ARCH	LC	SoL	13	CWA	218	66	82	51	85	AnP	Sum	NA	37.45	34.38	L	1.3	NNE	SW	70
BUFFALO ARCH	KB	Esc	11	FSA	446	18	73	24	82	Obj	Sum	DB	47.46	40.52	D	.1	SW	E	118
BULL ARCH	SA	SBo	46	JHA	401	18	84	18	84	Obj	SiH	NA	36.85	36.27	M	.8	E	E	170
BURNT CEILING ARCH	GW	GrW	26	JHA	403	88	85	88	85	Chr	SiC	KA	40.15	32.88	J	1.4	SSW	SE	75
BUTTONHOOK ARCH	GW	GrW	17	CWA	188	23	77	23	77	Obj	SiC	SR	40.12	35.69	J	1.1	SW	E	135
BYPASS ARCH	ND	BrC	52	CWA	41	36	83	23	83	Sit	ObF	SR	48.68	37.23	B	.8	NNE	SW	125
CACTUS ARCH	CA	WS	3	PFA	199	44	85	51	86	AnP	SiH	NA	41.92	32.57	I	.8	NNW	N	60
CAMEL LEG ARCH	SD	FiC	25	SAA	484	18	84	18	84	Obj	SiC	SR	47.92	36.75	C	1.4	NW	NW	41
CAMOUFLAGE TWINS NORTH	ND	IHG	16	FSA	213	51	84	51	84	Sit	ObF	SR	48.80	38.00	B	.9	NNW	SW	135
CAMOUFLAGE TWINS SOUTH	ND	IHG	17	ECA	404	51	84	51	84	Sit	ObF	SR	48.80	38.00	B	.9	NNW	SW	135
CAN OPENER ARCH	SA	SBo	52	PFA	273	51	84	51	84	Obj	SiH	NA	36.59	35.96	M	1.2	ESE	N	80
CANINE ARCH	ND	GoC	66	CWA	433	52	84	52	84	Obj	ObF	SR	48.34	37.48	B	.3	NNE	SW	130
CANOPY ARCH	SD	SVS	59	CWA	434	52	84	52	84	Obj	ObF	NA	47.38	38.58	C	.9	WNW	SW	140
CANTILEVER ARCH	ND	BrC	48	CWA	202	52	84	18	84	Obj	ObF	SR	48.62	37.19	B	.7	NNE	NE	140
CANYON BRIDGE	ND	BrC	54	NB	179	23	77	23	77	Sit	CBt	SR	48.73	37.26	B	.8	NNE	SW	122
CANYON WREN BRIDGE	ND	BrC	42	NB	289	51	84	51	84	Vic	CBt	SR	48.67	37.49	B	.7	N	NE	135
CAPPED ARCH	SA	SBo	36	FSA	383	26	82	66	82	Obj	SiH	NA	37.06	36.91	M	.2	ENE	S	75
CARLING ARCH	EP	SVE	45	CWA	311	90	86	51	86	Obj	SiH	NA	48.89	39.98	A	1.0	E	S	120
CAT EYE ARCH	ND	DkA	38	CWA	117	18	73	24	82	Obj	SiC	SR	48.58	37.88	B	.6	NNW	SW	110
CAT HEAD ARCH	ND	BrC	44	FSA	521	23	77	24	82	Obj	SiC	SR	48.62	37.44	B	.6	N	SW	130
CATERPILLAR ARCH	SD	DOS	2	ECA	478	24	82	24	82	Obj	Sum	SR	48.34	36.70	C	1.8	NNW	SW	140

129

NAME	AREA	SEC	NO	TYPE	RANK	RB	YR	NB	YR	DER	GEOG	GEOL	'LAT	'LONG	MP	MAP LOC DIS	DIR	EXP	CMP
CATHEDRAL ARCH	LC	NoL	9	CWA	335	66	81	51	85	Obj	Sum	NA	37.73	34.16	L	1.7	NNE	W	0
CAVE ARCH	SA	SBo	37	CWA	245	66	82	18	84	Obj	SiH	NA	37.05	36.89	M	.3	ENE	SE	103
CAVITY ARCH	KB	Twr	8	CWA	304	18	86	18	86	Obj	SiC	SR	47.41	41.11	D	.6	W	E	170
CHAMBER ARCH NORTH	ND	IHG	18	ECA	285	24	83	51	84	Obj	ObF	SR	48.79	38.04	B	.9	NNW	SW	135
CHAMBER ARCH SOUTH	ND	IHG	19	ECA	456	24	83	51	84	Obj	ObF	SR	48.79	38.04	B	.9	NNW	SW	135
CHEATGRASS ARCH	ND	SVN	78	SAA	405	67	85	24	86	AnP	SiH	KA	48.30	38.74	B	1.1	WNW	W	10
CHRISTMAS TREE ARCH	CA	WS	19	FSA	68	1	69	24	77	Obj	SiC	SR	41.51	32.19	I	.2	NNE	SW	175
CHUNK ARCH	KB	SoK	17	CWA	19	30	85	71	86	Chr	ObF	SR	45.41	39.73	D	2.5	SSE	W	10
CLAM SHELL ARCH	CA	PB	17	SAA	515	54	84	54	84	Obj	Sum	WI	43.23	32.29	H	.8	E	W	95
CLEAR VIEW ARCH	GW	GrW	19	FSA	251	18	73	24	85	Sit	Sum	SR	39.26	35.83	J	2.0	SSW	NW	75
CLIFF ARCH	FF	Lwr	26	CWA	74	12	58	12	59	Sit	ObF	SR	44.85	33.59	E	.4	NE	SW	165
CLIFF CREST ARCH	KB	Esc	2	PFA	247	63	84	18	84	Sit	Sum	SR	47.82	41.22	D	.8	WNW	E	130
CLIFF TOP ARCH	SW	WCW	17	FSA	299	22	80	24	82	Sit	Sum	KA	44.92	29.30	F	1.9	ENE	S	80
CLIFFHANGER ARCH	SA	CtT	2	CWA	377	22	84	24	85	Sit	SiC	SR	38.54	36.00	M	2.1	NNE	NE	65
CLIFFROSE ARCH	EP	SVE	48	ECA	506	18	86	24	86	AnP	SiH	WI	48.66	39.97	A	1.1	ESE	NE	140
CLIFFSIDE STRIP ARCH	UC	SoU	11	CWA	163	23	78	23	78	Sit	SiC	SR	38.90	38.03	K	1.9	W	SE	45
CLINGING ARCH	EP	SVE	20	CWA	183	58	84	58	84	Sit	SiH	NA	49.95	41.94	A	1.6	WNW	S	103
CLOISTER ARCH	FF	Lwr	43	CWA	190	10	61	10	61	Sit	ObF	SR	44.63	33.57	E	.3	E	S	154
CLOVER CANYON ARCH	FF	Upr	1	CWA	65	76	83	66	84	Sit	SiC	SD	46.91	32.71	E	2.9	NNE	NE	115
COBBLESTONE BRIDGE	SW	Del	10	NB	171	66	81	66	81	Chr	CBt	SW	44.32	30.94	F	.3	NE	S	80
COFFIN ARCH	ND	IHG	22	FSA	283	17	81	17	83	Obj	ObF	SR	48.75	37.85	B	.8	NNW	E	140
COKE OVEN ARCH	SD	LdT	57	CWA	71	23	77	23	77	Obj	ObF	SR	47.40	36.42	C	.8	NW	NE	147
COLUMBINE ARCH	ND	GoC	70	PAA	329	36	84	36	84	AnP	ObF	SR	48.31	37.33	B	.3	NE	SW	135
CONCEALED BRIDGE	HP	WiF	15	NB	191	17	80	24	81	Sit	CBt	SR	42.06	36.40	G	.2	NNW	E	77
CONFLUENCE ARCH	UC	NoU	2	CWA	96	66	83	66	83	Sit	SiC	SR	40.00	37.18	K	2.4	WNW	SW	127
CONTOURED ARCH	SD	FiC	23	CWA	110	23	77	23	77	Obj	ObF	SR	48.00	36.75	C	1.5	NW	SW	126
CORRIDOR ARCH	ND	DON	73	ECA	415	66	83	51	84	Sit	Sum	SR	48.36	37.19	B	.5	NE	NE	140
COTTONTAIL ARCH	SA	SBo	49	CWA	501	18	84	18	84	Vic	SiH	NA	36.84	36.28	M	.8	E	W	0

130

NAME	AREA	SEC	NO	TYPE	RANK	RB	YR	NB	YR	DER	GEOG	GEOL	'LAT	'LONG	MP	MAP LOC DIS	DIR	EXP	CMP
COUGAR ARCH	EP	SVE	25	JHA	487	60	84	51	84	AnP	SiC	WI	49.58	41.50	A	.8	NNW	SW	177
COVE ARCH	CA	WS	9	FSA	29	1	48	1	48	Sit	SiC	SD	41.65	32.52	I	.5	NNW	NW	122
CRACKER ARCH	EP	SVE	34	SAA	417	30	82	30	82	Vic	SiH	KA	49.04	40.64	A	.4	ENE	SW	80
CRACKER JACK ARCH	EP	SEF	27	CWA	165	24	83	18	84	Oth	SiH	SD	49.65	40.36	A	1.1	NE	S	128
CRAWL THRU ARCH	FF	Lwr	44	ECA	310	24	83	18	84	Oth	ObF	SR	44.63	33.57	E	.3	E	E	163
CROCODILE ARCH	FF	Upr	17	CWA	220	66	83	55	84	Obj	Sum	SR	45.18	34.18	E	.7	NNW	SW	157
CROSSBED ARCH	SA	SBo	42	SAA	288	18	84	18	84	Obj	SiH	NA	36.87	36.38	M	.7	E	E	80
CROSSBOW ARCH	SD	SVS	61	CWA	172	52	84	52	84	Obj	SiC	NA	47.38	36.58	C	.9	WNW	SW	135
CROW ARCH	EP	NWF	8	CWA	39	30	83	22	83	Oth	SiC	SR	50.51	42.15	A	2.1	NNW	S	105
CRY BABY ARCH	EP	SVE	42	CWA	390	23	78	23	78	Vic	SiH	KA	48.96	40.13	A	.9	E	SW	138
CRYSTAL ARCH NORTH	SD	Cst	40	FSA	60	10	69	10	69	Obj	SiC	SR	47.75	36.12	C	1.0	NNW	SW	103
CRYSTAL ARCH SOUTH	SD	Cst	39	FSA	231	10	69	10	69	Obj	SiC	SR	47.75	36.18	C	1.0	NNW	SW	103
CUP ARCH	ND	GoC	63	FSA	211	23	77	24	81	Obj	ObF	SR	48.43	37.40	B	.4	NNE	SW	140
DAH ARCH	SD	FiC	9	FSA	328	53	84	53	84	Sit	SiH	SR	48.20	36.71	C	1.7	NNW	SW	140
DAM ARCH	HP	WiF	16	FSA	242	17	85	17	85	Vic	SiH	SR	41.98	36.61	G	.3	WNW	N	105
DEAD END ARCH	UC	NoU	9	FSA	225	23	79	23	80	Sit	Sum	SR	39.43	35.04	K	.6	N	SE	65
DEAD JUNIPER ARCH	SD	SVS	16	ECA	513	66	85	66	85	Vic	SiH	KA	47.88	37.45	C	1.9	WNW	SE	60
DEBRIS ARCH	SD	FiC	35	FSA	10	21	77	23	77	Chr	ObF	SR	47.83	36.52	C	1.3	NW	NE	135
DECEPTION ARCH	UC	SoU	12	PHA	224	23	78	23	78	Oth	Sum	SR	38.90	37.80	K	1.7	W	E	140
DEEP ARCH	GW	PtD	9	ECA	318	66	84	51	84	Chr	Sum	NA	40.94	34.42	J	.5	E	W	175
DEER MOUSE ARCH	SA	SBo	53	FSA	263	51	84	51	84	Obj	SiH	NA	36.58	35.94	M	1.2	ESE	NW	75
DELICATE ARCH	SW	Del	14	FSA	34	1	32	2	34	Chr	Sum	SR	44.61	29.92	F	1.3	ENE	NW	73
DEMON ARCH	SA	RBM	29	FSA	278	34	82	24	83	Obj	Sum	MT	37.14	37.65	M	.5	WNW	N	110
DESTRUCTION ARCH	ND	SVN	86	CWA	495	52	85	18	85	Chr	SiH	KA	47.93	37.65	B	.2	SSW	S	125
DEVILS EYE ARCH	SD	SVS	58	CWA	357	18	84	18	84	Obj	SiH	KA	47.42	36.68	C	1.0	WNW	SW	140
DEVILS JUGHANDLE	SD	LdT	65	JHA	352	24	78	24	78	Sit	Sum	SR	47.33	35.83	C	.4	NNW	S	95
DIAMOND ARCH	SD	Cmg	76	FSA	97	10	70	10	77	Obj	SiC	SR	46.61	35.47	C	.5	SSE	W	140
DICTIONARY ARCH	LC	SoL	10	ECA	370	17	82	51	84	Obj	SiH	NA	37.45	34.65	L	1.2	N	SE	60

131

NAME	AREA	SEC	NO	TYPE	RANK	RB	YR	NB	YR	DER	GEOG	GEOL	'LAT	'LONG	MP	MAP DIS	LOC DIR	EXP	CMP
DIGGER ARCH	ND	BrC	59	CWA	375	53	84	53	84	Sit	ObF	SR	48.81	37.12	B	.9	NNE	SW	125
DIVING BOARD ARCH	SW	WCW	22	CWA	474	23	83	18	84	Obj	SiC	SR	44.56	29.80	F	1.4	ENE	S	100
DOG HEAD ARCH	SA	CtT	3	SAA	347	30	85	24	85	Obj	SiC	SR	38.45	36.89	M	1.7	N	NE	160
DOGBONE ARCH	SD	Cmg	82	CWA	219	34	85	66	85	Obj	SiC	SR	46.26	35.06	C	1.0	SE	N	85
DONUT ARCH	SW	WCW	19	CWA	512	22	80	24	82	Obj	SiC	KA	44.82	29.32	F	1.9	ENE	W	150
DOO ARCH	SD	FiC	8	ECA	361	53	84	53	84	Sit	SiH	SR	48.20	36.71	C	1.7	NNW	SW	140
DOUBLE ARCH SOUTH	CA	WS	16	FSA	3	3	34	3	34	Chr	Sum	SD	41.47	32.40	I	.2	NNW	S	70
DOUBLE ARCH WEST	CA	WS	15	FSA	9	3	34	3	34	Chr	Sum	SD	41.47	32.40	I	.2	NNW	W	32
DOUBLE O ARCH LOWER	SD	DOS	18	FSA	90	8	48	8	48	Obj	SiC	SR	47.95	37.16	C	1.8	NW	NE	112
DOUBLE O ARCH UPPER	SD	DOS	17	FSA	17	8	48	8	48	Obj	SiC	SR	47.95	37.16	C	1.8	NW	NE	112
DOVE FEATHER ARCH	LC	SoL	30	CWA	109	22	85	18	85	Vic	SiC	NA	36.46	34.34	L	.5	E	NE	135
DRAGON ARCH	FF	Lwr	34	CWA	54	36	83	24	83	Obj	SiC	SR	44.73	33.64	E	.3	NE	SW	160
DREAM ARCH	FF	Lwr	33	CWA	140	22	79	23	79	Oth	ObF	SR	44.74	33.68	E	.3	NE	NE	165
DRUMSTICK ARCH	CA	WS	24	CWA	222	18	84	18	84	Obj	Sum	SR	41.44	32.08	I	.2	NE	S	105
DRY FALLS ARCH	CA	WS	37	CWA	518	59	86	51	86	Obj	SiH	NA	40.79	33.05	I	.9	SW	W	175
DUAL ARCH NORTHEAST	FF	Lwr	30	ECA	399	18	84	51	84	Chr	CBt	SR	44.74	38.78	E	.2	NE	NE	155
DUAL ARCH SOUTHWEST	FF	Lwr	31	ECA	420	18	84	51	84	Chr	CBt	SR	44.74	33.78	E	.2	NE	NE	155
DUCK ARCH	EP	SEF	17	CWA	330	59	84	18	84	Obj	SiC	SR	50.11	40.17	A	1.6	NNE	NW	50
DUMBBELL ARCH LOWER	ND	BrC	46	CWA	412	51	84	51	84	Obj	ObF	SR	48.65	37.44	B	.7	N	NE	137
DUMBBELL ARCH UPPER	ND	BrC	45	CWA	363	51	84	51	84	Obj	ObF	SR	48.65	37.44	B	.7	N	NE	137
DUPLEX ARCH LOWER	CA	WS	39	CWA	324	51	86	24	86	Chr	SiH	NA	40.76	33.10	I	1.0	SW	W	0
DUPLEX ARCH UPPER	CA	WS	38	CWA	325	51	86	24	86	Chr	SiH	NA	40.76	33.10	I	1.0	SW	W	0
E ARCH	FF	Lwr	36	FSA	344	24	81	24	81	Obj	FlO	SR	44.71	33.90	E	.1	N	W	160
E T ARCH	CA	PB	3	JHA	392	54	84	54	84	Obj	SiH	WI	43.30	32.32	H	.8	ENE	N	10
EAGLE ARCH	EP	NWF	4	CWA	241	18	84	18	84	Obj	Sum	SR	50.56	42.06	A	2.1	NNW	N	70
EAGLE HEAD ARCH	CA	WS	11	PHA	81	22	79	22	79	Obj	Sum	SR	41.59	32.22	I	.3	N	W	20
EAST TUNNEL ARCH	SD	LdT	73	PHA	158	10	70	10	70	Fet	SiC	SR	47.08	37.73	C	.2	NNW	NE	114
ECHO ARCH	SW	Del	15	FSA	114	10	89	36	82	Evt	Sum	SR	44.74	29.86	F	1.4	ENE	SW	155

132

NAME	AREA	SEC	NO	TYPE	RANK	RB	YR	NB	YR	DER	GEOG	GEOL	'LAT	'LONG	MP	MAP LOC DIS	DIR	EXP	CMP
EDGE ARCH	SA	RBM	23	NB	156	30	83	30	83	Sit	Sum	SR	37.21	36.62	M	.5	ENE	N	90
EIFFEL TOWER BRIDGE	FF	Lwr	47	NB	483	43	85	43	85	Obj	CBt	SR	44.60	33.50	E	.4	E	SE	50
ELEPHANT CHIN ARCH	FF	Upr	19	FSA	146	10	70	23	79	Obj	Sum	SR	45.12	34.10	E	.6	NNW	NE	165
EMBLEM ARCH	ND	ALG	28	FSA	444	17	82	17	82	Obj	Sum	SR	48.78	37.78	B	.9	NNW	SW	130
EPHEDRA ARCH	GW	BIR	1	CWA	426	18	84	18	84	AnP	SiH	NA	42.26	34.19	J	1.7	NNE	S	10
EVIL EYE ARCH	ND	BrC	49	JHA	388	62	84	62	84	Obj	ObF	SR	48.73	37.38	B	.8	NNE	NW	50
EXCAVATION ARCH	ND	DkA	68	ECA	322	82	82	82	82	Chr	Sum	SR	48.29	37.44	B	.2	NNE	NE	115
EXFOLIATION ARCH	SD	Utr	48	PFA	205	51	84	18	84	Chr	SiC	SR	47.55	36.65	C	1.1	NW	NE	98
EYE OF THE WHALE	HP	RrO	8	FSA	47	1	58	11	58	Obj	SiC	SR	42.82	36.20	G	1.1	N	W	125
EYEBALL ARCH	ND	DkA	39	JHA	89	23	77	23	81	Oth	ObF	SR	48.61	37.84	B	.6	NNW	SE	140
FALCON ARCH	HP	RrO	14	ECA	459	24	83	51	84	AnP	Sum	SR	42.42	36.45	G	.6	N	SW	145
FALLEN SLAB BRIDGE	SD	SVS	45	NB	198	23	77	23	77	Chr	SiH	KA	47.54	36.94	C	1.3	WNW	SW	140
FALLING ROCK ARCH	ND	ALG	34	FSA	264	17	81	17	81	Chr	ObF	SR	48.72	37.72	B	.7	N	NE	135
FANTASY ARCH	ND	SVN	87	JHA	435	24	82	51	85	Oth	SiC	KA	47.93	37.62	B	.2	S	NE	150
FAR OUT ARCH	ND	YCW	7	FSA	70	21	77	23	77	Sit	Sum	SR	49.40	39.05	B	2.0	NW	W	120
FAWN ARCH	ND	BrC	58	ECA	287	53	84	53	84	Vic	SiC	SR	48.82	37.16	B	.9	NNE	SW	130
FESTOON ARCH	EP	NWF	10	CWA	510	89	86	18	86	Chr	SiC	SR	50.42	41.91	A	1.9	NNW	N	65
FIGURE ARCH	HP	RrO	12	CWA	244	66	82	23	82	Obj	ObF	SR	42.48	37.03	G	.9	NW	N	90
FILAGREE ARCH	ND	DkA	69	CWA	207	24	83	36	83	Chr	ObF	SR	48.30	37.37	B	.2	NE	NE	106
FISHTAIL ARCH	GW	PtD	8	ECA	184	66	84	51	84	Obj	SiH	NA	40.98	34.33	J	.6	E	E	170
FIVE HUNDRED BRIDGE	KB	Twr	4	NB	300	30	85	24	86	Oth	CBt	MT	47.78	41.55	D	1.0	WNW	SW	148
FIVE TWELVE ARCH	EP	NWF	9	CWA	290	40	86	40	86	Oth	Sum	SR	50.49	42.09	A	2.0	NNW	N	85
FLAME ARCH	CA	PB	19	FSA	136	66	83	24	83	Obj	SiH	KA	43.19	32.05	H	1.0	E	S	93
FLAPJACK ARCH	ND	YCW	3	ECA	353	61	84	18	84	Obj	ObF	SR	49.67	39.23	B	2.3	NW	N	105
FLAT ARCH	SA	RBM	8	PFA	277	51	84	51	84	Obj	FlO	MT	38.03	36.81	M	1.2	NNE	SE	20
FLATIRON ARCH	FF	Lwr	37	FSA	139	10	69	10	69	Obj	ObF	SR	44.71	33.76	E	.2	NE	E	163
FLEDGLING ARCH	ND	YCW	5	CWA	234	22	80	22	80	Fet	SiC	SR	49.61	38.17	B	1.8	NNW	NE	128
FLYING BUTTRESS ARCH	HP	RrO	4	JHA	92	22	78	22	83	Obj	ObF	SR	42.78	36.88	G	1.1	NNW	SW	118

133

NAME	AREA	SEC	NO	TYPE	RANK	RB	YR	NB	YR	DER	GEOG	GEOL	°LAT	°LONG	MAP LOC MP DIS DIR	EXP	CMP
FLYING HAT ARCH	ND	YCW	10	CWA	67	23	78	30	84	Evt	SiC	SR	48.85	38.69	B 1.4 NW	SW	122
FORGOTTEN ARCH	EP	NWF	5	FSA	132	30	83	30	83	Evt	ObF	SR	50.53	42.13	A 2.1 NNW	S	100
FOUR HUNDRED ARCH	SA	RBM	7	FSA	380	51	84	51	84	Oth	Sum	MT	38.05	37.17	M 1.3 N	E	155
FRAGILE ARCH	FF	Upr	8	JHA	475	52	84	51	84	Obj	SiC	SR	45.59	34.66	E 1.3 NNW	N	90
FRAME ARCH	SW	Del	13	FSA	134	10	70	24	79	Sit	Sum	SR	44.65	29.96	F 1.3 ENE	NW	65
FUNNEL ARCH	ND	BrC	43	FSA	226	23	77	23	81	Obj	SiC	SR	48.62	37.48	B .6 N	S	135
GAP ARCH	SA	SBo	44	FSA	343	18	84	18	84	Obj	SiC	NA	36.88	36.36	M .7 E	S	73
GARBAGE ARCH	FF	Upr	4	ECA	402	17	82	17	82	Sit	SiH	NA	45.48	35.94	E 2.1 WNW	N	110
GAUGE ARCH	LC	SoL	28	CWA	170	66	82	66	82	Fet	Sum	KA	36.81	34.68	L .5 NNE	N	20
GHOST ARCH	CA	WS	5	CWA	215	18	73	24	78	Obj	SiC	SR	41.88	32.48	I .7 NNW	N	90
GIMPY ARCH	CA	WS	27	PFA	366	75	85	24	85	Evt	SiH	NA	41.28	32.74	I .4 W	S	90
GOBLET ARCH	SD	Cmg	80	JHA	382	66	83	18	84	Obj	SiC	SR	46.44	34.72	C 1.1 SE	NW	121
GOOSEHEAD ARCH	SW	WCW	23	CWA	258	23	83	23	83	Obj	SiC	SR	44.54	29.75	F 1.4 ENE	W	8
GOSSIPS ARCH	SA	CtT	6	CWA	129	23	78	23	78	Fet	SiC	SR	38.12	36.24	M 1.5 NNE	NE	130
GOTHIC ARCH	ND	GoC	67	CWA	23	17	70	20	72	Chr	SiC	SR	48.36	37.42	B .3 NNE	NE	138
GRACEFUL ARCH	SA	SBo	35	CWA	203	23	83	23	83	Obj	SiH	NA	37.09	36.94	M .2 ENE	S	102
GREASEWOOD ARCH	EP	SVE	46	FSA	511	90	86	24	86	AnP	SiH	NA	48.88	39.93	A 1.1 E	SW	140
GREY FOX ARCH	ND	GoC	75	CWA	504	51	84	51	84	AnP	ObF	SR	48.38	37.22	B .5 NE	NE	137
GUANO ARCH	SD	UTr	51	CWA	78	17	78	17	78	Vic	SiC	SR	47.48	36.54	C 1.0 NW	NE	133
HALF MOON ARCH	LC	SoL	16	CWA	429	23	83	23	83	Obj	SiC	NA	37.13	34.46	L .9 NNE	NW	60
HAMBURGER ARCH	ND	IHG	21	ECA	430	51	84	51	84	Obj	ObF	SR	48.76	37.86	B .8 NNW	SW	150
HAMMER ARCH	EP	NWF	11	FSA	443	89	86	18	86	Obj	SiH	SD	50.24	41.75	A 1.6 NNW	W	25
HANGING ARCH	EP	SEF	29	JHA	194	59	84	59	84	Obj	SiC	DB	49.46	40.13	A 1.1 NE	S	20
HELMET ARCH	ND	DON	71	FSA	210	21	77	17	80	Obj	SiC	SR	48.32	37.21	B .4 NE	SW	138
HIDDEN ARCH	ND	DON	82	FSA	49	10	61	10	61	Sit	SiC	SR	48.24	37.26	B .3 ENE	NE	130
HIDDEN CANYON ARCH	HP	RrO	2	PAA	255	23	78	23	78	Sit	ObF	SR	42.95	36.79	G 1.3 NNW	S	107
HIP JOINT ARCH	EP	NWF	7	CWA	298	58	84	18	84	Obj	Sum	SR	50.51	42.17	A 2.1 NNW	W	179
HOLE IN FIN	FF	Lwr	29	FSA	145	23	77	23	77	Chr	ObF	SR	44.76	33.78	E .2 NNE	SW	170

134

NAME	AREA	SEC	NO	TYPE	RANK	RB	YR	NB	YR	DER	GEOG	GEOL	'LAT	'LONG	MAP LOC MP DIS DIR	EXP	CMP
HOLEY ARCH	ND	ALG	30	ECA	505	56	84	51	84	Chr	ObF	SR	48.86	37.70	B .9 N	SW	125
HOOF ARCH	FF	Upr	9	CWA	500	17	83	18	84	Obj	SiC	SR	45.52	34.60	E 1.2 NNW	SE	155
HOOP ARCH	GW	SiC	22	SAA	502	51	84	51	84	Obj	SiC	KA	39.93	33.64	J 1.6 SE	SE	55
HORN OF PLENTY ARCH	CA	PB	2	PAA	334	54	84	18	84	Obj	SiH	WI	43.31	32.52	H .6 ENE	N	90
HOURGLASS ARCH	EP	SEF	26	FSA	154	17	83	18	84	Obj	SiC	SD	49.65	40.38	A 1.1 NE	S	32
HUG ARCH	ND	ALG	37	PFA	367	24	84	51	84	Obj	ObF	SR	48.77	37.66	B .8 N	NE	122
HUMMINGBIRD ARCH	LC	NoL	7	CWA	416	51	84	18	84	AnP	SiC	NA	38.24	34.08	L 2.2 NNE	S	180
ILLUSION ARCH	HP	WiF	19	FSA	237	30	82	30	82	Oth	ObF	SR	41.70	36.33	G .2 S	S	65
INDIAN HEAD ARCH	ND	IHG	20	FSA	398	18	73	18	73	Obj	Sum	SR	48.80	37.91	B .9 NNW	SW	130
INNER SANCTUM BRIDGE	FF	Lwr	46	NB	137	10	69	23	81	Sit	ObF	SR	44.63	33.48	E .4 E	W	128
INSIDE OUT ARCH INNER	EP	SVE	36	CWA	153	22	81	24	82	Chr	SiC	KA	49.10	40.38	A .7 ENE	SW	125
INSIDE OUT ARCH OUTER	EP	SVE	35	CWA	64	21	77	24	82	Chr	SiC	KA	49.10	40.38	A .7 ENE	SW	125
IVY ARCH	SW	Del	11	CWA	72	83	81	24	81	Vic	SiC	SR	44.52	30.70	F .6 NE	S	87
JACK RABBIT ARCH	SA	RBM	21	JHA	465	51	84	51	84	AnP	Sum	MT	37.31	36.88	M .5 NNE	E	10
JICAMA ARCH	CA	WS	18	JHA	195	66	81	24	84	Obj	SiC	SR	41.47	32.28	I .2 N	E	0
JOGGERS ARCH	SA	SBo	40	JHA	374	42	85	42	85	Evt	ObF	NA	37.01	36.69	M .4 E	NE	145
JUNIPER ARCH	SA	RBM	22	FSA	454	30	83	30	83	AnP	ObF	MT	37.38	36.68	M .6 NE	SW	140
KEYHOLE ARCH	ND	DkA	26	ECA	354	23	77	24	82	Obj	Sum	SR	48.82	37.97	B .8 NNW	SW	132
KIDS ARCH EAST	SA	SBo	39	CWA	452	66	85	51	86	Vic	SiH	NA	37.08	36.85	M .3 ENE	S	100
KIDS ARCH WEST	SA	SBo	38	CWA	111	26	82	66	82	Vic	SiH	NA	37.08	36.85	M .3 ENE	S	100
KISSING TURTLES	FF	Lwr	39	FSA	293	18	73	20	75	Obj	Sum	SR	44.70	33.68	E .3 NE	NE	162
LANDMARK ARCH	FF	Lwr	49	FSA	468	23	82	24	82	Sit	ObF	SR	44.56	33.59	E .3 E	W	45
LANDSCAPE ARCH	SD	LdT	56	FSA	1	3	34	2	34	Sit	FlO	SR	47.43	36.42	C .8 NW	NE	147
LATTICE ARCH	ND	DON	80	ECA	286	52	84	52	84	Obj	ObF	SR	48.17	37.46	B .2 ENE	NE	128
LAUGHING COYOTE ARCH	GW	GrW	14	CWA	95	23	79	23	79	Obj	SiC	SR	40.25	35.51	J .9 SSW	S	125
LAYER ARCH	EP	NWF	15	ECA	448	91	86	91	86	Chr	SiH	SR	50.13	41.57	A 1.5 NNW	N	100
LAZY ARCH	SD	FiC	26	CWA	235	23	83	23	83	Obj	Sum	SR	47.89	36.64	C 1.4 NW	NE	116
LEAN TO ARCH	EP	SEF	28	JHA	522	59	84	18	84	Obj	SiC	SD	49.57	40.27	A 1.1 NE	SW	60

NAME	AREA	SEC	NO	TYPE	RANK	RB	YR	NB	YR	DER	GEOG	GEOL	'LAT	'LONG	MP	MAP DIS	LOC DIR	EXP	CMP
LEAPING ARCH	HP	RrO	3	FSA	28	1	70	17	74	Obj	Sum	SR	42.99	36.39	G	1.3	N	NE	142
LEAST ARCH	SD	SVS	69	ECA	397	23	84	23	84	Oth	ObF	NA	47.17	36.24	C	.5	WNW	NE	155
LEDGE ARCH	SD	LdT	62	CWA	11	23	77	23	77	Sit	SiC	SR	47.31	36.32	C	.7	NW	NE	151
LEECH ARCH	SA	SBo	33	CWA	476	18	84	18	84	Obj	SiC	SR	37.01	37.33	M	.2	W	E	20
LEGBONE ARCH	HP	RrO	11	JHA	508	66	84	24	85	Obj	SiC	SR	42.56	36.72	G	.8	NNW	NE	135
LENS ARCH	ND	BrC	57	CWA	391	53	84	53	84	Obj	ObF	SR	48.84	37.17	B	.9	NNE	NW	137
LICHEN ARCH	SD	Cst	44	FSA	350	23	83	66	83	Vic	ObF	SR	47.62	36.40	C	1.0	NW	NE	125
LIGHTNING BOLT ARCH	FF	Lwr	35	JHA	94	23	83	18	84	Obj	SiC	SR	44.72	33.64	E	.3	NE	SW	28
LIMBO ARCH	SD	FiC	34	CWA	196	23	77	66	81	Oth	SiC	SR	47.82	36.62	C	1.3	NW	SW	121
LITTLE DUCK WINDOW	CA	WS	25	FSA	233	23	77	23	77	Obj	SiC	SD	41.45	31.96	I	.3	ENE	S	73
LITTLE GOTHIC ARCH	GW	GrW	18	CWA	26	23	77	23	77	Oth	SiC	SR	39.78	35.60	J	1.4	SSW	E	35
LITTLE POTHOLE ARCH	GW	BIR	2	PHA	462	18	73	23	77	Obj	Sum	SR	41.94	34.36	J	1.3	NNE	E	0
LIZARD ARCH	LC	SoL	17	SAA	409	18	73	18	82	Obj	SiH	NA	37.11	34.51	L	.9	NNE	SE	42
LOST AND FOUND BRIDGE	HP	RrO	9	NB	133	23	77	23	83	Evt	ObF	SR	42.60	36.97	G	1.0	NW	W	45
LOUVER ARCH	FF	Lwr	38	FSA	169	18	84	18	84	Obj	SiC	SR	44.68	33.75	E	.2	NE	SW	165
MAGIC MYSTERY ARCH	SD	Cmg	85	NB	21	80	62	20	75	Oth	SiC	MT	46.20	34.30	C	1.5	SE	NE	130
MAGPIE ARCH NORTH	SD	UTr	52	CWA	197	17	82	18	84	AnP	SiC	SR	47.46	36.49	C	.9	NW	NE	138
MAGPIE ARCH SOUTH	SD	UTr	53	CWA	496	17	82	18	84	AnP	SiC	SR	47.46	36.49	C	.9	NW	NE	138
MAHOGANY ARCH	SA	RBM	25	CWA	307	66	83	24	84	AnP	Sum	SR	37.29	36.44	M	.7	ENE	S	109
MANDOLIN ARCH	SA	CtT	14	CWA	212	24	78	24	78	Obj	SiC	SR	38.81	36.09	M	1.4	NE	E	5
MICROPHONE ARCH	HP	WiF	20	FSA	379	25	80	22	81	Obj	ObF	SR	41.69	36.30	G	.3	S	SE	170
MINI SPECTACLES NORTH	FF	Upr	15	FSA	503	23	83	24	83	Obj	Sum	SD	45.20	34.20	E	.7	NNW	SW	140
MINI SPECTACLES SOUTH	FF	Upr	16	FSA	386	23	83	24	83	Obj	Sum	SD	45.20	34.20	E	.7	NNW	SW	140
MIRROR ARCH	SW	WCW	20	SAA	316	18	84	18	84	Obj	SiC	KA	44.62	29.30	F	1.8	ENE	N	100
MONOCLE ARCH	FF	Upr	14	FSA	400	23	85	51	86	Obj	SiH	SD	45.25	34.22	E	.8	NNW	W	0
MORRISON BRIDGE	SW	2JB	6	NB	451	24	82	24	82	Chr	CBt	BB	44.25	31.88	F	.6	W	W	0
MOSS ARCH	LC	SoL	19	SAA	467	51	84	18	84	Vic	SiH	NA	36.91	34.55	L	.7	NNE	N	160
MUKLUK ARCH	FF	Upr	12	FSA	442	18	73	24	84	Obj	Sum	DB	45.36	34.40	E	1.0	NNW	SW	145

NAME	AREA	SEC	NO	TYPE	RANK	RB	YR	NB	YR	DER	GEOG	GEOL	'LAT	'LONG	MAP LOC MP DIS DIR	EXP	CMP
MULE DEER ARCH	CA	WS	23	ECA	376	24	83	18	84	Vic	SiC	DB	41.38	32.38	I .1 NW	SW	25
MUSHROOM ARCH	ND	IHG	25	FSA	471	51	84	18	84	Obj	ObF	SR	48.70	37.97	B .8 NNW	N	130
NAND ARCH INNER	SD	FiC	20	CWA	38	23	77	66	82	Sit	SiC	SR	47.93	37.05	C 1.7 NW	E	107
NAND ARCH OUTER	SD	FiC	19	CWA	2	18	84	51	84	Sit	SiC	SR	47.93	37.05	C 1.7 NW	E	107
NARROW ARCH	CA	WS	17	ECA	240	24	83	24	84	Obj	Sum	SR	41.47	32.40	I .2 NNW	S	70
NAVAJO ARCH	SD	UTr	49	FSA	43	13	58	13	58	Obj	ObF	SR	47.55	36.56	C 1.0 NW	SW	90
NEGLECTED ARCH	CA	PB	16	CWA	181	54	84	24	84	Evt	SiH	WI	43.21	32.29	H .8 E	N	80
NORTH WINDOW	CA	WS	31	FSA	8	1	32	5	40	Sit	SiC	SD	41.15	31.94	I .4 ESE	SW	148
NUTCRACKER ARCH	UC	NoU	3	JHA	236	23	82	23	82	Obj	SiC	SR	39.81	37.11	K 2.2 WNW	SW	150
ON THE MONEY ARCH	EP	SVE	22	CWA	407	22	83	76	83	Sit	SiH	KA	49.68	41.60	A 1.0 NNW	SW	127
ONE BLOCK ARCH	ND	ALG	31	FSA	178	17	83	17	83	Chr	Sum	SR	48.82	37.66	B .9 N	SW	135
ONE LEGGED ARCH	SW	2JB	3	JHA	525	20	81	24	81	Obj	Sum	SW	44.12	32.59	F 1.3 W	NE	165
OVAL ARCH	ND	BrC	61	CWA	50	23	77	23	77	Obj	SiC	SR	48.39	37.58	B .3 N	E	138
OVERHANG ARCH	ND	BrC	40	SAA	155	52	84	52	84	Chr	ObF	SR	48.56	37.55	B .5 N	SW	138
OWL EYE ARCH	GW	SiC	20	SAA	281	35	82	24	82	Obj	CBt	NA	39.59	34.92	J 1.5 S	W	28
PACK RAT ARCH	EP	SVE	32	CWA	327	58	84	18	84	AnP	SiH	KA	49.05	40.60	A .4 E	SW	95
PAGODA ARCH	FF	Upr	11	FSA	256	17	82	17	82	Obj	Sum	SR	45.48	34.26	E 1.1 NNW	E	120
PAN ARCH	SD	SVS	68	CWA	177	56	84	24	84	Obj	SiC	NA	47.26	36.88	C .7 WNW	SW	125
PANORAMA BLUFFS ARCH	CA	PB	14	PAA	369	22	78	23	78	Sit	Sum	WI	43.16	32.36	H .7 E	S	70
PARADE OF ELEPHANTS NORTH	CA	WS	21	FSA	91	5	34	6	38	Fet	SiC	SD	41.40	32.42	I .2 WNW	SE	22
PARADE OF ELEPHANTS SOUTH	CA	WS	22	CWA	15	5	34	6	38	Fet	SiC	SD	41.36	32.41	I .2 WNW	E	0
PARALLEL ARCH INNER	KB	Twr	10	CWA	87	10	69	18	73	Chr	SiC	SR	47.38	41.16	D .7 W	SW	162
PARALLEL ARCH OUTER	KB	Twr	9	CWA	56	10	69	18	73	Chr	SiC	SR	47.38	41.16	D .7 W	SW	162
PARK AVENUE ARCH	SA	CtT	15	CWA	271	18	73	23	77	Fet	SiC	SR	37.53	35.71	M 1.4 ENE	SW	110
PARTITION ARCH NORTH	SD	UTr	54	FSA	66	8	48	8	48	Chr	SiC	SR	47.47	36.47	C .9 NW	NE	155
PARTITION ARCH SOUTH	SD	UTr	55	FSA	206	8	48	8	48	Chr	SiC	SR	47.47	36.47	C .9 NW	NE	155
PEDESTAL ARCH	SA	SBo	50	SAA	485	18	84	18	84	Obj	SiH	NA	36.81	36.38	M .7 ESE	S	123
PEEPHOLE ARCH	EP	SEF	18	CWA	84	22	83	73	83	Evt	SiC	SR	49.95	40.13	A 1.5 NE	S	105

137

NAME	AREA	SEC	NO	TYPE	RANK	RB	YR	NB	YR	DER	GEOG	GEOL	°LAT	°LONG	MP	MAP DIS	LOC DIR	EXP	CMP
PELLET ARCH	EP	SVE	40	FSA	445	65	84	65	84	Evt	SiH	KA	49.02	40.21	A	.8	E	S	90
PENGUIN ARCH	SA	SBo	34	CWA	275	18	84	18	84	Fet	SiC	SR	37.18	37.04	M	.3	NNE	W	165
PERFORATED PILLAR ARCH	CA	PB	5	SAA	461	66	83	66	83	Chr	SiH	WI	43.28	32.19	H	.8	E	N	175
PERSEVERANCE ARCH	SD	LdT	63	CWA	284	17	81	17	81	Oth	SiC	SR	47.30	36.08	C	.5	NW	NE	125
PET ARCH	ND	DkA	83	CWA	360	24	77	24	77	Obj	SiH	NA	48.02	37.65	B	.1	SW	SW	126
PHANTOM ARCH	ND	IHG	24	CWA	42	23	78	23	78	Oth	SiC	SR	48.71	38.03	B	.8	NNW	NE	132
PIANO ARCH	CA	PB	6	SAA	520	54	84	54	84	Obj	Sum	WI	43.27	31.97	H	1.1	E	W	125
PIANO LEG ARCH	ND	ALG	32	FSA	193	23	78	23	78	Obj	ObF	SR	48.84	37.54	B	.9	N	SW	120
PILLAR ARCH	GW	SiC	21	SAA	333	51	84	51	84	Obj	SiC	KA	39.96	33.81	J	1.6	SE	NW	30
PINCHED JUGHANDLE	GW	PtD	12	JHA	227	23	77	23	77	Obj	SiC	SR	40.47	35.61	J	.8	SW	N	100
PINE TREE ARCH	SD	LdT	64	FSA	36	8	45	8	45	Vic	SiC	SR	47.27	35.89	C	.4	NNW	N	120
PINYON JAY ARCH	SA	RBM	12	ECA	486	66	83	51	84	AnP	ObF	SM	37.83	36.83	M	1.0	NNE	W	5
PISTOL ARCH	ND	DON	79	CWA	83	18	73	24	83	Obj	SiC	SR	48.20	37.47	B	.2	ENE	E	155
PLANE BRIDGE	SD	SVS	38	NB	119	66	85	66	85	Obj	SiH	KA	47.73	37.28	C	1.6	WNW	SW	145
PLANK ARCH	GW	PtD	10	CWA	516	66	84	51	84	Obj	CBt	NA	40.93	34.34	J	.6	E	NE	140
POISON IVY ARCH	UC	NoU	1	CWA	30	66	83	24	83	Vic	SiC	SR	40.33	37.56	K	2.9	NW	NE	135
POLYPILLAR ARCH NORTH	CA	PB	7	SAA	428	54	84	18	84	Obj	Sum	WI	43.26	31.95	H	1.1	E	E	163
POLYPILLAR ARCH SOUTH	CA	PB	8	SAA	473	54	84	18	84	Obj	Sum	WI	43.26	31.95	H	1.1	E	E	163
POOL ARCH	SD	LFC	3	CWA	259	24	83	53	84	Vic	SiH	MT	48.32	35.30	C	1.6	NNE	NE	120
PORCUPINE ARCH	CA	WS	7	CWA	427	18	84	18	84	AnP	SiH	NA	41.87	32.02	I	.7	NNE	NE	125
PORTHOLE CAVE ARCH	SA	RBM	26	SAA	232	18	73	23	77	Obj	SiC	SD	37.28	37.45	M	.7	ENE	E	30
POSTULATION ARCH	ND	YCW	9	CWA	51	61	84	18	84	Oth	SiC	SR	49.19	39.31	B	2.0	NW	SW	115
POT ARCH	SD	SVS	67	CWA	200	56	84	24	84	Obj	SiC	NA	47.26	36.37	C	.7	WNW	SW	125
POTATO ARCH	CA	PB	13	CWA	477	54	84	54	84	Obj	Sum	WI	43.28	31.81	H	1.2	E	N	95
POTHOLE ARCH LOWER	CA	WS	1	PHA	46	1	69	1	69	Obj	Sum	SR	42.04	33.26	I	1.2	NW	N	120
POTHOLE ARCH UPPER	CA	WS	2	PHA	141	1	69	1	69	Obj	Sum	SR	42.04	33.26	I	1.2	NW	N	120
PRETZEL ARCH	LC	NoL	1	PFA	395	51	84	51	84	Obj	FlO	NA	37.10	34.80	L	2.6	N	W	25
PUNCH BOWL ARCH	SD	LdT	66	FSA	385	24	78	24	78	Obj	Sum	SR	47.40	35.72	C	.5	N	S	80

NAME	AREA	SEC	NO	TYPE	RANK	RB	YR	NB	YR	DER	GEOG	GEOL	°LAT	°LONG	MAP LOC MP DIS DIR	EXP	CMP
QUEUE JUGHANDLE	FF	Upr	24	JHA	524	28	79	23	79	Obj	Sum	SR	44.96	33.59	E .5 NE	N	90
QUICKSAND ARCH	UC	NoU	4	JHA	438	51	84	51	84	Vic	SiH	SR	39.67	37.28	K 2.3 WNW	W	0
RABBIT TRAP ARCH	SD	UTr	28	SAA	270	31	81	31	81	Obj	FlO	SR	47.83	36.96	C 1.5 NW	N	100
RAINDROP ARCH	KB	Esc	1	CWA	180	70	84	18	84	Chr	SiC	SR	47.86	41.20	D .8 WNW	E	128
RAVEN ARCH	CA	WS	20	ECA	269	18	73	18	84	AnP	SiC	SD	41.41	32.41	I .2 NW	E	162
RECON BRIDGE	KB	Twr	14	NB	498	36	86	86	86	Evt	CBt	SR	46.49	40.80	D 1.1 SSW	W	20
RECTANGULAR ARCH	ND	BrC	53	FSA	252	17	81	24	83	Obj	SiC	SR	48.73	37.28	B .8 NNE	SW	122
REDTAIL ARCH	ND	BrC	55	ECA	230	67	83	53	84	AnP	Sum	SR	48.77	37.25	B .8 NNE	SW	122
REFLEX ARCH	HP	RrO	10	CWA	131	23	78	23	82	Obj	ObF	SR	42.59	36.97	G 1.0 NW	W	5
REGAINED ARCH	GW	GrW	5	CWA	238	23	81	23	81	Evt	Sum	DB	41.05	35.33	J .3 WNW	S	170
REGAP ARCH	SA	SBo	45	ECA	355	18	84	18	84	Fet	SiC	NA	36.89	36.32	M .8 E	S	60
REPTILE ARCH	FF	Upr	20	ECA	394	55	84	55	84	Obj	ObF	SR	45.10	34.08	E .6 NNW	E	163
REVEREND ARCH	CA	WS	41	JHA	371	36	85	36	85	Chr	SiH	NA	40.56	33.17	I 1.2 SW	SE	60
RIBBON ARCH	CA	WS	12	FSA	40	5	39	5	39	Obj	Sum	SR	41.64	32.18	I .4 N	NE	150
RIM ARCH	SW	WCW	24	CWA	48	77	82	23	82	Sit	Sum	MT	44.37	30.00	F 1.1 ENE	S	98
RING ARCH	UC	SoU	19	PHA	37	2	40	10	61	Obj	SiC	SR	38.93	37.37	K 1.3 W	E	0
RINGTAIL ARCH LOWER	SD	FiC	14	FSA	144	23	77	24	82	Vic	SiC	SR	48.09	36.36	C .9 NNW	SW	130
RINGTAIL ARCH UPPER	SD	FiC	15	ECA	493	24	82	24	82	Vic	SiC	SR	48.09	36.36	C .9 NNW	SW	130
RINKY DINK ARCH	SD	Cmg	81	SAA	469	22	85	74	85	Chr	SiC	SD	46.32	35.30	C .8 SSE	NE	25
ROADSIDE ARCH	FF	Upr	13	CWA	32	18	73	23	79	Sit	SiC	SD	45.38	34.40	E 1.0 NNW	SW	115
ROCK CATCHER ARCH	SD	LdT	71	CWA	356	18	84	18	84	Obj	SiC	SR	47.21	36.20	C .5 WNW	NE	140
ROCK IN THE HOLE ARCH	KB	SoK	18	ECA	272	51	84	18	84	Chr	SiC	SR	45.39	39.64	D 2.5 SSE	E	8
ROLLED ARCH	ND	DON	81	CWA	305	24	83	23	83	Chr	ObF	SR	48.20	37.34	B .3 ENE	NE	140
RUBBLE ARCH NORTHWEST	ND	SVN	84	FSA	492	82	82	82	82	Chr	SiH	KA	47.92	37.88	B .2 SSW	N	70
RUBBLE ARCH SOUTHEAST	ND	SVN	85	ECA	321	82	82	82	82	Chr	SiH	KA	47.92	37.88	B .2 SSW	NW	25
RUIN ARCH	SD	Cmg	78	CWA	22	18	73	24	81	Obj	ObF	MT	46.70	34.88	C .8 ESE	W	135
RUNNING COYOTE ARCH	UC	NoU	8	CWA	173	23	78	23	78	Vic	SiC	SR	39.42	35.27	K .7 NNW	W	15
RUPTURE ARCH	LC	SoL	29	CWA	368	23	85	24	85	Obj	SiH	KA	36.43	34.86	L .1 NE	N	112

139

NAME	AREA	SEC	NO	TYPE	RANK	RB	YR	NB	YR	DER	GEOG	GEOL	'LAT	'LONG	MAP LOC MP DIS DIR	EXP	CMP
SAGE ARCH	CA	WS	8	FSA	373	18	84	18	84	AnP	Sum	KA	41.83	31.90	I .7 NNE	NE	0
SALAMANDER ARCH	EP	NWF	13	CWA	127	30	81	22	81	Obj	SiC	SR	50.16	41.56	A 1.5 NNW	S	115
SALT WASH ARCH	SW	UpW	2	PHA	315	27	79	24	81	Sit	Sum	MT	44.92	31.68	F 1.0 NNW	E	0
SALTBUSH ARCH	EP	SVE	47	ECA	359	18	86	24	86	AnP	SiH	WI	48.66	39.97	A 1.1 ESE	S	80
SAND ARCH INNER	SD	FiC	22	CWA	16	23	77	66	82	Sit	SiC	SR	47.91	37.02	C 1.6 NW	E	107
SAND ARCH OUTER	SD	FiC	21	CWA	101	23	77	66	82	Sit	SiC	SR	47.91	37.02	C 1.6 NW	E	107
SAND DUNE ARCH	FF	Upr	2	FSA	77	1	65	1	65	Sit	ObF	SR	45.86	34.84	E 1.7 NNW	NE	140
SAND HILL ARCH	KB	SoK	16	CWA	31	21	77	24	78	Sit	SiC	SR	45.58	39.96	D 2.2 SSE	E	0
SAUCER ARCH	ND	GoC	64	FSA	254	23	77	24	81	Obj	ObF	SR	48.43	37.40	B .4 NNE	SW	140
SCAB ARCH	CA	WS	28	PFA	437	51	84	18	84	Obj	SiH	NA	41.25	32.55	I .3 W	S	105
SCOOP ARCH	EP	SVE	19	CWA	268	23	78	23	81	Obj	SiC	KA	49.95	42.00	A 1.5 NW	S	113
SCREECH OWL ARCH	ND	YCW	4	CWA	55	22	80	22	80	Vic	SiC	MT	49.61	38.17	B 1.8 NNW	NE	128
SEA SHELL ARCH	EP	SVE	24	ECA	490	58	84	18	84	Obj	SiH	WI	49.64	41.56	A .9 NNW	W	108
SEAGULL ARCH	CA	WS	29	FSA	85	1	69	23	77	Obj	SiC	SD	41.24	31.96	I .3 ESE	SE	130
SEARCH PARTY ARCH	SD	Cst	27	CWA	440	18	84	18	84	Evt	Sum	SR	47.84	37.04	C 1.6 NW	SW	114
SECRETIVE ARCH	FF	Upr	21	ECA	499	24	85	24	85	Sit	ObF	SR	45.08	34.11	E .6 NNW	SW	145
SEE SAW ARCH	CA	PB	1	SAA	447	54	84	54	84	Obj	SiH	WI	43.34	32.60	H .6 ENE	N	153
SERPENTINE ARCH	CA	WS	4	FSA	69	1	69	23	79	Obj	SiC	SD	41.84	32.79	I .8 NW	NW	63
SERVICEBERRY ARCH	GW	PtD	7	PFA	274	75	85	24	85	Vic	FlO	NA	41.15	34.30	J .7 ENE	NE	100
SHADOW BOX ARCH	SD	DOS	10	FSA	228	18	73	23	77	Obj	SiC	SR	48.07	37.21	C 1.9 NW	SW	113
SHELF ARCH	SD	LFC	6	CWA	262	23	83	23	83	Sit	Sum	MT	48.30	35.31	C 1.6 NNE	N	90
SHELTER ARCH	ND	IHG	11	FSA	297	18	73	18	81	Obj	ObF	SR	48.88	38.00	B 1.0 NNW	SW	125
SHIELD ARCH	ND	YCW	8	FSA	185	23	77	24	80	Obj	SiC	SR	49.28	39.26	B 2.1 NW	N	112
SHOE ARCH	SA	CtT	4	ECA	250	18	73	24	83	Fet	FlO	DB	38.30	35.72	M 2.0 NE	NW	54
SHOTGUN ARCH	SA	SBo	43	ECA	411	18	84	18	84	Obj	SiC	NA	36.88	36.36	M .7 E	E	155
SIBLING ARCH CENTER	EP	NWF	1	CWA	24	78	83	22	83	Oth	ObF	SR	50.56	42.28	A 2.2 NNW	N	102
SIBLING ARCH NORTH	EP	NWF	2	CWA	151	78	83	22	83	Oth	ObF	SR	50.56	42.28	A 2.2 NNW	N	102
SIBLING ARCH SOUTH	EP	NWF	3	PAA	338	40	86	51	86	Oth	ObF	SR	50.56	42.28	A 2.2 NNW	N	102

NAME	AREA	SEC	NO	TYPE	RANK	RB	YR	NB	YR	DER	GEOG	GEOL	'LAT	'LONG	MP	MAP LOC DIS	DIR	EXP	CMP
SIDE FIN ARCH	ND	BrC	41	FSA	82	29	80	29	80	Sit	SiC	SR	48.56	37.50	B	.6	N	SW	134
SINK ARCH	CA	WS	42	FSA	514	88	85	88	85	Obj	FlO	NA	40.56	32.45	I	.9	S	N	100
SIT DOWN ARCH	HP	RrO	13	CWA	164	23	77	74	85	Evt	ObF	SR	42.42	36.66	G	.6	NNW	S	115
SKATE KEY ARCH	SA	RBM	13	FSA	453	51	84	51	84	Obj	Sum	SM	37.76	36.81	M	.9	NNE	S	70
SKEPTICAL ARCH	SD	LFC	5	JHA	362	71	83	51	84	Oth	SiC	MT	48.31	35.29	C	1.6	NNE	N	5
SKYLINE ARCH	SD	Cmg	79	FSA	13	3	34	10	58	Sit	Sum	SR	46.51	35.39	C	.6	SSE	SW	120
SLANT ARCH LOWER	SA	CtF	10	FSA	491	30	83	24	83	Obj	FlO	NA	37.92	34.93	M	2.3	ENE	SW	130
SLANT ARCH UPPER	SA	CtF	9	FSA	348	30	83	24	83	Obj	FlO	NA	37.92	34.93	M	2.3	ENE	SW	130
SLANTED EYE ARCH	HP	WiF	17	PFA	128	22	78	24	81	Obj	Sum	SR	41.97	36.43	G	.1	WNW	N	100
SLAT ARCH	HP	RrO	6	ECA	303	52	84	52	84	Fet	ObF	SR	42.75	36.88	G	1.1	NNW	N	100
SLEEPING ARCH	EP	SVE	33	CWA	457	30	82	24	82	Evt	SiH	KA	49.04	40.66	A	.4	ENE	W	145
SLIPPER ARCH	LC	NoL	6	ECA	319	24	81	51	84	Obj	FlO	NA	38.20	34.52	L	2.1	N	SW	150
SLIT ARCH	FF	Upr	3	ECA	103	30	83	71	83	Obj	ObF	SR	45.82	34.81	E	1.6	NNW	NE	140
SLIVER ARCH	FF	Lwr	42	CWA	308	36	83	36	83	Obj	ObF	SR	44.70	33.54	E	.3	ENE	E	160
SLOPE ARCH	CA	PB	18	CWA	464	23	78	23	78	Sit	Sum	WI	43.20	32.09	H	1.0	E	SE	68
SLOT ARCH	HP	RrO	5	ECA	323	23	78	23	78	Obj	ObF	SR	42.75	36.88	G	1.1	NNW	N	100
SNAKEHEAD ARCH	ND	GoC	65	CWA	189	31	81	31	81	Obj	ObF	SR	48.33	37.52	B	.3	NNE	NE	135
SNOUT ARCH	SA	CtF	16	PFA	326	24	85	51	85	Obj	FlO	NA	37.35	35.05	M	1.9	ENE	N	85
SNOWY ARCH	EP	SVE	37	CWA	121	65	84	18	84	Evt	SiC	KA	49.06	40.26	A	.8	E	SW	145
SOLO ARCH	SW	WCW	21	JHA	523	18	84	18	84	Oth	SiC	KA	44.58	29.28	F	1.8	ENE	SW	145
SOUTH WINDOW	CA	WS	32	FSA	5	1	32	1	32	Sit	SiC	SD	41.10	31.91	I	.4	SE	SW	155
SPALLING ARCH	CA	PB	11	CWA	143	66	83	23	83	Chr	SiH	WI	43.30	31.89	H	1.2	E	N	110
SPATULA ARCH	SA	SBo	54	CWA	261	51	84	51	84	Obj	SiH	NA	36.58	35.77	M	1.4	ESE	SW	143
SPIDER ARCH	EP	NWF	16	CWA	257	89	86	18	86	Vic	SiH	DB	50.15	41.67	A	1.5	NNW	S	125
SPINDLE ARCH	LC	SoL	27	CWA	479	51	84	18	84	Obj	SiH	KA	36.83	34.68	L	.5	NNE	NW	35
SPLIT BOTTOM ARCH	SA	RBM	24	CWA	57	23	83	23	83	Obj	Sum	SR	37.22	36.51	M	.6	ENE	E	148
SPLIT TOP ARCH	SA	RBM	27	CWA	102	23	77	23	77	Obj	Sum	SR	37.29	36.31	M	.8	ENE	S	115
SPRING ARCH	GW	SiC	23	CWA	175	68	84	23	84	Vic	SiH	KA	39.82	33.38	J	1.9	SE	NW	62

141

NAME	AREA	SEC	NO	TYPE	RANK	RB	YR	NB	YR	DER	GEOG	GEOL	'LAT	'LONG	MP	MAP LOC DIS	DIR	EXP	CMP
SQUAWBUSH ARCH	LC	SoL	24	JHA	396	51	84	51	84	AnP	SiH	KA	36.93	34.52	L	.7	NNE	N	0
SQUEEZED JUGHANDLE	SD	Cmg	83	JHA	187	18	73	24	82	Obj	SiC	SR	35.12	46.19	C	1.0	SSE	SW	135
SQUIRREL ARCH	SA	CtF	17	CWA	276	24	85	24	85	Vic	SiH	NA	36.98	35.00	M	1.9	E	E	23
STALE ARCH	ND	GoC	62	CWA	52	21	77	24	84	Obj	ObF	SR	48.38	37.46	B	.4	NNE	NE	135
STALE CRACKER ARCH	UC	SoU	20	CWA	267	51	84	51	84	Vic	SiH	SR	38.60	37.51	K	1.5	WSW	W	178
STEEP SLOPE ARCH	UC	NoU	5	CWA	113	66	83	51	84	Sit	SiC	SR	39.62	37.05	K	2.1	WNW	E	153
STEM ARCH	SD	SVS	47	JHA	364	52	84	18	84	Obj	SiC	KA	47.50	36.88	C	1.2	WNW	S	85
STILT ARCH	CA	PB	12	CWA	436	52	85	52	85	Obj	SiH	WI	43.31	31.81	H	1.2	E	N	122
STRAP ARCH	FF	Upr	18	CWA	439	55	84	55	84	Obj	Sum	SR	45.12	34.15	E	.6	NNW	SW	147
STREAKED ARCH	LC	NoL	8	CWA	44	23	81	66	83	Chr	SiC	NA	38.21	33.92	L	2.2	NNE	N	75
STYLED ARCH	SD	Cmg	74	PAA	105	22	76	23	78	Obj	ObF	MT	47.11	35.11	C	.6	ENE	SW	125
SUBTLE ARCH	GW	SiC	24	CWA	372	51	84	51	84	Oth	SiH	KA	39.82	33.32	J	1.9	SE	N	85
SUNGLASS ARCH	CA	WS	40	SAA	422	51	86	18	86	Obj	SiH	NA	40.77	33.05	I	.9	SW	N	3
SUNLIGHT ARCH	CA	WS	35	ECA	481	87	85	87	85	Evt	SiC	SR	40.86	32.28	I	.5	S	E	15
SUNSHINE ARCH	UC	SoU	14	CWA	147	66	82	66	82	Evt	SiC	SR	38.77	37.00	K	1.9	W	SW	160
SUPERSTITION ARCH	EP	SVE	23	SAA	480	60	84	18	84	Oth	SiH	WI	49.65	41.59	A	1.0	NNW	SW	38
SURPRISE ARCH	FF	Lwr	27	FSA	20	10	64	79	64	Evt	ObF	SR	44.83	33.86	E	.3	NNE	SW	162
SWAN ARCH	EP	SVE	21	FSA	123	23	78	24	82	Obj	SiH	KA	49.93	41.94	A	1.5	WNW	NW	132
SWANKY ARCH	SW	UpW	1	FSA	99	39	83	51	85	Obj	SiC	SR	45.95	30.80	F	2.1	N	SW	130
SWEPT ARCH	FF	Upr	10	JHA	150	23	82	23	82	Obj	Sum	SR	45.42	34.62	E	1.2	NNW	SW	125
TAIL ARCH	FF	Upr	5	JHA	488	66	85	18	86	Obj	Sum	NA	45.55	35.19	E	1.6	NW	NW	35
TALUS ARCH	FF	Lwr	50	CWA	342	36	83	36	86	Sit	ObF	SR	44.53	33.50	E	.5	E	N	100
TANDEM ARCH NORTH	LC	SoL	15	SAA	148	23	85	18	85	Chr	SiC	NA	37.48	34.38	L	1.3	NNE	N	120
TANDEM ARCH SOUTH	LC	SoL	14	SAA	314	23	85	18	85	Chr	SiC	NA	37.48	34.38	L	1.3	NNE	S	120
TAPERED ARCH	SW	Del	16	PHA	414	23	82	23	82	Obj	ObF	SR	44.70	29.80	F	1.4	ENE	NW	165
TAPESTRY ARCH	SD	Cmg	77	FSA	35	1	66	1	66	Chr	SiC	SR	46.67	35.07	C	.7	ESE	SW	132
TARGET ARCH	LC	NoL	2	CWA	125	66	83	23	83	Obj	SiC	NA	38.49	34.55	L	2.4	N	N	110
TEA KETTLE ARCH	LC	SoL	18	CWA	45	66	82	52	85	Obj	SiC	NA	37.01	34.72	L	.7	NNE	SW	100

142

NAME	AREA	SEC	NO	TYPE	RANK	RB	YR	NB	YR	DER	GEOG	GEOL	'LAT	'LONG	MAP LOC MP DIS DIR	EXP	CMP
TEARDROP ARCH	FF	Upr	23	FSA	112	23	77	23	77	Obj	ObF	SR	45.01	33.78	E .5 NNE	NE	150
TEATIME ARCH NORTH	ND	BrC	50	FSA	253	21	77	23	77	Obj	ObF	SR	48.71	37.35	B .7 NNE	SW	130
TEATIME ARCH SOUTH	ND	BrC	51	FSA	166	21	77	23	77	Obj	ObF	SR	48.71	37.35	B .7 NNE	SW	130
TEE ARCH	SD	SVS	60	FSA	317	52	84	52	84	Obj	SiC	NA	47.38	36.58	C .9 WNW	SE	20
TENSION ARCH	ND	BrC	60	CWA	229	37	83	24	83	Obj	SiC	MT	48.95	36.95	B 1.1 NNE	NE	112
TEPEE ARCH	SA	RBM	31	FSA	455	32	82	24	82	Obj	Sum	MT	37.16	37.44	M .3 NW	NW	75
TERMINAL ARCH	SD	Cst	43	ECA	431	53	84	53	84	Sit	ObF	SR	47.66	36.41	C 1.0 NW	S	133
TEXTBOOK ARCH EAST	ND	YCW	1	FSA	116	22	83	73	83	Oth	Sum	SR	49.87	39.37	B 2.6 NW	S	102
TEXTBOOK ARCH WEST	ND	YCW	2	FSA	266	22	83	73	83	Oth	Sum	SR	49.87	39.37	B 2.6 NW	S	102
THANKSGIVING BRIDGE	CA	WS	26	NB	336	30	84	18	84	Evt	CBt	NA	41.29	32.73	I .4 W	NE	172
THE TUNNEL	UC	NoU	7	NT	331	23	79	66	80	Oth	SiC	SR	39.58	35.38	K .9 NNW	W	10
THEORY ARCH	ND	YCW	6	CWA	365	61	84	18	84	Oth	SiC	SR	49.38	39.22	B 2.1 NW	NE	116
THIGH IN THE SKY	KB	Esc	6	JHA	135	57	84	40	84	Obj	SiC	SR	47.69	40.94	D .5 WNW	E	150
THREE HUNDRED ARCH	GW	SiC	25	CWA	100	33	84	66	84	Oth	SiC	KA	39.85	33.26	J 2.0 SE	NW	75
THUNDER ARCH	SA	SBo	55	CWA	217	18	84	18	84	Evt	SiH	NA	36.50	35.94	M 1.3 ESE	SW	140
TIP TOP ARCH	SD	FiC	36	FSA	378	58	84	58	84	Sit	ObF	SR	47.83	36.52	C 1.3 NW	SW	135
TONGUE ARCH	SD	DOS	1	FSA	449	17	81	24	82	Oth	SiC	MT	48.35	36.72	C 1.8 NNW	W	115
TOP OF THE SLOPE ARCH	HP	RrO	1	CWA	246	23	77	23	81	Sit	Sum	SR	42.95	36.89	G 1.3 NNW	SE	150
TOP STORY WINDOW	ND	DON	72	FSA	108	10	61	14	63	Sit	SiC	SR	48.32	37.21	B .4 NE	SW	150
TORNADO ARCH	EP	SVE	39	JHA	320	65	84	18	84	Obj	SiH	KA	49.02	40.21	A .8 E	SW	125
TORTOISE ARCH	EP	SVE	31	CWA	432	58	84	18	84	Obj	SiH	KA	49.06	40.65	A .4 ENE	S	122
TOWER ARCH	KB	Twr	7	FSA	6	4	36	4	36	Obj	SiC	SR	47.43	41.18	D .7 W	S	160
TRAIL ARCH	SD	UTr	29	CWA	260	66	83	66	83	Sit	FlO	SR	47.83	36.93	C 1.5 NW	NE	112
TRAIL END ARCH	UC	NoU	10	ECA	497	69	80	24	84	Sit	Sum	SR	39.43	35.04	K .6 N	NE	130
TRAP DOOR ARCH	LC	SoL	25	PAA	421	51	84	18	84	Obj	SiH	KA	36.93	34.52	L .7 NNE	SW	70
TRAVERSE ARCH	EP	SVE	43	CWA	124	17	83	76	84	Oth	SiH	NA	48.96	39.83	A 1.1 E	S	129
TRIANGLE ARCH	CA	WS	10	FSA	208	17	80	18	84	Obj	Sum	SR	41.60	32.30	I .3 N	SW	145
TROUBLED WATER BRIDGE	SW	2JB	5	NB	149	24	81	24	81	Oth	CBt	SW	44.28	32.45	F 1.1 W	SW	160

143

NAME	AREA	SEC	NO	TYPE	RANK	RB	YR	NB	YR	DER	GEOG	GEOL	'LAT	'LONG	MAP LOC MP DIS DIR	EXP	CMP
TROUGH ARCH	CA	WS	14	CWA	345	34	82	24	82	Vic	Sum	KA	41.60	31.81	I .5 NE	N	100
TUB ARCH	ND	IHG	12	ECA	221	18	73	24	78	Obj	ObF	SR	48.83	38.03	B .9 NNW	SW	140
TUBA ARCH	CA	PB	20	SAA	494	54	84	54	84	Obj	Sum	KA	43.19	32.05	H 1.0 E	W	143
TUMBLEWEED ARCH	ND	SVN	77	FSA	410	17	83	67	85	AnP	SiH	KA	48.28	38.79	B 1.1 WNW	W	15
TUNNEL ARCH	SD	LdT	72	FSA	76	5	40	5	40	Chr	SiC	SR	47.09	35.75	C .2 NNW	NE	115
TURBAN HEAD ARCH	ND	ALG	33	FSA	248	23	78	23	78	Obj	ObF	SR	48.76	37.73	B .7 N	E	90
TURKEY ARCH	ND	BrC	56	FSA	340	84	83	24	83	Obj	Sum	SR	48.82	37.24	B .9 NNE	NE	137
TURRET ARCH NORTH	CA	WS	33	FSA	18	3	34	3	34	Obj	Sum	SD	41.06	32.06	I .3 SE	E	0
TURRET ARCH SOUTH	CA	WS	34	FSA	157	3	34	3	34	Obj	Sum	SD	41.06	32.06	I .3 SE	E	0
TURTLE SHELL ARCH	KB	Esc	5	CWA	381	70	84	18	84	Vic	SiC	SR	47.69	40.96	D .5 WNW	NE	102
TWIG ARCH	EP	SVE	38	CWA	489	65	84	18	84	Vic	SiC	KA	49.06	40.28	A .8 E	SW	145
TWIN ARCH NORTH	FF	Lwr	41	FSA	73	10	69	10	69	Chr	Sum	SR	44.69	33.54	E .3 ENE	E	85
TWIN ARCH SOUTH	FF	Lwr	40	FSA	33	10	69	10	69	Chr	Sum	SR	44.69	33.54	E .3 ENE	E	177
TWIN SPANS EAST	ND	IHG	15	FSA	332	18	73	18	73	Obj	Sum	SR	48.82	38.00	B .9 NNW	E	0
TWIN SPANS WEST	ND	IHG	14	FSA	413	18	73	18	73	Obj	Sum	SR	48.82	38.00	B .9 NNW	E	152
TWO BLOCKS ARCH	SD	DOS	12	FSA	98	21	77	17	81	Chr	Sum	SR	48.08	37.04	C 1.8 NW	NE	145
TWO HUNDRED ARCH	SA	RBM	28	FSA	280	24	82	24	82	Oth	Sum	MT	37.23	37.82	M .7 WNW	N	90
TYRANNOSAURUS ARCH	LC	SoL	20	ECA	302	51	84	51	84	Obj	SiH	NA	36.92	34.54	L .7 NNE	NW	60
UGLY ARCH	GW	GrW	16	CWA	75	23	79	23	79	Obj	SiC	SR	40.19	34.59	J 1.0 SSW	NE	150
UNSEEN ARCH	FF	Lwr	28	FSA	295	23	77	23	77	Evt	ObF	SR	44.76	33.78	E .2 NNE	NE	140
URN ARCH	SD	LdT	70	PHA	186	18	84	18	84	Obj	Sum	SR	47.19	36.20	C .5 WNW	NE	145
UTE BRIDGE	SA	RBM	30	NB	214	32	82	24	82	Oth	CBt	MT	37.22	37.43	M .4 NW	SW	140
VALLEY VIEW ARCH	EP	SVE	41	SAA	470	65	84	18	84	Sit	SiH	KA	49.02	40.22	A .8 E	SW	20
VISITOR CENTER ARCH	SA	SBo	32	CWA	424	46	78	23	78	Sit	SiC	SR	37.01	37.33	M .2 W	E	20
VISOR ARCH	CA	PB	15	CWA	509	54	84	54	84	Obj	SiH	WI	43.19	32.29	H .8 E	NW	70
VULTURE ARCH	FF	Upr	7	FSA	309	30	83	66	83	Vic	Sum	SR	45.57	34.87	E 1.4 NW	E	150
WALK THRU BRIDGE	FF	Lwr	45	NB	223	10	69	23	80	Oth	ObF	SR	44.63	33.57	E .3 E	S	65
WALL ARCH	SD	UTr	50	FSA	12	8	48	8	48	Sit	ObF	SR	47.56	36.41	C .9 NW	SW	115

144

NAME	AREA	SEC	NO	TYPE	RANK	RB	YR	NB	YR	DER	GEOG	GEOL	°LAT	°LONG	MAP LOC MP DIS DIR	EXP	CMP
WASH BASIN ARCH	ND	IHG	13	ECA	507	51	84	51	84	Fet	ObF	SR	48.83	38.03	B .9 NNW	NE	160
WASHBOARD ARCH	SD	SVS	46	CWA	482	56	84	51	84	Obj	SiC	KA	47.51	36.87	C 1.2 WNW	SW	135
WATER TANK ARCH	SA	SBo	41	CWA	63	35	82	24	82	Fet	SiC	NA	36.87	36.38	M .7 E	W	140
WEBBING ARCH	FF	Upr	22	CWA	130	23	77	23	77	Chr	SiC	SR	45.06	33.95	E .5 N	SW	165
WEDGE ARCH	SD	FiC	37	FSA	279	23	77	24	80	Obj	ObF	SR	48.81	36.49	C 1.2 NW	SW	135
WEEPING ARCH	EP	SVE	30	CWA	526	24	82	24	82	Obj	SiH	KA	49.06	40.68	A .4 ENE	W	60
WEST BOUNDARY ARCH	UC	SoU	15	FSA	27	85	77	23	78	Sit	SiC	SR	38.59	38.21	K 2.1 W	W	15
WHALE ARCH NORTH	LC	NoL	5	CWA	389	18	84	24	81	Obj	Sum	NA	38.38	34.48	L 2.2 N	E	0
WHALE ARCH SOUTH	LC	NoL	4	CWA	161	66	81	24	81	Obj	Sum	NA	38.38	34.48	L 2.2 N	E	0
WHIPPED CREAM ARCH	FF	Lwr	48	ECA	517	23	82	23	82	Obj	Sum	SR	44.54	33.78	E .1 ESE	NE	135
WHITE FIN ARCH	SD	Cst	42	FSA	88	21	77	23	77	Chr	ObF	SR	47.65	36.42	C 1.0 NW	NE	155
WILDFLOWER ARCH	LC	NoL	3	CWA	306	23	84	66	84	Vic	ObF	NA	38.44	34.65	L 2.3 N	E	0
WILLOW ARCH	SD	LFC	4	CWA	107	30	83	30	83	Vic	SiC	MT	48.31	35.29	C 1.6 NNE	N	115
WILLOW SPRINGS BRIDGE	HP	WiF	18	NB	239	17	81	66	84	Sit	CBt	MT	41.87	37.75	G 1.3 W	E	0
WIMPY ARCH	EP	SVE	44	PFA	358	18	86	18	86	Oth	SiH	NA	48.96	39.68	A 1.3 E	S	115
WINDOW ARCH	ND	ALG	27	FSA	192	23	78	22	78	Obj	SiC	SR	48.82	37.78	B .9 NNW	SW	137
WINE BOTTLE ARCH	KB	Twr	15	ECA	301	66	82	66	82	Obj	SiH	SR	46.35	40.78	D 1.3 SSW	NW	65
WINE GLASS ARCH	FF	Lwr	25	CWA	243	23	77	23	77	Obj	SiC	SR	44.86	33.60	E .4 NE	NE	165
WINTER CAMP ARCH	SW	WCW	18	SAA	466	66	82	24	82	Sit	SiC	KA	44.79	29.41	F 1.8 ENE	E	50
WOLFE BLUFFS ARCH	SW	Del	12	CWA	4	21	77	23	78	Sit	SiC	SR	44.52	30.62	F .7 NE	S	85
WOLFE RANCH ARCH	SW	Del	9	CWA	182	23	81	23	81	Sit	SiC	SW	44.19	30.97	F .2 ENE	S	95
WRINKLED ARCH	SA	RBM	18	CWA	176	66	83	23	83	Obj	Sum	MT	37.34	37.49	M .5 NW	E	168
Y ARCH	SA	SBo	51	JHA	174	18	84	18	84	Obj	SiH	NA	36.78	36.38	M .7 ESE	N	100
YUCCA ARCH	UC	SoU	18	CWA	339	66	83	51	84	AnP	ObF	SR	38.98	37.34	K 1.3 W	NE	145

145

Table 3

KEY TO RANKING LIST

RANK:

This rank order was determined by using the largest of the two "light openings". If there was a tie the "light opening index" (width plus depth of light opening) was used as a tie breaker. If a tie still existed, the following tie breakers were used in the order shown:
1. Opening beneath the span
2. Opening beneath the span index (length plus width)
3. Other span dimensions

IDENT: (Identification)

The "area", or in the case of the "Central Area", the "Section" is used in conjunction with the arch number.

EP	= Eagle Park		ND	= North Devils Garden
SD	= South Devils Garden		KB	= Klondike Bluffs
FF	= Fiery Furnace		SW	= Salt Wash
HP	= Herdina Park		PB	= Panorama Bluffs
WS	= Windows Section		GW	= Great Wall
UC	= Upper Courthouse Wash		LC	= Lower Courthouse Wash
SA	= Southwestern Area			

TYPE:

FSA	= Free Standing Arch		CWA	= Cliff Wall Arch
PHA	= Pot Hole Arch		JHA	= Jug Handle Arch
PFA	= Platform Arch		ECA	= Expanded Crevice Arch
NB	= Natural Bridge		SAA	= Spanned Alcove Arch
PAA	= Perforated Alcove Arch		NT	= Natural Tunnel'

YM: Year measured

LOL: Light Opening Length in feet (see page 22)

HM: How measured.

The list below applies to all "HM" in the table.

Tp	= tape		Rf	= range finder
Rd	= rod		TR	= telefix & range finder
TT	= tape & transit		Es	= estimate
TE	= tape & estimate		RE	= rod and estimate
TX	= telefix, range finder, estimate			

LOD: Light Opening Depth in feet (see page 22)

DLO: Discontinuous Light Opening.

A "Yes" in this column indicates that the light opening is interrupted, but the arch is not considered a "multiple" opening because of the nature of the discontinuous opening. A "No" indicates that there is only one qualifying opening in the arch.

OBW: Opening Beneath the Span Width in feet (see page 22)

OBH: Opening Beneath the Span Height in feet (see page 22)

SVT: Vertical Thickness of the Span in feet (see page 22)

SHT: Horizontal Thickness of the Span in feet (see page 22)

SXT: Extent of the Span in feet (see page 22)

NA: Not Applicable

LISTING OF ARCHES BY RANK

RANK	IDENT	NAME	TYPE	YM	LOL	HM	LOD	HM	DLO	HM	OBW	HM	OBH	HM	SVT	HM	SHT	HM	SXT	HM
1	SD 56	LANDSCAPE ARCH	FSA	84	306.0	TT	88.6	Tp	NO	NA	306.0	TT	88.6	Tp	16.0	Tp	15.5	Tp	434.0	TT
2	SD 19	NAND ARCH OUTER	CWA	84	184.0	Tp	2.0	Tp	NO	NA	205.0	Rf	56.0	Rf	20.0	TE	11.0	Tp	250.0	Rf
3	WS 16	DOUBLE ARCH SOUTH	FSA	84	144.0	Rf	112.0	Rf	NO	NA	144.0	Rf	112.0	Rf	28.0	TR	26.0	TR	190.0	Rf
4	SW 12	WOLFE BLUFFS ARCH	CWA	84	141.0	Tp	.5	TE	NO	NA	190.0	Tp	28.5	Rd	33.4	TR	31.0	Tp	210.0	TE
5	WS 32	SOUTH WINDOW	FSA	84	115.0	Rf	56.0	Rf	NO	NA	115.0	Rf	56.0	Rf	37.0	Rd	32.0	TR	145.0	Rf
6	KB 7	TOWER ARCH	FSA	84	101.0	Tp	45.0	Rf	NO	NA	101.0	Tp	45.0	Rf	46.0	TR	28.0	TE	145.0	TR
7	WS 30	BICEPS ARCH	CWA	84	95.0	TR	2.7	Es	NO	NA	102.0	TR	95.0	TR	22.0	TR	33.0	TR	NA	NA
8	WS 31	NORTH WINDOW	FSA	84	90.0	Tp	48.0	Rf	NO	NA	90.0	Tp	48.0	Rf	49.0	TR	26.0	EX	113.0	Tp
9	WS 15	DOUBLE ARCH WEST	FSA	84	61.0	Rf	86.0	Rf	NO	NA	67.0	Rf	86.0	Rd	37.0	TR	34.0	TR	95.0	Tp
10	SD 35	DEBRIS ARCH	FSA	84	85.0	Tp	12.5	Rd	NO	NA	85.0	Tp	15.0	Rd	29.0	Rd	15.0	Rd	135.0	TE
11	SD 62	LEDGE ARCH	CWA	84	73.0	Tp	1.3	Tp	NO	NA	73.0	Tp	13.0	Rd	4.0	Tp	2.3	Tp	89.0	Tp
12	SD 50	WALL ARCH	FSA	84	71.0	Tp	33.5	Rd	NO	NA	71.0	Tp	33.5	Rd	8.0	Rd	7.0	Rd	115.0	Tp
13	SD 79	SKYLINE ARCH	FSA	84	71.0	Tp	33.5	Rd	NO	NA	71.0	Tp	33.5	Rd	13.2	TR	24.0	Rd	90.0	Tp
14	SD 24	BLACK ARCH	FSA	84	70.8	Tp	39.0	Rd	NO	NA	70.8	Tp	39.0	Rd	57.0	TR	12.0	Rd	71.0	Tp
15	WS 22	PARADE OF ELEPHANTS SOUTH	CWA	84	68.0	TR	10.0	TR	NO	NA	68.0	Tp	90.0	Rf	38.0	TR	24.0	TR	122.0	Tp
16	SD 22	SAND ARCH INNER	CWA	84	68.0	Tp	3.8	Tp	NO	NA	78.0	Rf	83.0	Rf	34.0	Tp	7.0	Tp	85.0	Rf
17	SD 17	DOUBLE O ARCH UPPER	FSA	84	66.5	Tp	35.3	Rd	NO	NA	66.5	Tp	35.3	Rd	9.5	Es	11.0	Rd	130.0	Tp
18	WS 33	TURRET ARCH NORTH	FSA	84	35.0	Tp	65.0	Rf	NO	NA	35.0	Tp	65.0	Rf	19.0	TR	16.0	TR	35.0	Tp
19	KB 17	CHUNK ARCH	CWA	86	65.0	Tp	1.0	Rd	NO	NA	65.0	Tp	23.0	Rd	12.0	TR	19.0	RE	127.0	Tp
20	FF 27	SURPRISE ARCH	FSA	84	63.0	TE	11.0	TE	NO	NA	63.0	TE	53.0	TE	5.0	RE	5.3	TE	87.0	TE
21	SD 85	MAGIC MYSTERY ARCH	NB	84	62.0	Tp	12.0	Rd	NO	NA	62.0	Tp	48.0	Rf	8.0	Tp	11.0	Tp	95.0	Tp
22	SD 78	RUIN ARCH	CWA	84	59.0	Tp	1.1	Tp	NO	NA	71.0	Tp	12.5	Tp	17.0	Tp	25.5	Tp	115.0	Tp
23	ND 67	GOTHIC ARCH	CWA	84	58.0	Tp	4.0	TR	NO	NA	80.0	Rf	78.0	Rf	39.0	TR	19.5	TR	88.0	Es
24	EP 1	SIBLING ARCH CENTER	CWA	84	55.2	Tp	5.9	Tp	NO	NA	55.2	Tp	16.0	Rd	11.0	Tp	4.0	TE	70.0	Tp
25	SD 84	BROKEN ARCH	FSA	84	53.0	Tp	41.0	Rd	NO	NA	53.0	Tp	41.0	Rd	12.0	TR	17.0	Rd	78.0	Tp
26	GW 18	LITTLE GOTHIC ARCH	CWA	84	53.0	Rf	1.0	Es	NO	NA	72.0	Rf	110.0	Rf	20.0	Es	8.0	Es	116.0	Rf
27	UC 15	WEST BOUNDARY ARCH	FSA	84	52.0	TR	6.0	Es	NO	NA	52.0	TR	34.0	TR	7.5	Es	5.0	Es	79.0	TR

148

RANK	IDENT	NAME	TYPE	YM	LOL	HM	LOD	HM	DLO	HM	OBW	HM	OBH	HM	SVT	HM	SHT	HM	SXT	HM
28	HP 3	LEAPING ARCH	FSA	84	47.0	Tp	50.0	Rf	NO	NA	68.0	Tp	52.0	Rf	7.0	Es	7.0	Es	100.0	Tp
29	WS 9	COVE ARCH	FSA	84	50.0	Rf	33.5	Rd	NO	NA	50.0	Rf	38.0	Rd	158.0	Rf	27.0	Es	65.0	Rf
30	UC 1	POISON IVY ARCH	CWA	84	49.0	Tp	3.0	Es	YES	Tp	145.0	Tp	53.0	Rf	42.0	TR	4.0	Es	145.0	Tp
31	KB 16	SAND HILL ARCH	CWA	84	48.0	Tp	1.5	Tp	NO	NA	55.0	Tp	34.0	Tp	13.0	TR	9.0	Es	60.0	TR
32	FF 13	ROADSIDE ARCH	CWA	84	48.0	Tp	1.0	Es	NO	NA	64.0	Tp	44.0	Rf	58.0	TR	29.0	Tp	96.0	Tp
33	FF 40	TWIN ARCH SOUTH	FSA	84	47.0	Tp	30.0	Rd	NO	NA	47.0	Tp	30.0	Rd	25.0	Es	20.0	Es	150.0	Es
34	SW 14	DELICATE ARCH	FSA	84	32.0	Tp	46.0	Rf	NO	NA	32.0	Tp	46.0	Rf	5.8	TR	14.2	TR	NA	NA
35	SD 77	TAPESTRY ARCH	FSA	84	46.0	Tp	13.0	Tp	NO	NA	50.5	Tp	30.5	Rd	14.0	TR	14.0	Tp	68.0	Tp
36	SD 64	PINE TREE ARCH	FSA	84	45.0	Tp	44.0	Tp	NO	NA	45.0	Tp	44.0	Tp	35.0	TR	23.0	Tp	120.0	Tp
37	UC 19	RING ARCH	PHA	84	45.0	Tp	39.0	Rd	NO	NA	56.0	Tp	39.0	Rd	4.6	Rd	4.9	Rd	61.0	Rf
38	SD 20	NAND ARCH INNER	CWA	84	45.0	Es	.3	Tp	YES	TE	170.0	Rf	57.0	Rf	20.0	TE	2.0	Rd	185.0	Rf
39	EP 8	CROW ARCH	CWA	84	44.0	Tp	.5	Es	NO	NA	44.0	Tp	20.8	Rd	7.8	Rd	13.0	Rd	NA	NA
40	WS 12	RIBBON ARCH	FSA	84	43.8	Tp	23.5	Tp	NO	NA	43.8	Tp	28.0	Tp	.7	Tp	3.0	Tp	59.0	Tp
41	ND 52	BYPASS ARCH	CWA	84	43.0	TE	1.0	Es	YES	Tp	58.0	Tp	35.0	Rf	17.0	Tp	3.8	Tp	69.0	Tp
42	ND 24	PHANTOM ARCH	CWA	84	42.0	Tp	6.0	TE	NO	NA	56.0	Tp	16.0	Tp	3.0	RE	7.0	TE	88.0	Tp
43	SD 49	NAVAJO ARCH	FSA	84	41.0	Tp	13.3	Rd	NO	NA	41.0	Tp	13.3	Rd	34.0	Rd	31.0	Tp	77.0	Tp
44	LC 8	STREAKED ARCH	CWA	84	41.0	Tp	1.0	Es	NO	NA	65.0	TR	67.0	Rf	18.0	TR	6.2	TR	82.0	TR
45	LC 18	TEA KETTLE ARCH	CWA	85	39.0	Es	.8	Tp	NO	NA	52.0	TE	65.0	Tp	16.0	Tp	8.0	Tp	NA	NA
46	WS 1	POTHOLE ARCH LOWER	PHA	84	37.0	Tp	20.0	Tp	NO	NA	67.0	Tp	24.0	Rd	1.9	Tp	4.5	Tp	76.0	Tp
47	HP 8	EYE OF THE WHALE	FSA	84	36.0	Tp	20.0	Tp	NO	NA	63.0	Tp	20.0	Rd	29.0	TR	43.0	Tp	89.0	Tp
48	SW 24	RIM ARCH	CWA	84	36.0	Tp	.5	Tp	NO	NA	36.0	Tp	2.0	Tp	1.1	Tp	3.5	TE	45.0	TE
49	ND 82	HIDDEN ARCH	FSA	84	35.0	Tp	26.4	Rd	NO	NA	41.0	Tp	26.4	Rd	22.0	TR	26.0	Rd	61.0	Tp
50	ND 61	OVAL ARCH	CWA	84	35.0	TR	1.0	Es	NO	NA	35.0	Tp	12.0	TR	13.0	TR	10.0	Es	40.0	Es
51	ND 9	POSTULATION ARCH	CWA	84	35.0	Tp	.8	TE	NO	NA	44.0	Tp	8.0	Rd	4.5	TR	1.2	TR	64.0	Tp
52	ND 62	STALE ARCH	CWA	84	34.0	Tp	2.0	Tp	NO	NA	40.0	Tp	14.0	Rd	6.0	Tp	12.0	Tp	67.0	Tp
53	UC 21	BRAND A ARCH	CWA	84	33.0	Tp	1.2	Tp	NO	NA	52.5	Tp	13.0	Tp	6.0	Es	4.5	Es	53.0	Tp
54	FF 34	DRAGON ARCH	CWA	84	32.5	TE	.3	Rd	NO	NA	42.0	Tp	24.7	Rd	8.7	TR	4.0	TR	55.0	Tp
55	ND 4	SCREECH OWL ARCH	CWA	84	32.0	Tp	4.0	Tp	NO	NA	32.0	Tp	16.1	Tp	10.0	Tp	9.0	Tp	NA	NA

RANK	IDENT	NAME	TYPE	YM	LOL	HM	LOD	HM	DLO	HM	OBW	HM	OBH	HM	SVT	HM	SHT	HM	SXT	HM
56	KB 9	PARALLEL ARCH OUTER	CWA	84	32.0	Tp	1.0	TE	NO	NA	36.0	Tp	40.0	Rd	4.5	TR	4.0	Tp	68.0	Tp
57	SA 24	SPLIT BOTTOM ARCH	CWA	84	32.0	Tp	.3	Tp	YES	Tp	79.0	TR	27.0	TR	8.3	TR	3.5	Tp	79.0	TR
58	SD 30	BLACK CAVE ARCH OUTER	CWA	84	32.0	Tp	.2	Tp	YES	Tp	76.0	Tp	22.9	Rd	12.5	Tp	14.0	Tp	88.0	Tp
59	ND 23	BIG EYE ARCH	FSA	84	31.5	Tp	5.5	Tp	NO	NA	31.5	Tp	5.5	Tp	53.0	RE	16.0	Tp	50.0	Tp
60	SD 40	CRYSTAL ARCH NORTH	FSA	84	31.0	Tp	27.2	Rd	NO	NA	31.0	Tp	27.2	Rd	44.0	RE	23.5	Tp	125.0	Rf
61	FF 51	BENCH ARCH	PHA	84	31.0	Tp	19.0	Tp	NO	NA	36.0	Tp	33.3	RE	24.0	RE	17.5	Tp	62.0	Tp
62	SD 13	BOX ARCH	FSA	84	31.0	Tp	14.5	Rd	NO	NA	31.0	Tp	14.5	Tp	8.5	Rd	13.0	Tp	69.0	Tp
63	SA 41	WATER TANK ARCH	CWA	84	31.0	Tp	12.0	Tp	NO	NA	32.0	Tp	31.0	Rd	11.0	Rd	5.5	Tp	39.0	Tp
64	EP 35	INSIDE OUT ARCH OUTER	CWA	84	31.0	Tp	5.0	Tp	NO	NA	31.5	Tp	15.0	Rd	7.8	Tp	3.5	Tp	47.0	Tp
65	FF 1	CLOVER CANYON ARCH	CWA	85	31.0	Tp	1.5	Tp	YES	Tp	88.0	Tp	30.0	Rd	26.0	Tp	13.0	TE	88.0	Tp
66	SD 54	PARTITION ARCH NORTH	FSA	84	29.8	Tp	30.0	Tp	NO	NA	76.0	Tp	30.6	Tp	38.0	Tp	24.0	Tp	135.0	Tp
67	ND 10	FLYING HAT ARCH	FSA	84	29.0	Tp	4.0	Es	NO	NA	69.0	Tp	43.0	Rd	72.0	TR	35.0	TE	170.0	Tp
68	WS 19	CHRISTMAS TREE ARCH	FSA	84	21.0	Rd	28.0	Rd	NO	NA	21.0	Rd	28.0	Rd	13.0	RE	11.0	Rd	36.0	Rd
69	WS 4	SERPENTINE ARCH	FSA	84	16.0	TR	28.0	TR	NO	NA	16.0	TR	28.0	TR	21.0	Tp	6.0	Tp	NA	NA
70	ND 7	FAR OUT ARCH	FSA	84	28.0	Tp	11.5	Rd	NO	NA	30.0	Tp	27.0	Rd	29.0	Tp	16.0	Tp	44.0	Tp
71	SD 57	COKE OVEN ARCH	CWA	84	28.0	Rd	5.5	Tp	NO	NA	28.0	Tp	14.0	Rd	8.9	Tp	7.0	Tp	37.0	Tp
72	SW 11	IVY ARCH	CWA	84	28.0	Rd	1.0	Es	NO	NA	31.0	Rd	10.0	Rd	9.0	Rd	1.5	Rd	32.0	Rd
73	FF 41	TWIN ARCH NORTH	FSA	84	27.8	Tp	27.0	Rd	NO	NA	27.8	Tp	27.0	Rd	28.0	Es	27.0	Es	35.0	Es
74	FF 26	CLIFF ARCH	CWA	84	27.5	Tp	3.5	Tp	NO	NA	38.0	Tp	12.0	Tp	11.0	Rd	15.0	Rd	39.0	Tp
75	GW 16	UGLY ARCH	CWA	84	27.0	Tp	1.0	Es	NO	NA	28.0	Tp	36.0	Rd	79.0	TR	10.0	Es	60.0	Tp
76	SD 72	TUNNEL ARCH	FSA	84	23.5	Tp	25.8	Rd	NO	NA	23.5	Tp	25.8	Rd	37.0	Tp	15.0	Tp	27.0	Tp
77	FF 2	SAND DUNE ARCH	FSA	84	25.0	Tp	11.5	Tp	NO	NA	34.0	Tp	11.5	Tp	2.5	Tp	8.0	Tp	45.0	Tp
78	SD 51	GUANO ARCH	CWA	84	25.0	Tp	1.2	Tp	NO	NA	29.0	Tp	8.9	Tp	8.0	Rd	6.0	Rd	45.0	Tp
79	SA 5	BABY ARCH	FSA	84	24.5	Tp	14.5	Tp	NO	NA	42.0	Tp	16.0	Tp	205.0	TR	22.5	Tp	61.0	Tp
80	GW 4	ARCH OF MOTION	CWA	84	24.5	Tp	10.0	Rd	NO	NA	24.5	Tp	10.0	Rd	11.5	Rd	9.5	Tp	42.0	Tp
81	WS 11	EAGLE HEAD ARCH	PHA	84	17.0	Tp	24.0	Tp	NO	NA	17.0	Tp	24.0	Rd	5.0	Tp	13.0	Tp	29.0	Tp
82	ND 41	SIDE FIN ARCH	FSA	84	24.0	Tp	12.0	Tp	NO	NA	24.0	Tp	12.0	Rd	80.0	Es	10.0	Es	29.0	Es
83	ND 79	PISTOL ARCH	CWA	84	23.0	Tp	1.5	Es	NO	NA	97.0	Tp	39.0	Rd	10.0	TR	9.0	RE	124.0	Tp

RANK	IDENT	NAME	TYPE	YM	LOL	HM	LOD	HM	DLO	HM	OBW	HM	OBH	HM	SVT	HM	SHT	HM	SXT	HM
84	EP 18	PEEPHOLE ARCH	CWA	84	23.0	Tp	.6	Tp	NO	NA	41.0	TR	37.0	TR	7.0	TR	7.0	Tp	58.0	TR
85	WS 29	SEAGULL ARCH	FSA	84	22.7	TR	18.2	TR	NO	NA	22.7	TR	18.2	TR	63.0	TR	30.0	Es	NA	NA
86	GW 13	BAR ROOM DOOR ARCH	CWA	84	22.6	EX	3.0	Es	NO	NA	50.0	TR	35.0	TR	22.5	TR	3.5	Es	51.0	TR
87	KB 10	PARALLEL ARCH INNER	CWA	84	22.0	Tp	5.0	Rd	NO	NA	36.0	Tp	29.5	Rd	5.5	TR	5.0	Tp	36.0	Tp
88	SD 42	WHITE FIN ARCH	FSA	84	22.0	Tp	5.0	Tp	NO	NA	22.0	Tp	5.0	Tp	3.5	Tp	7.5	Tp	35.0	Tp
89	ND 39	EYEBALL ARCH	JHA	84	.7	Es	22.0	Rd	NO	NA	.7	Es	22.0	Rd	4.5	TR	7.0	Tp	50.0	RE
90	SD 18	DOUBLE O ARCH LOWER	FSA	84	21.1	Tp	9.3	Rd	NO	NA	21.1	Tp	9.3	Rd	11.2	Rd	11.0	Tp	55.0	Tp
91	WS 21	PARADE OF ELEPHANTS NORTH	FSA	84	17.0	TR	21.0	TR	NO	NA	17.0	TR	21.0	TR	48.0	TR	22.0	Es	25.0	TR
92	HP 4	FLYING BUTTRESS ARCH	JHA	84	21.0	Tp	2.0	Tp	NO	NA	21.0	Tp	24.0	Tp	7.0	Tp	11.0	Tp	35.0	Es
93	GW 6	BEAN POT ARCH	PHA	84	20.0	Tp	18.0	Es	NO	NA	26.0	TR	29.0	TR	28.0	TR	14.0	Es	26.0	TR
94	FF 35	LIGHTNING BOLT ARCH	JHA	84	1.5	RE	20.0	Es	YES	RE	1.5	Es	40.0	RE	2.0	Es	5.0	Es	51.0	Es
95	GW 14	LAUGHING COYOTE ARCH	CWA	84	20.0	EX	.8	Es	NO	NA	55.0	TR	27.0	TR	26.0	TR	6.0	Es	73.0	TR
96	UC 2	CONFLUENCE ARCH	CWA	84	20.0	TE	.3	Es	YES	Tp	99.0	Tp	48.0	Rf	36.0	TR	12.0	Es	109.0	TE
97	SD 76	DIAMOND ARCH	FSA	84	19.7	Rd	14.0	Rd	NO	NA	19.7	Rd	14.0	Rd	21.0	Rd	11.0	Rd	38.0	Rd
98	SD 12	TWO BLOCKS ARCH	FSA	84	19.7	Tp	7.0	Tp	NO	NA	24.5	Tp	7.0	Tp	9.3	Rd	9.3	Tp	33.0	Tp
99	SW 1	SWANKY ARCH	FSA	85	19.5	TR	5.0	TR	NO	NA	19.5	TR	5.0	TR	25.0	TR	18.0	TR	48.0	TR
100	GW 25	THREE HUNDRED ARCH	CWA	84	19.0	Tp	5.5	Tp	NO	NA	46.0	Tp	5.5	Tp	2.0	Tp	9.0	Tp	64.0	Tp
101	SD 21	SAND ARCH OUTER	CWA	84	19.0	Tp	3.0	Tp	YES	Tp	87.0	Rf	78.0	Rf	29.0	Rf	6.0	Tp	104.0	Rf
102	SA 27	SPLIT TOP ARCH	CWA	84	19.0	Tp	1.5	Tp	YES	Tp	45.0	Tp	26.0	Tp	6.0	Tp	9.0	Tp	58.0	Tp
103	FF 3	SLIT ARCH	ECA	84	19.0	TE	1.3	TR	NO	NA	35.0	TE	1.3	TR	15.0	TE	16.0	TE	35.0	TE
104	EP 14	ALL THE WAY ARCH	CWA	84	19.0	TR	1.0	Es	NO	NA	22.0	TR	11.0	TR	4.0	TR	3.0	Es	31.0	TR
105	SD 74	STYLED ARCH	PAA	84	18.9	Tp	8.9	Rd	NO	NA	63.0	Tp	12.9	Rd	29.0	Tp	16.5	Tp	109.0	TE
106	EP 12	BIG BUCK ARCH	CWA	84	18.5	TE	2.0	Es	NO	NA	21.0	TR	28.0	Rd	1.1	TR	1.6	TR	21.0	TE
107	SD 4	WILLOW ARCH	CWA	84	18.5	Tp	.8	Tp	YES	Tp	54.0	Tp	2.5	Tp	2.5	Tp	5.7	Tp	78.0	Tp
108	ND 72	TOP STORY WINDOW	FSA	84	18.0	TR	12.5	TR	NO	NA	18.0	TR	12.5	TR	13.0	TR	14.0	Es	33.0	TR
109	LC 30	DOVE FEATHER ARCH	CWA	85	18.0	Tp	.8	Tp	YES	Tp	190.0	Tp	44.0	Tp	30.0	Tp	38.0	Tp	262.0	Tp
110	SD 23	CONTOURED ARCH	CWA	84	17.5	Tp	.5	Tp	NO	NA	17.5	Tp	8.8	Tp	3.2	Tp	2.3	Tp	19.0	Tp
111	SA 38	KIDS ARCH WEST	CWA	84	17.5	Tp	.3	Tp	NO	NA	30.0	Tp	3.0	Tp	.6	Tp	4.6	Tp	30.0	Tp

151

RANK	IDENT	NAME	TYPE	YM	LOL	HM	LOD	HM	DLO	HM	OBW	HM	OBH	HM	SVT	HM	SHT	HM	SXT	HM
112	FF 23	TEARDROP ARCH	FSA	84	17.0	Rd	3.2	Tp	NO	NA	17.0	Rd	21.0	Rd	6.0	Tp	3.2	Tp	24.0	Rd
113	UC 5	STEEP SLOPE ARCH	CWA	84	17.0	Tp	.2	Es	NO	NA	57.0	Tp	44.0	Rf	3.0	TR	3.0	Es	70.0	Es
114	SW 15	ECHO ARCH	FSA	84	16.5	Rd	13.2	Rd	NO	NA	43.0	Rd	26.0	TE	14.0	Tp	20.0	Rd	62.0	Rd
115	KB 12	ANNIVERSARY ARCH NORTH	FSA	84	16.0	Tp	11.0	Tp	NO	NA	16.0	Tp	11.0	Tp	40.0	Es	16.0	Tp	23.0	TE
116	ND 1	TEXTBOOK ARCH EAST	FSA	84	16.0	Tp	6.0	Tp	NO	NA	19.0	Tp	6.0	Tp	4.7	Tp	5.2	Tp	22.5	Tp
117	ND 38	CAT EYE ARCH	CWA	84	16.0	Tp	2.0	Tp	NO	NA	18.9	TR	31.5	Rd	8.5	Tp	12.3	TR	82.0	TR
118	ND 76	ARROW ARCH	FSA	84	16.0	TR	2.0	TR	NO	NA	16.0	TR	5.3	TR	8.6	TR	10.6	EX	26.0	TR
119	SD 38	PLANE BRIDGE	NB	85	16.0	Tp	1.3	Tp	NO	NA	26.5	Tp	3.8	Tp	2.7	Tp	3.5	Tp	32.5	Tp
120	WS 13	ALCOVE ARCH	CWA	84	16.0	TE	1.0	Es	YES	Tp	92.0	Rf	51.0	Rf	11.0	TR	20.0	TE	106.0	Rf
121	EP 37	SNOWY ARCH	CWA	84	16.0	Tp	.7	Tp	NO	NA	16.0	Tp	7.0	Tp	5.0	Tp	4.0	Tp	19.0	Tp
122	SD 31	BLACK CAVE ARCH INNER	CWA	84	16.0	Tp	.3	Tp	NO	NA	70.0	Tp	30.5	Rd	.9	Rd	2.5	Tp	70.0	Tp
123	EP 21	SWAN ARCH	FSA	84	15.0	Tp	6.0	Tp	NO	NA	15.0	Tp	10.5	Tp	10.0	Rd	8.5	Rd	18.0	Tp
124	EP 43	TRAVERSE ARCH	CWA	84	15.0	Tp	2.0	Tp	NO	NA	19.0	Tp	3.0	Tp	2.4	Tp	4.2	Tp	20.0	Tp
125	LC 2	TARGET ARCH	CWA	84	15.0	TR	1.0	Es	NO	NA	23.0	TR	14.0	TR	11.0	TR	9.0	Es	36.0	TR
126	SD 75	ARC DE TRIOMPHE	CWA	84	15.0	Tp	1.0	Tp	NO	NA	20.0	Tp	17.0	Tp	5.7	Tp	10.0	Tp	35.0	Tp
127	EP 13	SALAMANDER ARCH	CWA	84	15.0	TR	.8	TR	NO	NA	15.0	TR	22.5	TR	3.4	TR	2.5	TR	15.0	TE
128	HP 17	SLANTED EYE ARCH	PFA	84	15.0	Tp	.7	Tp	NO	NA	31.0	Tp	14.0	Tp	1.4	Tp	4.0	Tp	NA	NA
129	SA 6	GOSSIPS ARCH	CWA	84	15.0	Tp	.6	Tp	NO	NA	36.0	Tp	7.0	Tp	8.5	Tp	6.0	Tp	47.0	Tp
130	FF 22	WEBBING ARCH	CWA	84	15.0	Tp	.5	Tp	NO	NA	15.0	Tp	5.0	Tp	27.0	Rd	7.0	Tp	18.0	Tp
131	HP 10	REFLEX ARCH	CWA	84	15.0	Tp	.2	Tp	NO	NA	15.0	Tp	2.2	Tp	.9	Tp	4.2	Tp	28.0	Tp
132	EP 5	FORGOTTEN ARCH	FSA	84	14.6	Tp	5.2	Tp	NO	NA	14.6	Tp	5.2	Tp	6.0	Tp	5.8	Tp	NA	NA
133	HP 9	LOST AND FOUND BRIDGE	NB	84	14.6	Tp	2.5	Tp	NO	NA	14.6	Tp	2.5	Tp	.5	Tp	1.8	Tp	16.0	Tp
134	SW 13	FRAME ARCH	FSA	84	14.5	Rd	12.5	Rd	NO	NA	14.5	Rd	12.5	Rd	14.0	Rd	13.0	Rd	18.0	Rd
135	KB 6	THIGH IN THE SKY	JHA	84	14.5	Tp	2.0	Tp	NO	NA	14.5	Tp	2.0	Tp	1.4	Tp	2.8	Tp	18.0	Tp
136	PB 19	FLAME ARCH	FSA	84	7.5	Tp	14.2	Rd	NO	NA	7.5	Tp	14.2	Rd	9.5	Tp	19.0	Tp	15.0	Tp
137	FF 46	INNER SANCTUM BRIDGE	NB	84	11.5	Tp	14.0	Tp	NO	NA	11.5	Tp	20.0	Rd	5.0	Tp	7.8	Tp	30.0	Tp
138	ND 36	ALADDINS LAMP	FSA	84	14.0	TR	5.0	TR	NO	NA	14.0	TR	5.0	TR	9.3	TR	7.0	Es	NA	NA
139	FF 37	FLATIRON ARCH	FSA	84	14.0	Tp	4.5	Tp	NO	NA	14.0	Tp	5.5	Tp	7.0	Tp	8.0	Tp	19.0	Tp

RANK	IDENT	NAME	TYPE	YM	LOL	HM	LOD	HM	DLO	HM	OBW	HM	OBH	HM	SVT	HM	SHT	HM	SXT	HM
140	FF 33	DREAM ARCH	CWA	84	14.0	Tp	2.5	Tp	NO	NA	14.0	Tp	16.0	TR	8.0	Es	3.5	Tp	25.0	Es
141	WS 2	POTHOLE ARCH UPPER	PHA	84	14.0	Tp	1.0	Tp	NO	NA	63.0	Tp	29.0	Tp	15.0	Tp	10.5	Tp	76.0	Tp
142	SD 41	BLOCKED ARCH	CWA	84	14.0	Tp	.5	Tp	NO	NA	20.0	TR	17.0	TR	20.0	TR	9.0	TR	32.0	Tp
143	PB 11	SPALLING ARCH	CWA	85	13.5	Tp	2.5	Tp	NO	NA	15.0	Tp	4.0	Tp	9.0	Tp	5.0	Tp	17.0	Tp
144	SD 14	RINGTAIL ARCH LOWER	FSA	84	13.3	TR	4.8	TR	NO	NA	13.3	TR	4.8	TR	11.6	TR	4.5	TR	21.0	TR
145	FF 29	HOLE IN FIN	FSA	84	13.0	Tp	9.0	Tp	NO	NA	13.0	Tp	16.0	Tp	27.0	Tp	8.0	Tp	15.0	Tp
146	FF 19	ELEPHANT CHIN ARCH	FSA	84	13.0	Tp	8.0	Tp	NO	NA	13.0	Tp	8.0	Tp	35.0	Rd	9.0	Tp	20.0	Rd
147	UC 14	SUNSHINE ARCH	CWA	84	13.0	Tp	5.0	Es	NO	NA	27.0	Tp	10.0	Tp	43.0	TR	10.0	Es	40.0	Es
148	LC 15	TANDEM ARCH NORTH	SAA	85	3.0	TR	13.0	TR	NO	NA	3.0	TR	13.0	TR	9.0	TR	9.4	TR	24.0	TR
149	SW 5	TROUBLED WATER BRIDGE	NB	84	13.0	Tp	2.0	Tp	NO	NA	21.0	Tp	2.0	Tp	1.2	Tp	2.9	Tp	23.0	Tp
150	FF 10	SWEPT ARCH	JHA	84	13.0	Tp	1.2	Tp	NO	NA	13.0	Tp	1.2	Tp	1.5	Tp	4.2	Tp	33.0	Tp
151	EP 2	SIBLING ARCH NORTH	CWA	84	13.0	Tp	.9	Tp	NO	NA	55.2	Tp	15.0	Tp	11.0	Tp	8.0	TE	70.0	TR
152	UC 16	BOUNDARY TWINS OUTER	CWA	84	13.0	Tp	.6	Tp	NO	NA	14.0	Tp	4.0	Tp	1.4	Tp	.9	Tp	20.5	Tp
153	EP 36	INSIDE OUT ARCH INNER	CWA	84	13.0	Tp	.5	Tp	NO	NA	13.0	Tp	12.5	Rd	7.5	Tp	4.5	Tp	20.0	Tp
154	EP 26	HOURGLASS ARCH	FSA	84	9.0	Tp	12.5	Tp	NO	NA	9.0	Tp	12.5	Tp	1.8	Tp	1.9	Tp	24.3	Tp
155	ND 40	OVERHANG ARCH	SAA	84	12.5	Tp	2.5	Tp	NO	NA	12.5	Tp	2.5	Tp	1.9	Tp	1.7	Tp	23.5	Tp
156	SA 23	EDGE ARCH	NB	84	12.5	Tp	1.7	Tp	NO	NA	12.5	Tp	1.7	Tp	.8	Tp	7.5	Tp	17.0	Tp
157	WS 34	TURRET ARCH SOUTH	FSA	84	10.5	Tp	12.0	Tp	NO	NA	10.5	Tp	12.0	Tp	38.0	TR	18.0	Tp	NA	NA
158	SD 73	EAST TUNNEL ARCH	PHA	84	12.0	Tp	6.9	Tp	NO	NA	15.9	Tp	10.2	Tp	6.2	Tp	11.0	Tp	25.0	Tp
159	LC 12	BOULDER ARCH	FSA	84	12.0	Tp	3.0	Es	NO	NA	33.0	Tp	31.0	Rd	31.0	TR	23.0	TR	42.0	TR
160	LC 11	BIGFOOT ARCH	CWA	84	12.0	TR	1.5	Tp	NO	NA	14.3	TR	7.0	TR	2.0	Es	6.8	TR	14.3	TR
161	LC 4	WHALE ARCH SOUTH	CWA	84	12.0	Tp	1.5	Tp	NO	NA	12.0	Tp	8.0	TR	14.0	TR	13.0	Tp	15.0	TR
162	ND 29	BOW JUGHANDLE	JHA	84	1.0	TR	12.0	TR	NO	NA	1.0	TR	12.0	TR	5.0	TR	2.0	Es	NA	NA
163	UC 11	CLIFFSIDE STRIP ARCH	CWA	84	12.0	TR	.4	Es	YES	TR	205.0	Tp	31.0	EX	11.0	TR	11.0	TR	205.0	Tp
164	HP 13	SIT DOWN ARCH	CWA	86	12.0	Tp	.3	Tp	NO	NA	15.0	Tp	1.5	Tp	1.8	Tp	2.9	Tp	NA	NA
165	EP 27	CRACKER JACK ARCH	CWA	84	12.0	Tp	.1	Tp	NO	NA	16.0	Tp	4.2	Tp	2.2	Tp	2.0	Tp	21.0	Tp
166	ND 51	TEATIME ARCH SOUTH	FSA	84	10.9	Tp	11.2	Tp	NO	NA	10.9	Tp	11.2	Tp	17.0	Rd	17.0	Tp	41.0	Tp
167	EP 6	BELLY ARCH	ECA	86	1.1	TR	11.2	TR	NO	NA	1.1	TR	11.2	TR	13.4	TR	13.0	Es	37.0	TR

153

RANK	IDENT	NAME	TYPE	YM	LOL	HM	LOD	HM	DLO	HM	OBW	HM	OBH	HM	SVT	HM	SHT	HM	SXT	HM
168	SA 19	ABOVE THE ALCOVE ARCH SO.	FSA	85	5.5	Tp	11.0	Tp	NO	NA	21.0	Tp	19.0	Tp	38.0	Tp	35.0	Tp	NA	NA
169	FF 38	LOUVER ARCH	FSA	84	3.0	Es	11.0	Rd	NO	NA	3.0	Es	11.0	Rd	13.5	TR	5.0	Es	NA	NA
170	LC 28	GAUGE ARCH	CWA	84	11.0	Tp	2.0	Tp	NO	NA	11.0	Tp	3.5	Tp	2.2	Tp	8.8	Tp	13.0	Tp
171	SW 10	COBBLESTONE BRIDGE	NB	84	11.0	Tp	2.0	Tp	NO	NA	11.0	Tp	2.0	Tp	1.3	Tp	5.0	Tp	30.0	Tp
172	SD 61	CROSSBOW ARCH	CWA	84	11.0	Tp	1.0	Tp	NO	NA	11.2	Tp	3.5	Tp	15.0	Tp	6.0	Tp	14.0	Tp
173	UC 8	RUNNING COYOTE ARCH	CWA	84	11.0	Tp	.7	Tp	NO	NA	16.5	Tp	4.0	Tp	7.0	Rd	6.0	Tp	29.0	Tp
174	SA 51	Y ARCH	JHA	84	.5	Tp	11.0	Tp	NO	NA	.5	Tp	11.0	Tp	.7	Tp	4.6	Tp	20.0	Tp
175	GW 23	SPRING ARCH	CWA	84	11.0	Tp	.4	Tp	YES	Tp	23.0	Tp	2.5	Tp	1.7	Tp	1.2	Tp	32.0	Tp
176	SA 18	WRINKLED ARCH	CWA	84	11.0	Tp	.3	Tp	NO	NA	19.5	Tp	2.5	Tp	1.2	Tp	3.5	Tp	NA	NA
177	SD 68	PAN ARCH	CWA	84	11.0	Tp	.2	Tp	NO	NA	11.0	Tp	5.5	Tp	10.0	Rd	5.5	Tp	11.0	Tp
178	ND 31	ONE BLOCK ARCH	FSA	84	10.7	Tp	5.4	Tp	NO	NA	10.7	Tp	5.4	Tp	7.0	Tp	6.5	Tp	12.5	Tp
179	ND 54	CANYON BRIDGE	NB	84	10.7	Tp	4.5	Tp	NO	NA	10.7	Tp	4.5	Tp	3.1	Tp	2.5	Tp	24.0	Tp
180	KB 1	RAINDROP ARCH	CWA	84	10.6	Tp	1.7	Tp	NO	NA	10.6	Tp	1.7	Tp	9.0	Tp	5.5	Tp	18.0	Tp
181	PB 16	NEGLECTED ARCH	CWA	84	10.5	Tp	1.3	Tp	NO	NA	10.5	Tp	4.5	Tp	1.7	Tp	.8	Tp	14.0	Tp
182	SW 9	WOLFE RANCH ARCH	CWA	84	10.5	Tp	.5	Tp	NO	NA	10.5	Tp	7.0	Tp	5.5	Tp	4.5	Tp	NA	NA
183	EP 20	CLINGING ARCH	CWA	84	10.5	Tp	.1	Tp	NO	NA	23.0	Tp	2.6	Tp	2.0	Tp	1.9	Tp	28.0	Tp
184	GW 8	FISHTAIL ARCH	ECA	84	10.3	Tp	.4	Tp	NO	NA	10.3	Tp	.4	Tp	.7	Tp	2.5	Tp	12.0	Tp
185	ND 8	SHIELD ARCH	FSA	84	10.2	Tp	9.0	Tp	NO	NA	10.2	Tp	11.0	Tp	9.2	Tp	5.3	Tp	26.0	Tp
186	SD 70	URN ARCH	PHA	84	5.1	Tp	10.2	Tp	NO	NA	5.1	Tp	10.2	Tp	.2	Tp	.2	Tp	23.0	TE
187	SD 83	SQUEEZED JUGHANDLE	JHA	84	10.2	Tp	.6	Tp	NO	NA	13.0	Tp	.6	Tp	2.9	Tp	4.2	Tp	19.0	Tp
188	GW 17	BUTTONHOOK ARCH	CWA	84	10.1	TR	2.6	Tp	NO	NA	10.1	TR	50.0	Es	9.4	TR	15.5	TR	19.0	TR
189	ND 65	SNAKEHEAD ARCH	CWA	84	10.1	Tp	1.6	Tp	NO	NA	10.1	Tp	4.0	Tp	2.4	Tp	3.9	Tp	12.5	Tp
190	FF 43	CLOISTER ARCH	CWA	84	10.1	Tp	1.0	Tp	NO	NA	10.1	Tp	14.5	Rd	26.5	Rd	3.5	Tp	18.0	Tp
191	HP 15	CONCEALED BRIDGE	NB	84	9.5	Tp	10.0	Tp	NO	NA	14.0	Tp	12.2	Tp	1.9	Tp	2.2	Tp	21.0	Tp
192	ND 27	WINDOW ARCH	FSA	84	10.0	Tp	7.0	Tp	NO	NA	10.0	Tp	7.0	Tp	21.0	Es	8.0	Tp	30.0	Es
193	ND 32	PIANO LEG ARCH	FSA	84	10.0	Tp	3.0	Tp	NO	NA	10.0	Tp	5.9	Tp	.3	Tp	1.2	Tp	17.8	Tp
194	EP 29	HANGING ARCH	JHA	84	2.1	Tp	10.0	Tp	NO	NA	2.1	Tp	10.0	Tp	3.0	Es	6.5	Es	12.0	Es
195	WS 18	JICAMA ARCH	JHA	84	2.0	TR	10.0	TR	NO	NA	2.0	TR	10.0	TR	4.5	TR	5.6	TR	34.0	TR

RANK	IDENT	NAME	TYPE	YM	LOL	HM	LOD	HM	DLO	HM	OBW	HM	OBH	HM	SVT	HM	SHT	HM	SXT	HM
196	SD 34	LIMBO ARCH	CWA	84	10.0	Es	.5	Es	NO	NA	19.8	TR	9.9	TR	7.4	TR	6.0	Es	20.0	TR
197	SD 52	MAGPIE ARCH NORTH	CWA	84	10.0	Tp	.5	Tp	NO	NA	14.0	Tp	1.0	Tp	1.8	Tp	.6	Tp	19.0	Tp
198	SD 45	FALLEN SLAB BRIDGE	NB	84	10.0	Tp	.4	Tp	YES	Tp	48.0	Tp	11.3	Tp	6.0	Tp	2.0	Tp	48.0	Tp
199	WS 3	CACTUS ARCH	PFA	86	10.0	Tp	.3	Tp	NO	NA	10.0	Tp	.3	Tp	.5	Tp	7.5	Tp	35.0	Tp
200	SD 67	POT ARCH	CWA	84	10.0	Tp	.2	Tp	NO	NA	10.0	Tp	2.0	Tp	10.0	Tp	4.0	Tp	20.0	Tp
201	UC 13	BAR ARCH	CWA	84	9.5	TE	.8	Es	NO	NA	9.5	TE	5.0	Es	.8	Es	2.0	Es	NA	NA
202	ND 48	CANTILEVER ARCH	CWA	84	9.5	Tp	.6	Tp	NO	NA	11.5	Tp	3.5	Tp	4.6	Tp	6.8	Tp	18.0	Tp
203	SA 35	GRACEFUL ARCH	CWA	84	9.5	Tp	.1	Tp	NO	NA	17.0	Tp	1.9	Tp	.7	Tp	1.1	Tp	25.0	Tp
204	LC 21	BACKSIDE ARCH INNER	CWA	84	9.4	Tp	.4	Tp	NO	NA	9.4	Tp	4.1	Tp	1.1	Tp	1.4	Tp	12.0	Tp
205	SD 48	EXFOLIATION ARCH	PFA	84	9.2	Tp	.8	Tp	NO	NA	9.2	Tp	.8	Tp	.3	Tp	2.1	Tp	9.2	Tp
206	SD 55	PARTITION ARCH SOUTH	FSA	84	8.5	Tp	9.1	Tp	NO	NA	8.5	Tp	9.1	Tp	48.0	Tp	31.0	Tp	135.0	Tp
207	ND 69	FILAGREE ARCH	CWA	84	9.1	Tp	.7	Tp	NO	NA	9.1	Tp	7.2	Tp	10.5	Tp	3.3	Tp	14.3	Tp
208	WS 10	TRIANGLE ARCH	FSA	84	9.0	Es	8.0	Es	NO	NA	9.0	Es	8.0	Es	2.0	Es	7.0	Es	NA	NA
209	WS 36	BIGHORN ARCH	FSA	86	9.0	TR	8.0	EX	NO	NA	9.0	TR	8.0	EX	43.0	TR	4.0	Es	NA	NA
210	ND 71	HELMET ARCH	FSA	84	7.0	RE	9.0	Rd	NO	NA	7.0	RE	9.0	Rd	8.0	Rd	12.0	RE	22.0	RE
211	ND 63	CUP ARCH	FSA	84	9.0	RE	6.0	RE	NO	NA	9.0	RE	6.0	RE	12.0	RE	7.0	RE	NA	NA
212	SA 14	MANDOLIN ARCH	CWA	84	9.0	Tp	5.0	Es	NO	NA	22.0	TR	38.0	TR	78.0	Tp	8.0	Es	NA	NA
213	ND 16	CAMOUFLAGE TWINS NORTH	FSA	84	9.0	Tp	2.7	Tp	NO	NA	9.0	Tp	2.7	Tp	30.0	TE	21.0	Tp	14.0	Tp
214	SA 30	UTE BRIDGE	NB	84	9.0	Tp	1.8	Tp	NO	NA	13.5	Tp	6.0	Tp	1.7	Tp	3.8	Tp	17.0	Tp
215	WS 5	GHOST ARCH	CWA	84	9.0	TR	1.3	TR	NO	NA	32.0	TR	64.0	Rf	7.0	Tp	6.4	TR	36.0	TR
216	UC 17	BOUNDARY TWINS INNER	CWA	84	9.0	Tp	1.0	Tp	NO	NA	11.0	Tp	3.0	Tp	1.0	Tp	.6	Tp	20.5	Tp
217	SA 55	THUNDER ARCH	CWA	84	9.0	Tp	1.0	Tp	NO	NA	9.0	Tp	1.0	Tp	3.0	Tp	2.7	Tp	15.0	Tp
218	LC 13	BUCKTHORN ARCH	CWA	85	9.0	Tp	.3	Tp	NO	NA	32.0	Tp	12.0	Tp	4.2	Tp	3.5	Tp	45.0	Tp
219	SD 82	DOGBONE ARCH	CWA	86	8.8	TR	1.0	TR	NO	NA	11.5	TR	13.0	TR	1.5	Tp	1.2	TR	14.0	TR
220	FF 17	CROCODILE ARCH	CWA	84	8.8	Tp	.3	Tp	NO	NA	12.5	Tp	1.5	Tp	1.5	Tp	2.2	Tp	17.0	Tp
221	ND 12	TUB ARCH	ECA	84	8.6	Tp	1.7	Tp	NO	NA	8.6	Tp	1.7	Tp	5.0	Tp	7.0	Tp	NA	NA
222	WS 24	DRUMSTICK ARCH	CWA	84	8.6	TR	.1	TR	NO	NA	37.5	TR	12.0	TR	3.0	TR	2.6	TR	43.0	TR
223	FF 45	WALK THRU BRIDGE	NB	84	8.5	Tp	6.2	Tp	NO	NA	10.2	Tp	8.0	Tp	2.5	Tp	2.6	Tp	13.4	Tp

RANK	IDENT	NAME	TYPE	YM	LOL	HM	LOD	HM	DLO	HM	OBW	HM	OBH	HM	SVT	HM	SHT	HM	SXT	HM
224	UC 12	DECEPTION ARCH	PHA	84	8.5	Tp	4.5	Tp	NO	NA	15.0	Tp	5.0	Tp	.8	Tp	1.6	Tp	28.0	Tp
225	UC 9	DEAD END ARCH	FSA	84	8.5	Tp	2.4	Tp	NO	NA	8.5	Tp	2.4	Tp	2.5	Tp	3.5	Tp	10.0	Tp
226	ND 43	FUNNEL ARCH	FSA	84	7.5	TE	8.3	Tp	NO	NA	7.5	TE	8.3	Tp	23.5	TR	10.0	Es	12.0	TR
227	GW 12	PINCHED JUGHANDLE	JHA	84	.8	TR	8.3	TR	NO	NA	.8	TR	22.4	TR	.8	TR	2.7	TR	35.0	TR
228	SD 10	SHADOW BOX ARCH	FSA	84	8.2	TR	3.6	TR	NO	NA	8.2	TR	3.6	TR	21.0	TR	20.0	Es	25.0	TR
229	ND 60	TENSION ARCH	CWA	84	8.2	Tp	2.4	Tp	NO	NA	8.2	Tp	5.2	Tp	.3	Tp	.8	Tp	NA	NA
230	ND 55	REDTAIL ARCH	ECA	84	1.5	Es	8.2	TR	NO	NA	1.5	Es	8.2	TR	7.0	Tp	7.0	Es	NA	NA
231	SD 39	CRYSTAL ARCH SOUTH	FSA	84	5.5	Tp	8.0	Tp	NO	NA	5.5	Tp	8.0	TR	25.0	Rd	12.0	Tp	125.0	Rf
232	SA 26	PORTHOLE CAVE ARCH	SAA	84	5.0	TE	8.0	Rd	NO	NA	17.5	Rd	12.0	Rd	6.5	Rd	6.0	Tp	NA	NA
233	WS 25	LITTLE DUCK WINDOW	FSA	84	8.0	TR	3.5	TR	NO	NA	8.0	TR	3.5	TR	8.5	TR	6.0	Es	12.0	TR
234	ND 5	FLEDGLING ARCH	CWA	84	8.0	Tp	3.0	Tp	NO	NA	8.0	Tp	3.0	Tp	19.5	TR	9.2	Tp	19.0	Tp
235	SD 26	LAZY ARCH	CWA	84	8.0	Es	2.5	Tp	NO	NA	15.0	Es	3.2	Tp	1.2	Tp	1.8	Tp	22.0	TR
236	UC 3	NUTCRACKER ARCH	JHA	84	2.0	Es	8.0	TR	NO	NA	8.0	TR	8.0	TR	12.6	TR	7.0	TR	11.0	TR
237	HP 19	ILLUSION ARCH	FSA	84	2.0	Tp	8.0	Tp	NO	NA	2.0	TR	8.0	TR	4.5	TR	6.0	Tp	8.5	Tp
238	GW 5	REGAINED ARCH	CWA	85	8.0	Tp	1.5	Tp	NO	NA	8.5	Tp	1.5	Tp	3.1	Tp	2.6	Tp	NA	NA
239	HP 18	WILLOW SPRINGS BRIDGE	NB	84	8.0	Tp	1.2	Tp	NO	NA	11.5	Tp	1.2	Tp	.8	Tp	3.4	Tp	NA	NA
240	WS 17	NARROW ARCH	ECA	84	8.0	TR	1.0	TR	NO	NA	8.0	TR	1.0	TR	16.0	TR	26.0	TR	24.0	TR
241	EP 4	EAGLE ARCH	CWA	84	8.0	TR	1.0	TR	NO	NA	8.0	TR	1.0	TR	9.0	TR	8.0	TR	NA	NA
242	HP 16	DAM ARCH	FSA	86	8.0	Tp	.9	Tp	NO	NA	8.0	Tp	.9	Tp	3.2	Tp	5.5	Tp	NA	NA
243	FF 25	WINE GLASS ARCH	CWA	84	8.0	EX	.8	Es	NO	NA	27.0	TR	16.0	TR	6.4	TR	6.0	Es	34.0	TR
244	HP 12	FIGURE ARCH	FSA	84	8.0	TR	.5	Es	NO	NA	8.4	TR	15.0	TR	1.5	TR	1.0	Es	11.5	TR
245	SA 37	CAVE ARCH	CWA	84	8.0	Tp	.3	Tp	NO	NA	8.0	Tp	2.5	Tp	3.8	Tp	12.0	Tp	21.0	Tp
246	HP 1	TOP OF THE SLOPE ARCH	CWA	84	8.0	Tp	.2	Tp	NO	NA	11.0	Tp	6.0	Tp	7.3	Tp	4.8	Tp	25.0	Tp
247	KB 2	CLIFF CREST ARCH	PFA	84	7.9	Tp	.6	Tp	NO	NA	7.9	Tp	.6	Tp	.3	Tp	2.1	Tp	14.0	Tp
248	ND 33	TURBAN HEAD ARCH	FSA	84	7.8	Tp	3.0	Tp	NO	NA	7.8	Tp	3.0	Tp	2.4	Tp	3.3	Tp	11.0	Tp
249	LC 22	BACKSIDE ARCH OUTER	CWA	84	7.8	Tp	1.0	Tp	NO	NA	15.8	Tp	5.0	Tp	2.7	Tp	.8	Tp	19.5	Tp
250	SA 4	SHOE ARCH	ECA	84	7.6	TR	2.0	TR	NO	NA	7.6	TR	2.0	TR	16.5	TR	7.5	TR	NA	NA
251	GW 19	CLEAR VIEW ARCH	FSA	84	7.5	Tp	7.5	Tp	NO	NA	7.5	Tp	7.5	Tp	3.0	Tp	2.9	Tp	10.0	Tp

RANK	IDENT	NAME	TYPE	YM	LOL	HM	LOD	HM	DLO	HM	OBW	HM	OBH	HM	SVT	HM	SHT	HM	SXT	HM
252	ND 53	RECTANGULAR ARCH	FSA	84	7.5	Tp	5.8	Tp	NO	NA	7.5	Tp	5.8	Tp	60.0	Es	17.0	Tp	NA	NA
253	ND 50	TEATIME ARCH NORTH	FSA	84	7.5	Rd	5.5	Rd	NO	NA	7.5	Rd	5.5	Rd	18.0	Rd	20.0	Rd	41.0	Tp
254	ND 64	SAUCER ARCH	FSA	84	7.5	RE	4.0	RE	NO	NA	7.5	RE	4.0	RE	19.0	RE	8.0	RE	NA	NA
255	HP 2	HIDDEN CANYON ARCH	PAA	84	7.5	Tp	2.5	Tp	NO	NA	20.0	Tp	3.2	Tp	22.0	TE	39.0	Tp	75.0	Tp
256	FF 11	PAGODA ARCH	FSA	84	7.5	Tp	1.9	Tp	NO	NA	7.5	Tp	1.9	Tp	3.1	Tp	7.5	Tp	NA	NA
257	EP 16	SPIDER ARCH	CWA	86	7.5	Tp	1.8	Tp	NO	NA	13.5	Tp	2.5	Tp	.5	Tp	.9	Tp	13.5	Tp
258	SW 23	GOOSEHEAD ARCH	CWA	84	7.5	TR	1.0	Es	NO	NA	7.5	TR	21.0	TR	10.7	TR	7.0	Es	37.5	Tp
259	SD 3	POOL ARCH	CWA	84	7.5	Tp	.4	Tp	NO	NA	12.0	Tp	1.3	Tp	.9	Tp	2.9	Tp	17.0	Tp
260	SD 29	TRAIL ARCH	CWA	84	7.5	Tp	.3	Tp	NO	NA	10.0	Tp	2.0	Tp	3.0	Tp	2.5	Tp	10.0	Tp
261	SA 54	SPATULA ARCH	CWA	84	7.5	Tp	.2	Tp	NO	NA	8.5	Tp	1.5	Tp	1.0	Tp	.3	Tp	12.0	Tp
262	SD 6	SHELF ARCH	CWA	84	7.5	Tp	.1	Tp	NO	NA	7.5	Tp	3.2	Tp	.5	Tp	1.5	Tp	13.0	Tp
263	SA 53	DEER MOUSE ARCH	FSA	84	7.0	Tp	7.3	Tp	NO	NA	7.0	Tp	7.3	Tp	.4	Tp	.6	Tp	NA	NA
264	ND 34	FALLING ROCK ARCH	FSA	84	7.3	Tp	4.3	Tp	NO	NA	7.3	Tp	4.3	Tp	3.5	Tp	2.5	Tp	9.0	Tp
265	KB 13	ANNIVERSARY ARCH SOUTH	FSA	84	7.2	Tp	6.5	Tp	NO	NA	14.0	Tp	7.0	Tp	8.0	TT	15.0	Tp	19.0	Tp
266	ND 2	TEXTBOOK ARCH WEST	FSA	84	7.2	Tp	4.1	Tp	NO	NA	7.2	Tp	4.1	Tp	7.3	Tp	10.8	Tp	22.5	Tp
267	UC 20	STALE CRACKER ARCH	CWA	84	7.2	Tp	1.8	Tp	NO	NA	8.5	Tp	2.1	Tp	.7	Tp	1.4	Tp	NA	NA
268	EP 19	SCOOP ARCH	CWA	84	7.2	Tp	.8	Tp	NO	NA	7.2	Tp	3.5	Tp	6.5	Tp	3.0	Tp	9.5	Tp
269	WS 20	RAVEN ARCH	ECA	84	7.0	TR	2.5	TR	NO	NA	7.0	TR	2.5	TR	26.0	TR	7.0	TR	NA	NA
270	SD 28	RABBIT TRAP ARCH	SAA	84	7.0	Tp	2.0	Tp	NO	NA	7.0	Tp	2.0	Tp	.6	Tp	.8	Tp	7.0	Tp
271	SA 15	PARK AVENUE ARCH	CWA	84	7.0	TE	.5	TE	NO	NA	70.0	Tp	62.0	Rf	8.5	TR	8.0	TR	73.0	Tp
272	KB 18	ROCK IN THE HOLE ARCH	ECA	84	7.0	Tp	.4	Tp	NO	NA	9.5	Tp	3.7	Tp	12.0	Es	13.0	Es	NA	NA
273	SA 52	CAN OPENER ARCH	PFA	84	7.0	Tp	.4	Tp	NO	NA	7.0	Tp	.4	Tp	.2	Tp	1.4	Tp	8.0	Tp
274	GW 7	SERVICEBERRY ARCH	PFA	85	7.0	Tp	.2	Tp	NO	NA	7.0	Tp	.2	Tp	.3	Tp	3.1	Tp	7.8	Tp
275	SA 34	PENGUIN ARCH	CWA	84	7.0	Tp	.1	Tp	YES	Tp	51.0	Tp	11.0	Tp	2.5	Tp	3.7	Tp	58.0	Tp
276	SA 17	SQUIRREL ARCH	CWA	85	7.0	Tp	.1	Tp	NO	NA	9.5	Tp	2.3	Tp	1.5	Tp	.8	Tp	9.5	Tp
277	SA 8	FLAT ARCH	PFA	84	7.0	Tp	.1	Tp	NO	NA	7.0	Tp	.2	Tp	.3	Tp	1.9	Tp	NA	NA
278	SA 29	DEMON ARCH	FSA	84	6.8	Tp	2.5	Tp	NO	NA	6.8	Tp	3.0	Tp	9.0	Tp	5.5	Tp	10.0	Tp
279	SD 37	WEDGE ARCH	FSA	84	6.7	TR	2.0	TR	NO	NA	11.7	TR	10.0	TR	8.8	TR	7.0	TR	NA	NA

157

RANK	IDENT	NAME	TYPE	YM	LOL	HM	LOD	HM	DLO	HM	OBW	HM	OBH	HM	SVT	HM	SHT	HM	SXT	HM
280	SA 28	TWO HUNDRED ARCH	FSA	84	6.5	Tp	5.0	Tp	NO	NA	6.5	Tp	5.0	Tp	3.5	Tp	4.6	Tp	14.0	Tp
281	GW 20	OWL EYE ARCH	SAA	84	6.5	Tp	4.1	Tp	NO	NA	6.5	Tp	4.1	Tp	2.2	Tp	3.5	Tp	10.0	Tp
282	SW 7	BRUSHY BASIN BRIDGE	NB	84	6.5	Tp	3.2	Tp	NO	NA	7.0	Tp	3.4	Tp	5.5	Tp	10.0	Tp	NA	NA
283	ND 22	COFFIN ARCH	FSA	84	6.5	Tp	2.8	Tp	NO	NA	6.5	Tp	2.8	Tp	2.8	Tp	5.0	Tp	14.0	Tp
284	SD 63	PERSEVERANCE ARCH	CWA	84	6.5	Es	2.0	Es	NO	NA	6.5	TR	2.0	TR	5.0	Es	4.0	Es	11.5	Es
285	ND 18	CHAMBER ARCH NORTH	ECA	84	6.5	Tp	1.5	Tp	NO	NA	6.5	Tp	1.5	Tp	4.0	Tp	9.0	Tp	10.0	Tp
286	ND 80	LATTICE ARCH	ECA	84	6.5	Tp	1.1	Tp	NO	NA	6.5	Tp	1.1	Tp	7.3	Tp	3.8	Tp	20.5	Tp
287	ND 58	FAWN ARCH	ECA	84	6.5	Tp	1.0	Tp	NO	NA	6.5	Tp	1.0	Tp	15.0	Es	7.0	Tp	NA	NA
288	SA 42	CROSSBED ARCH	SAA	84	6.4	Tp	1.0	Tp	NO	NA	6.4	Tp	1.0	Tp	.7	Tp	.9	Tp	NA	NA
289	ND 42	CANYON WREN BRIDGE	NB	84	6.3	Tp	.1	Tp	NO	NA	8.0	Tp	2.0	Tp	1.7	Tp	1.2	Tp	9.0	Tp
290	EP 9	FIVE TWELVE ARCH	CWA	86	6.3	Tp	.9	TE	NO	NA	6.3	Tp	3.1	Tp	.3	TE	.7	TE	8.2	Tp
291	SW 8	BLUE ARCH	NB	84	6.2	Tp	5.0	Tp	NO	NA	6.2	Tp	5.0	Tp	1.8	Tp	2.3	Tp	NA	NA
292	ND 47	BOBCAT ARCH	FSA	84	3.9	Tp	6.2	Tp	NO	NA	7.0	Tp	7.0	Tp	1.1	Tp	1.9	Tp	9.5	Tp
293	FF 39	KISSING TURTLES	FSA	84	6.1	Tp	4.5	Tp	NO	NA	7.3	Tp	5.2	Tp	4.5	Tp	3.5	Tp	11.0	Tp
294	SD 33	BOOST ARCH	SAA	84	6.0	Tp	5.0	Tp	NO	NA	6.0	Tp	5.0	Tp	6.3	Tp	.7	Tp	10.0	Tp
295	FF 28	UNSEEN ARCH	FSA	84	5.0	TE	6.0	TE	NO	NA	5.0	TE	6.0	TE	4.5	Es	5.0	Es	14.0	Es
296	FF 32	APOSTROPHE ARCH	FSA	84	3.9	Tp	6.0	Tp	NO	NA	3.9	Tp	6.0	Tp	6.0	Tp	2.9	Tp	7.0	Tp
297	ND 11	SHELTER ARCH	FSA	84	6.0	Tp	3.7	Tp	NO	NA	15.0	Tp	6.0	Tp	29.0	Rd	16.0	Tp	35.0	Tp
298	EP 7	HIP JOINT ARCH	CWA	84	3.5	Es	6.0	Rd	NO	NA	3.5	Es	6.0	Rd	2.0	Es	4.0	Es	NA	NA
299	SW 17	CLIFF TOP ARCH	FSA	84	6.0	TR	2.8	TR	NO	NA	6.0	TR	2.8	TR	3.1	Tp	7.0	TR	8.0	TR
300	KB 4	FIVE HUNDRED BRIDGE	NB	86	6.0	Tp	2.3	Tp	NO	NA	6.0	Tp	2.3	Tp	3.2	Tp	4.7	Tp	9.0	Tp
301	KB 15	WINE BOTTLE ARCH	ECA	86	1.5	Tp	6.0	Tp	NO	NA	9.8	Tp	6.0	Tp	4.2	Tp	4.0	Tp	NA	NA
302	LC 20	TYRANNOSAURUS ARCH	ECA	84	6.0	Tp	1.2	Tp	NO	NA	7.0	Tp	3.0	Tp	2.4	Tp	2.0	Tp	14.0	Tp
303	HP 6	SLAT ARCH	ECA	84	6.0	Tp	1.0	Tp	NO	NA	6.0	Tp	1.5	Tp	3.7	Tp	4.7	Tp	16.0	Tp
304	KB 8	CAVITY ARCH	CWA	86	6.0	TR	.6	TR	NO	NA	43.0	Tp	34.0	TR	12.0	TR	9.0	TR	43.0	Tp
305	ND 81	ROLLED ARCH	CWA	84	6.0	Tp	.5	Tp	NO	NA	34.0	Tp	.5	Tp	1.6	Tp	3.8	Tp	45.0	Tp
306	LC 3	WILDFLOWER ARCH	CWA	85	6.0	Tp	.2	Tp	NO	NA	33.0	Tp	11.8	Tp	2.5	Tp	4.8	Tp	44.0	Tp
307	SA 25	MAHOGANY ARCH	CWA	84	6.0	Tp	.2	Tp	NO	NA	10.0	Tp	3.7	Tp	2.3	Tp	2.0	Tp	16.0	Tp

RANK	IDENT	NAME	TYPE	YM	LOL	HM	LOD	HM	DLO	HM	OBW	HM	OBH	HM	SVT	HM	SHT	HM	SXT	HM
308	FF 42	SLIVER ARCH	CWA	84	6.0	RE	.2	Rd	NO	NA	6.0	Rd	14.5	Rd	3.5	Rd	1.1	Rd	8.3	Rd
309	FF 7	VULTURE ARCH	FSA	84	5.9	Tp	1.8	Tp	NO	NA	5.9	Tp	1.8	Tp	.1	Tp	.4	Tp	5.9	Tp
310	FF 44	CRAWL THRU ARCH	ECA	84	5.9	Tp	1.4	Tp	NO	NA	5.9	Tp	1.4	Tp	12.8	Tp	7.5	Tp	NA	NA
311	EP 45	CARLING ARCH	CWA	86	5.9	Tp	.5	Tp	NO	NA	5.9	Tp	3.6	Tp	4.0	Tp	4.5	Tp	8.0	Tp
312	ND 35	ALADDINS BRIDGE	NB	84	5.9	Tp	.4	Tp	NO	NA	5.9	Tp	.4	Tp	.2	Tp	1.5	Tp	6.0	Tp
313	SA 48	AIRFOIL ARCH LOWER	ECA	84	5.6	Tp	.8	Tp	NO	NA	5.6	TR	1.5	Tp	1.0	Tp	1.2	Tp	NA	NA
314	LC 14	TANDEM ARCH SOUTH	SAA	85	5.0	TR	5.5	TR	NO	NA	5.0	TR	5.5	TR	4.5	TR	6.0	TR	11.0	TR
315	SW 2	SALT WASH ARCH	PHA	84	5.5	Tp	4.5	Tp	NO	NA	80.0	Tp	34.0	Tp	3.0	Es	10.8	Tp	104.0	Tp
316	SW 20	MIRROR ARCH	SAA	84	5.5	Tp	4.0	Tp	NO	NA	5.5	Tp	4.0	Tp	8.0	Tp	2.1	Tp	NA	NA
317	SD 60	TEE ARCH	FSA	84	5.5	Tp	2.0	Tp	NO	NA	5.5	Tp	2.0	Tp	4.0	Tp	7.0	Tp	7.0	Tp
318	GW 9	DEEP ARCH	ECA	84	5.5	Tp	1.8	Tp	NO	NA	9.5	Tp	2.0	Tp	5.5	Tp	17.0	Tp	16.0	Tp
319	LC 6	SLIPPER ARCH	ECA	84	5.5	Tp	1.5	TR	NO	NA	5.5	TR	1.5	Tp	8.5	TR	2.5	TR	NA	NA
320	EP 39	TORNADO ARCH	JHA	84	5.5	Tp	1.4	Tp	NO	NA	5.5	Tp	1.4	Tp	.4	Tp	1.1	Tp	6.6	Tp
321	ND 85	RUBBLE ARCH SOUTHEAST	ECA	85	5.5	Tp	1.4	Tp	NO	NA	5.5	Tp	1.4	Tp	.7	Tp	3.1	Tp	5.5	Tp
322	ND 68	EXCAVATION ARCH	ECA	84	5.5	Tp	.8	Tp	NO	NA	5.5	Tp	.8	Tp	1.7	Tp	6.0	Tp	27.0	Tp
323	HP 5	SLOT ARCH	ECA	84	5.5	Tp	.5	Tp	NO	NA	19.0	Tp	1.0	Tp	3.5	Tp	5.8	Tp	22.5	Tp
324	WS 39	DUPLEX ARCH LOWER	CWA	86	5.5	Tp	.5	Tp	NO	NA	6.0	Tp	.5	Tp	.2	Tp	.6	Tp	9.0	Tp
325	WS 38	DUPLEX ARCH UPPER	CWA	86	5.5	Tp	.3	Tp	NO	NA	5.5	Tp	.6	Tp	.4	Tp	.8	Tp	9.0	Tp
326	SA 16	SNOUT ARCH	PFA	85	5.5	Tp	.3	Tp	NO	NA	5.5	Tp	.3	Tp	.2	Tp	.8	Tp	5.8	Tp
327	EP 32	PACK RAT ARCH	CWA	84	5.4	Tp	2.0	Tp	NO	NA	10.0	Tp	5.0	Tp	5.0	Tp	7.0	Tp	11.5	Tp
328	SD 9	DAH ARCH	FSA	84	5.4	Tp	2.0	Tp	NO	NA	5.4	Tp	2.0	Tp	12.0	Rd	12.0	Rd	NA	NA
329	ND 70	COLUMBINE ARCH	PAA	84	5.3	Tp	2.8	Tp	NO	NA	13.0	Tp	4.5	Tp	70.0	TR	25.0	Rd	NA	NA
330	EP 17	DUCK ARCH	CWA	84	5.3	Tp	.6	Tp	NO	NA	5.3	Tp	3.2	Tp	3.5	Tp	8.0	Tp	13.0	Tp
331	UC 7	THE TUNNEL	NT	84	5.2	Tp	4.0	Tp	NO	NA	6.0	Tp	7.0	Tp	12.0	EX	53.0	Tp	NA	NA
332	ND 15	TWIN SPANS EAST	FSA	84	5.2	Tp	4.0	Tp	NO	NA	5.2	Tp	4.0	Tp	2.7	Tp	8.0	Tp	10.0	Tp
333	GW 21	PILLAR ARCH	SAA	84	3.1	Tp	5.2	Tp	NO	NA	3.1	Tp	5.2	Tp	3.5	Tp	1.6	Tp	8.0	Tp
334	PB 2	HORN OF PLENTY ARCH	PAA	84	5.2	Tp	1.3	Tp	NO	NA	9.0	Tp	2.5	Tp	17.0	Tp	15.0	Tp	14.0	Tp
335	LC 9	CATHEDRAL ARCH	CWA	85	5.2	TR	1.0	TR	NO	NA	44.0	TR	19.0	TR	5.0	TR	5.0	Es	57.0	Es

RANK	IDENT	NAME	TYPE	YM	LOL	HM	LOD	HM	DLO	HM	OBW	HM	OBH	HM	SVT	HM	SHT	HM	SXT	HM
336	WS 26	THANKSGIVING BRIDGE	NB	84	5.2	Tp	.7	Tp	NO	NA	6.2	Tp	2.1	Tp	.5	Tp	1.3	Tp	11.0	Tp
337	LC 23	BACKSIDE ARCH UPPER	CWA	84	5.2	Tp	.7	Tp	NO	NA	5.2	Tp	1.6	Tp	1.2	Tp	4.2	Tp	NA	NA
338	EP 3	SIBLING ARCH SOUTH	PAA	86	5.2	Tp	.1	Tp	NO	NA	41.0	Tp	11.0	TE	22.0	TE	12.0	Tp	50.0	TE
339	UC 18	YUCCA ARCH	CWA	84	5.2	Tp	.1	Tp	NO	NA	16.5	Tp	6.2	Tp	1.2	Tp	2.1	Jp	18.0	Tp
340	ND 56	TURKEY ARCH	FSA	84	5.1	TR	4.8	TR	NO	NA	5.1	TR	4.8	TR	7.4	TR	3.0	Es	12.3	TR
341	GW 11	ARTISTIC ARCH	FSA	84	5.1	Tp	1.8	Tp	NO	NA	5.1	Tp	1.8	Tp	1.0	Tp	2.3	Tp	10.0	Tp
342	FF 50	TALUS ARCH	CWA	84	5.1	Rd	.8	Rd	NO	NA	5.1	Rd	1.5	Rd	1.9	Rd	2.0	Es	7.0	Rd
343	SA 44	GAP ARCH	FSA	84	3.5	Tp	5.0	Tp	NO	NA	3.5	Tp	5.0	Tp	1.4	Tp	4.0	Tp	3.5	Tp
344	FF 36	E ARCH	FSA	84	3.1	Tp	5.0	Tp	NO	NA	3.1	Tp	5.0	Tp	10.0	Tp	4.0	Tp	7.0	Tp
345	WS 14	TROUGH ARCH	CWA	84	5.0	Tp	3.0	Tp	NO	NA	6.5	Tp	9.0	Tp	3.5	Tp	5.0	Tp	11.0	Tp
346	HP 7	ATTIC ARCH	FSA	86	5.0	TR	2.5	TR	NO	NA	7.0	TR	6.0	TR	10.0	TR	6.0	TR	NA	NA
347	SA 3	DOG HEAD ARCH	SAA	86	5.0	RE	2.5	RE	NO	NA	5.0	Rd	2.5	Rd	2.5	Rd	2.5	Rd	7.0	Rd
348	SA 9	SLANT ARCH UPPER	FSA	84	5.0	Tp	2.2	Tp	NO	NA	5.0	Tp	2.2	Tp	2.5	Tp	9.0	Tp	14.0	Tp
349	SA 20	ABOVE THE ALCOVE ARCH NO.	FSA	85	2.0	Tp	5.0	Tp	NO	NA	21.0	Tp	19.0	Tp	38.0	Tp	35.0	Tp	NA	NA
350	SD 44	LICHEN ARCH	FSA	84	5.0	TR	2.0	TR	NO	NA	5.0	TR	2.0	TR	5.1	TR	3.5	TR	NA	NA
351	SW 4	BOOT ARCH	FSA	84	2.0	Tp	5.0	Tp	NO	NA	4.5	Tp	5.0	Tp	.8	Tp	2.2	Tp	6.5	Tp
352	SD 65	DEVILS JUGHANDLE	JHA	84	2.0	TR	5.0	TR	NO	NA	2.0	TR	5.0	TR	2.0	TR	1.0	TR	18.0	TR
353	ND 3	FLAPJACK ARCH	ECA	84	5.0	Tp	1.5	Tp	NO	NA	5.0	Tp	1.5	Tp	.4	Tp	1.4	Tp	NA	NA
354	ND 26	KEYHOLE ARCH	ECA	84	1.5	Rd	5.0	Rd	NO	NA	1.5	Rd	5.0	Rd	1.3	Es	8.0	Es	8.0	Es
355	SA 45	REGAP ARCH	ECA	84	5.0	Tp	1.3	Tp	NO	NA	5.0	Tp	1.3	Tp	3.0	Tp	3.9	Tp	NA	NA
356	SD 71	ROCK CATCHER ARCH	CWA	84	5.0	Tp	1.0	Tp	YES	Tp	21.5	Tp	16.9	Rd	3.5	Rd	2.0	Tp	29.0	Tp
357	SD 58	DEVILS EYE ARCH	CWA	84	5.0	Tp	.8	Tp	NO	NA	5.0	Tp	2.8	Tp	2.0	Tp	1.0	TR	14.0	TR
358	EP 44	WIMPY ARCH	PFA	86	5.0	Tp	.7	Tp	NO	NA	7.3	Tp	.7	Tp	.3	Tp	.8	Tp	9.0	Tp
359	EP 47	SALTBUSH ARCH	ECA	86	5.0	Tp	.6	Tp	NO	NA	5.0	Tp	.6	Tp	1.1	Tp	.9	Tp	6.0	Tp
360	ND 83	PET ARCH	CWA	84	5.0	Tp	.5	Tp	NO	NA	7.2	Tp	4.5	Tp	21.0	Tp	10.0	Tp	21.5	Tp
361	SD 8	DOO ARCH	ECA	84	5.0	Tp	.5	Tp	NO	NA	5.0	Tp	.5	Tp	.5	Rd	1.0	Tp	6.0	Tp
362	SD 5	SKEPTICAL ARCH	JHA	84	.5	Tp	5.0	Tp	NO	NA	1.5	Tp	15.0	Tp	.4	Tp	1.5	Tp	15.0	Tp
363	ND 45	DUMBBELL ARCH UPPER	CWA	84	5.0	Tp	.4	Tp	YES	Tp	10.2	Tp	2.5	Tp	.4	Tp	.7	Tp	10.2	Tp

RANK	IDENT	NAME	TYPE	YM	LOL	HM	LOD	HM	DLO	HM	OBW	HM	OBH	HM	SVT	HM	SHT	HM	SXT	HM
364	SD 47	STEM ARCH	JHA	84	.4	Tp	5.0	Tp	NO	NA	.4	Tp	5.0	Tp	.5	Tp	.8	Tp	6.5	Tp
365	ND 6	THEORY ARCH	CWA	84	5.0	Tp	.1	Tp	NO	NA	11.0	Tp	3.5	Tp	1.1	Tp	2.0	Tp	14.0	Tp
366	WS 27	GIMPY ARCH	PFA	85	5.0	Tp	.1	Tp	NO	NA	5.0	Tp	.1	Tp	.7	Tp	4.5	Tp	16.0	Tp
367	ND 37	HUG ARCH	PFA	84	5.0	Tp	.1	Tp	NO	NA	5.0	Tp	.1	Tp	.1	Tp	.7	Tp	6.0	Tp
368	LC 29	RUPTURE ARCH	CWA	85	4.9	Tp	1.5	Tp	NO	NA	9.0	Tp	3.0	Tp	.7	Tp	.2	Tp	10.0	Tp
369	PB 14	PANORAMA BLUFFS ARCH	PAA	84	4.9	Tp	1.3	Tp	NO	NA	8.7	Tp	6.0	Tp	14.7	Tp	5.5	Tp	10.5	Tp
370	LC 10	DICTIONARY ARCH	ECA	84	4.9	Tp	1.2	Tp	NO	NA	4.9	Tp	1.2	Tp	2.6	Tp	3.0	Tp	NA	NA
371	WS 41	REVEREND ARCH	JHA	86	.9	Tp	4.9	Tp	NO	NA	.9	Tp	4.9	Tp	.3	Tp	1.2	Tp	7.0	Tp
372	GW 24	SUBTLE ARCH	CWA	84	4.9	Tp	.2	Tp	NO	NA	4.9	Tp	.3	Tp	.3	Tp	.8	Tp	6.1	Tp
373	WS 8	SAGE ARCH	FSA	84	4.8	Tp	3.0	Tp	NO	NA	4.8	Tp	3.0	Tp	4.0	Tp	3.5	Tp	NA	NA
374	SA 40	JOGGERS ARCH	JHA	86	2.8	Tp	4.8	Tp	NO	NA	3.5	Tp	5.5	Tp	.7	Tp	1.1	Tp	7.0	Tp
375	ND 59	DIGGER ARCH	CWA	84	4.8	Tp	.8	Tp	NO	NA	4.8	Tp	1.0	Tp	4.0	Tp	2.1	Tp	8.0	Tp
376	WS 23	MULE DEER ARCH	ECA	84	4.8	TR	.6	TR	NO	NA	4.8	TR	.6	TR	6.3	TR	3.0	TR	NA	NA
377	SA 2	CLIFFHANGER ARCH	CWA	85	4.8	TR	.2	TR	NO	NA	6.1	TR	3.2	TR	.4	Es	.8	TR	7.0	TR
378	SD 36	TIP TOP ARCH	FSA	84	4.3	TR	4.6	TR	NO	NA	4.3	TR	4.6	TR	8.2	TR	3.0	Es	NA	NA
379	HP 20	MICROPHONE ARCH	FSA	84	4.5	Tp	4.5	Tp	NO	NA	4.5	Tp	4.5	Tp	2.0	Tp	2.5	Tp	6.0	Tp
380	SA 7	FOUR HUNDRED ARCH	FSA	84	2.5	Tp	4.5	Tp	NO	NA	2.5	Tp	4.5	Tp	6.5	Tp	3.9	Tp	13.0	Tp
381	KB 5	TURTLE SHELL ARCH	CWA	84	4.5	Tp	1.5	Tp	NO	NA	4.5	Tp	1.8	Tp	2.0	Tp	5.0	Tp	19.0	Tp
382	SD 80	GOBLET ARCH	JHA	84	1.5	Rd	4.5	Rd	NO	NA	1.5	Rd	4.5	Rd	2.2	Rd	3.0	Rd	6.0	Rd
383	SA 36	CAPPED ARCH	FSA	84	4.5	Tp	1.4	Tp	NO	NA	8.0	Tp	1.5	Tp	4.0	Tp	7.5	Tp	NA	NA
384	PB 9	BIG TOP ARCH	ECA	85	4.5	Tp	1.1	Tp	NO	NA	4.5	Tp	1.1	Tp	1.4	Tp	3.5	Tp	6.0	Tp
385	SD 66	PUNCH BOWL ARCH	FSA	84	4.5	Tp	1.1	Tp	NO	NA	4.5	Tp	1.1	Tp	1.2	Tp	3.5	Tp	5.5	Tp
386	FF 16	MINI SPECTACLES SOUTH	FSA	84	4.5	Tp	1.1	Tp	NO	NA	4.5	Tp	1.1	Tp	3.1	Tp	1.4	Tp	NA	NA
387	PB 10	BLACKBRUSH ARCH	CWA	85	4.5	Tp	1.0	Tp	NO	NA	4.5	Tp	1.9	Tp	1.0	Tp	6.0	Tp	NA	NA
388	ND 49	EVIL EYE ARCH	JHA	84	4.5	Tp	1.0	Es	NO	NA	4.5	Tp	1.0	Es	2.0	Es	23.0	TE	9.0	Es
389	LC 5	WHALE ARCH NORTH	CWA	84	4.5	Tp	1.0	Tp	NO	NA	4.5	Tp	1.0	Tp	16.0	TR	13.0	Tp	7.0	Tp
390	EP 42	CRY BABY ARCH	CWA	84	4.5	Tp	.9	Tp	NO	NA	14.0	Tp	6.2	Tp	3.0	Tp	6.2	Tp	15.0	Tp
391	ND 57	LENS ARCH	CWA	84	4.5	Tp	.6	Tp	NO	NA	4.5	Tp	.6	Tp	5.5	Tp	1.8	Tp	7.0	Tp

RANK	IDENT	NAME	TYPE	YM	LOL HM	LOD HM	DLO HM	OBW HM	OBH HM	SVT HM	SHT HM	SXT HM
392	PB 3	E T ARCH	JHA	84	.6 Tp	4.5 Tp	NO NA	.6 Tp	4.5 Tp	.9 Tp	3.1 Tp	7.0 Tp
393	SD 11	AROUND BACK ARCH	ECA	86	4.5 Tp	.5 Tp	NO NA	17.0 Tp	3.5 Tp	3.3 Tp	5.2 Tp	17.0 Tp
394	FF 20	REPTILE ARCH	ECA	84	4.5 Tp	.5 Tp	NO NA	4.5 Tp	.5 Tp	2.7 Tp	3.7 Tp	9.0 Tp
395	LC 1	PRETZEL ARCH	PFA	84	4.5 Tp	.2 Tp	NO NA	5.5 Tp	.2 Tp	.1 Tp	1.2 Tp	7.0 Tp
396	LC 24	SQUAWBUSH ARCH	JHA	84	.2 Tp	4.5 Tp	NO NA	3.0 Tp	4.5 Tp	.1 Tp	1.5 Tp	7.8 Tp
397	SD 69	LEAST ARCH	ECA	84	4.5 Tp	.1 Tp	NO NA	4.5 Tp	.1 Tp	4.5 Tp	.8 Tp	8.0 Tp
398	ND 20	INDIAN HEAD ARCH	FSA	84	3.9 Tp	4.4 Tp	NO NA	3.9 Tp	4.4 Tp	3.7 Tp	2.9 Tp	NA NA
399	FF 30	DUAL ARCH NORTHEAST	ECA	84	4.4 Tp	1.8 Tp	NO NA	2.8 Tp	5.3 Tp	11.0 Tp	4.5 Tp	8.0 Tp
400	FF 14	MONOCLE ARCH	FSA	86	4.4 Tp	1.4 Tp	NO NA	4.4 Tp	1.4 Tp	3.0 Tp	.9 Tp	7.0 Tp
401	SA 46	BULL ARCH	JHA	84	4.4 Tp	1.0 Tp	NO NA	4.4 Tp	14.0 Tp	3.0 Tp	3.8 Tp	6.5 Tp
402	FF 4	GARBAGE ARCH	ECA	84	4.4 Tp	1.0 Tp	NO NA	4.4 Tp	1.5 Tp	1.5 Tp	3.0 Tp	NA NA
403	GW 26	BURNT CEILING ARCH	JHA	86	4.4 Tp	.9 Tp	NO NA	4.4 Tp	.9 Tp	1.1 Tp	2.8 Tp	5.0 Tp
404	ND 17	CAMOUFLAGE TWINS SOUTH	ECA	84	4.3 Tp	1.7 Tp	NO NA	4.3 Tp	1.7 Tp	30.0 Tp	21.0 Tp	9.0 Tp
405	ND 78	CHEATGRASS ARCH	SAA	86	4.3 Tp	1.5 Tp	NO NA	4.3 Tp	1.8 Tp	1.2 Tp	1.8 Tp	9.0 Tp
406	UC 6	BEND ARCH	CWA	84	4.3 Tp	.3 Tp	YES Tp	20.0 Rd	12.0 Rd	3.3 Rd	3.7 Tp	30.0 RE
407	EP 22	ON THE MONEY ARCH	CWA	84	4.3 Tp	.3 Tp	NO NA	9.2 Tp	2.6 Tp	1.7 Tp	1.5 Tp	12.0 Tp
408	SD 32	BEAM ARCH	CWA	84	4.3 Tp	.3 Tp	NO NA	5.3 Tp	.6 Tp	.7 Tp	.8 Tp	8.4 Tp
409	LC 17	LIZARD ARCH	SAA	84	4.2 Tp	4.1 Tp	NO NA	4.2 Tp	4.1 Tp	.9 Tp	1.9 Tp	10.0 Tp
410	ND 77	TUMBLEWEED ARCH	FSA	86	4.2 Tp	2.5 Tp	NO NA	4.5 Tp	3.0 Tp	2.0 Tp	1.8 Tp	5.5 Tp
411	SA 43	SHOTGUN ARCH	ECA	84	4.2 Tp	.7 Tp	NO NA	7.0 Tp	1.0 Tp	.7 Tp	1.5 Tp	12.0 Tp
412	ND 46	DUMBBELL ARCH LOWER	CWA	84	4.2 Tp	.5 Tp	NO NA	6.0 Tp	2.1 Tp	1.0 Tp	.9 Tp	7.5 Tp
413	ND 14	TWIN SPANS WEST	FSA	84	4.1 Tp	2.8 Tp	NO NA	4.1 TR	2.8 Tp	.8 Tp	2.5 Tp	6.2 Tp
414	SW 16	TAPERED ARCH	PHA	84	4.1 TR	2.3 TR	NO NA	4.1 TR	2.3 TR	3.6 TR	3.5 TR	15.0 TR
415	ND 73	CORRIDOR ARCH	ECA	84	4.1 TR	.7 Es	NO NA	4.1 TR	.7 Es	11.7 TR	12.0 TR	NA NA
416	LC 7	HUMMINGBIRD ARCH	CWA	84	4.0 Tp	.5 Es	NO NA	160.0 TR	13.0 TR	7.0 TR	5.0 TR	160.0 TR
417	EP 34	CRACKER ARCH	SAA	84	4.0 Tp	3.7 Tp	NO NA	4.0 Tp	3.7 Tp	1.2 Tp	3.5 Tp	11.0 Tp
418	SA 11	BADGER ARCH	FSA	84	4.0 Tp	2.7 Tp	NO NA	4.0 Tp	2.7 Tp	7.0 Tp	22.0 Tp	NA NA
419	GW 15	BIRDS EYE ARCH	SAA	84	4.0 Tp	1.9 Tp	NO NA	4.0 Tp	1.9 Tp	2.2 Tp	2.3 Tp	5.2 Tp

RANK	IDENT	NAME	TYPE	YM	LOL	HM	LOD	HM	DLO	HM	OBW	HM	OBH	HM	SVT	HM	SHT	HM	SXT	HM
420	FF 31	DUAL ARCH SOUTHWEST	ECA	84	4.0	Tp	1.7	Tp	NO	NA	4.0	Tp	4.5	Tp	11.0	Tp	4.5	Tp	8.0	Tp
421	LC 25	TRAP DOOR ARCH	PAA	84	1.6	Tp	4.0	Tp	NO	NA	17.5	Tp	6.0	Tp	1.5	Tp	4.0	Tp	17.5	Tp
422	WS 40	SUNGLASS ARCH	SAA	86	4.0	Tp	1.3	Tp	NO	NA	4.6	Tp	1.4	Tp	.7	Tp	.7	Tp	4.6	Tp
423	KB 3	BUCKLE ARCH	FSA	84	4.0	TR	1.2	TR	NO	NA	4.0	TR	1.2	TR	.5	TR	.5	Es	4.0	TR
424	SA 32	VISITOR CENTER ARCH	CWA	84	4.0	Tp	1.0	Tp	YES	Tp	21.5	Tp	30.5	Rd	16.0	Tp	10.5	Tp	57.0	Tp
425	WS 6	BOW TIE ARCH	CWA	84	4.0	TR	1.0	TR	NO	NA	13.6	TR	14.0	TR	6.4	TR	2.0	EX	20.0	TR
426	GW 1	EPHEDRA ARCH	CWA	84	4.0	Tp	1.0	Tp	NO	NA	8.0	Tp	9.0	Tp	.8	Tp	3.6	Tp	9.0	Tp
427	WS 7	PORCUPINE ARCH	CWA	84	4.0	Tp	1.0	Tp	NO	NA	8.0	Tp	1.5	Tp	.4	Tp	2.4	Tp	8.0	Tp
428	PB 7	POLYPILLAR ARCH NORTH	SAA	84	4.0	Tp	.8	Tp	NO	NA	4.1	Tp	1.1	Tp	1.0	Tp	16.0	Tp	16.0	Tp
429	LC 16	HALF MOON ARCH	CWA	85	4.0	TE	.5	TE	YES	TE	26.0	Tp	21.0	TE	15.0	TR	8.0	Tp	28.0	Tp
430	ND 21	HAMBURGER ARCH	ECA	84	4.0	Tp	.5	Tp	NO	NA	6.0	Tp	.5	Tp	1.0	Tp	6.0	Tp	6.0	Tp
431	SD 43	TERMINAL ARCH	ECA	84	4.0	Tp	.5	Tp	YES	Tp	5.5	Tp	1.5	Tp	4.0	Tp	4.0	Tp	8.5	Tp
432	EP 31	TORTOISE ARCH	CWA	84	4.0	Tp	.5	Tp	NO	NA	4.5	Tp	.5	Tp	.8	Tp	2.6	Tp	6.3	Tp
433	ND 66	CANINE ARCH	CWA	84	4.0	Tp	.5	Tp	NO	NA	4.4	Tp	1.2	Tp	.9	Tp	1.1	Tp	25.0	Tp
434	SD 59	CANOPY ARCH	CWA	84	4.0	Tp	.5	Tp	NO	NA	4.0	Tp	3.5	Tp	10.0	Tp	3.0	Tp	5.0	Tp
435	ND 87	FANTASY ARCH	JHA	85	.5	Es	4.0	TE	YES	TE	.5	Es	4.0	TE	5.5	Tp	6.0	Tp	30.0	Es
436	PB 12	STILT ARCH	CWA	85	4.0	Tp	.3	Tp	NO	NA	7.0	Tp	2.0	Tp	1.5	Tp	2.0	Tp	7.0	Tp
437	WS 28	SCAB ARCH	PFA	84	4.0	Tp	.3	Tp	NO	NA	5.3	Tp	.3	Tp	.2	Tp	.9	Tp	8.0	Tp
438	UC 4	QUICKSAND ARCH	JHA	84	.2	Tp	4.0	Tp	NO	NA	3.5	Tp	5.0	Tp	1.2	Tp	3.9	Tp	6.0	Tp
439	FF 18	STRAP ARCH	CWA	84	4.0	Tp	.1	Tp	NO	NA	6.5	Tp	.5	Tp	.2	Tp	.5	Tp	7.8	Tp
440	SD 27	SEARCH PARTY ARCH	CWA	84	4.0	Tp	.1	Tp	NO	NA	6.0	Tp	1.2	Tp	1.3	Tp	.9	Tp	12.0	Tp
441	ND 74	BOOMERANG ARCH	CWA	84	4.0	Tp	.1	Tp	NO	NA	4.0	Tp	.7	Tp	.3	Tp	.3	Tp	4.5	Tp
442	FF 12	MUKLUK ARCH	FSA	84	3.9	Tp	3.7	Tp	NO	NA	3.9	Tp	3.7	Tp	2.9	Tp	3.0	Tp	7.0	Tp
443	EP 11	HAMMER ARCH	FSA	86	3.9	Tp	3.6	Tp	NO	NA	3.9	Tp	3.6	Tp	.4	Tp	.8	Tp	NA	NA
444	ND 28	EMBLEM ARCH	FSA	84	3.9	Tp	3.0	Tp	NO	NA	3.9	Tp	3.0	Tp	4.0	Tp	9.0	Tp	10.5	Tp
445	EP 40	PELLET ARCH	FSA	84	3.9	Tp	3.0	Tp	NO	NA	3.9	Tp	3.0	Tp	2.8	Tp	7.0	Tp	8.0	Tp
446	KB 11	BUFFALO ARCH	FSA	84	3.9	Tp	2.8	Tp	NO	NA	3.9	Tp	2.8	Tp	1.2	Tp	.5	Tp	6.9	Tp
447	PB 1	SEE SAW ARCH	SAA	84	3.9	Tp	.9	Tp	NO	NA	3.9	Tp	.9	Tp	.6	Tp	1.7	Tp	7.0	Tp

RANK	IDENT	NAME	TYPE	YM	LOL	HM	LOD	HM	DLO	HM	OBW	HM	OBH	HM	SVT	HM	SHT	HM	SXT	HM
448	EP 15	LAYER ARCH	ECA	86	3.9	Tp	.3	Tp	NO	NA	7.5	Tp	.6	Tp	1.3	Tp	4.0	Tp	7.5	Tp
449	SD 1	TONGUE ARCH	FSA	84	3.8	Tp	3.0	Tp	NO	NA	7.9	Tp	3.0	Tp	1.5	Tp	1.5	Tp	10.0	Tp
450	SA 1	BABEL ARCH	FSA	85	3.8	Tp	1.5	Tp	NO	NA	3.8	Tp	1.5	Tp	16.5	Tp	5.0	Tp	NA	NA
451	SW 6	MORRISON BRIDGE	NB	84	3.8	Tp	1.3	Tp	NO	NA	3.8	Tp	3.0	Tp	5.2	Tp	51.0	Tp	NA	NA
452	SA 39	KIDS ARCH EAST	CWA	86	3.8	Tp	.7	Tp	NO	NA	6.0	Tp	.8	Tp	4.5	Tp	15.0	Tp	NA	NA
453	SA 13	SKATE KEY ARCH	FSA	84	3.7	Tp	3.5	Tp	NO	NA	3.7	Tp	3.5	Tp	1.2	Tp	3.5	Tp	NA	NA
454	SA 22	JUNIPER ARCH	FSA	84	3.1	Tp	3.7	Tp	NO	NA	3.1	Tp	3.7	Tp	1.5	Tp	.5	Tp	NA	NA
455	SA 31	TEPEE ARCH	FSA	84	3.0	Tp	3.7	Tp	NO	NA	4.1	Tp	4.8	Tp	1.8	Tp	6.0	Tp	NA	NA
456	ND 19	CHAMBER ARCH SOUTH	ECA	84	3.7	Tp	1.8	Tp	NO	NA	3.7	Tp	1.8	Tp	4.0	Tp	9.0	Tp	10.0	Tp
457	EP 33	SLEEPING ARCH	CWA	84	3.7	Tp	1.5	Tp	NO	NA	9.5	Tp	3.2	Tp	6.0	Tp	1.8	Tp	16.0	Tp
458	PB 4	BALL ARCH	CWA	85	3.7	Tp	1.4	Tp	NO	NA	3.7	Tp	1.9	Tp	1.5	Tp	.8	Tp	4.5	Tp
459	HP 14	FALCON ARCH	ECA	84	3.7	TR	.8	Es	NO	NA	3.7	TR	.8	Es	1.0	Es	1.0	Es	NA	NA
460	LC 26	BALCONY ARCH	PAA	84	3.7	Tp	.3	Tp	NO	NA	5.0	Tp	2.2	Tp	4.0	Tp	3.0	Tp	7.0	Tp
461	PB 5	PERFORATED PILLAR ARCH	SAA	84	3.6	Tp	3.6	Tp	NO	NA	3.6	Tp	3.6	Tp	.5	Tp	2.5	Tp	8.0	Tp
462	GW 2	LITTLE POTHOLE ARCH	PHA	84	3.5	Tp	3.6	Tp	NO	NA	5.5	Tp	4.5	Tp	5.8	Tp	4.0	Tp	10.0	Tp
463	GW 3	BARBED ARCH	FSA	84	3.5	Tp	3.6	Tp	NO	NA	3.5	Tp	3.6	Tp	3.0	Tp	3.0	Tp	18.0	Tp
464	PB 18	SLOPE ARCH	CWA	84	3.6	Tp	1.2	Tp	YES	Tp	19.8	Tp	4.7	Tp	2.0	Tp	7.0	Tp	19.8	Tp
465	SA 21	JACK RABBIT ARCH	JHA	84	1.0	Tp	3.6	Tp	NO	NA	1.0	Tp	3.6	Tp	.3	Tp	.3	Tp	5.0	Tp
466	SW 18	WINTER CAMP ARCH	SAA	84	3.5	Tp	2.4	Tp	NO	NA	3.5	Tp	2.4	Tp	.5	Tp	.3	Tp	5.2	Tp
467	LC 19	MOSS ARCH	SAA	84	3.5	Tp	2.0	Tp	NO	NA	5.0	Tp	4.5	Tp	2.0	Tp	1.4	Tp	6.0	Tp
468	FF 49	LANDMARK ARCH	FSA	84	3.5	Tp	2.0	Tp	NO	NA	4.0	Tp	5.3	Tp	.9	Tp	1.9	Tp	8.0	Tp
469	SD 81	RINKY DINK ARCH	SAA	86	3.5	Tp	1.5	Tp	NO	NA	4.1	Tp	1.8	Tp	2.0	Tp	1.4	Tp	NA	NA
470	EP 41	VALLEY VIEW ARCH	SAA	84	3.5	Tp	1.3	Tp	NO	NA	3.5	Tp	1.3	Tp	.4	Tp	.5	Tp	NA	NA
471	ND 25	MUSHROOM ARCH	FSA	84	3.5	Tp	1.0	Tp	NO	NA	3.5	Tp	1.0	Tp	.5	Tp	.7	Tp	7.0	Tp
472	SD 7	ANTEATER ARCH	ECA	84	3.5	Tp	1.0	Tp	NO	NA	3.5	Tp	1.0	Tp	.4	Tp	.4	Tp	7.0	Tp
473	PB 8	POLYPILLAR ARCH SOUTH	SAA	84	3.5	Tp	.8	Tp	NO	NA	4.0	Tp	1.1	Tp	1.0	Tp	16.0	Tp	16.0	Tp
474	SW 22	DIVING BOARD ARCH	CWA	84	3.5	TR	.7	Es	YES	TR	77.0	Rf	5.0	TR	4.0	TR	5.0	TR	135.0	Rf
475	FF 8	FRAGILE ARCH	JHA	84	3.5	Tp	.7	Tp	NO	NA	3.5	Tp	1.5	Tp	.3	Tp	.4	Tp	4.5	Tp

RANK	IDENT	NAME	TYPE	YM	LOL	HM	LOD	HM	DLO	HM	OBW	HM	OBH	HM	SVT	HM	SHT	HM	SXT	HM
476	SA 33	LEECH ARCH	CWA	84	3.5	Tp	.5	Tp	NO	NA	5.0	Tp	21.0	Rd	.4	Tp	.4	Tp	12.0	Tp
477	PB 13	POTATO ARCH	CWA	84	3.5	Tp	.4	Tp	NO	NA	5.0	Tp	2.5	Tp	4.5	Tp	3.0	Tp	9.0	Tp
478	SD 2	CATERPILLAR ARCH	ECA	84	3.5	Tp	.4	Tp	NO	NA	3.5	Tp	.4	Tp	2.0	Tp	.7	Tp	7.0	Tp
479	LC 27	SPINDLE ARCH	CWA	84	3.5	Tp	.3	Tp	NO	NA	4.2	Tp	1.4	Tp	.1	Tp	.3	Tp	5.0	Tp
480	EP 23	SUPERSTITION ARCH	SAA	84	3.5	Tp	.3	Tp	YES	Tp	3.5	Tp	3.4	Tp	1.0	Tp	1.1	Tp	7.0	Tp
481	WS 35	SUNLIGHT ARCH	ECA	86	.3	Tp	3.5	Tp	NO	NA	.3	Tp	3.5	Tp	2.0	Tp	7.0	Tp	9.0	Tp
482	SD 46	WASHBOARD ARCH	CWA	84	3.5	Tp	.2	Tp	NO	NA	6.9	Tp	5.0	Tp	4.0	Tp	1.5	Tp	7.0	Tp
483	FF 47	EIFFEL TOWER BRIDGE	NB	85	3.4	Tp	3.0	Tp	NO	NA	3.4	Tp	3.1	Tp	28.5	Rd	6.5	Tp	5.0	Tp
484	SD 25	CAMEL LEG ARCH	SAA	84	3.4	Tp	2.0	Tp	NO	NA	4.3	Tp	2.0	Tp	1.3	Tp	.8	Tp	4.8	Tp
485	SA 50	PEDESTAL ARCH	SAA	84	3.4	Tp	1.2	Tp	NO	NA	3.4	Tp	1.2	Tp	.4	Tp	.3	Tp	NA	NA
486	SA 12	PINYON JAY ARCH	ECA	84	.9	Tp	3.4	Tp	NO	NA	.9	Tp	3.4	Tp	5.5	Tp	3.3	Tp	NA	NA
487	EP 25	COUGAR ARCH	JHA	84	.5	Tp	3.4	Tp	NO	NA	.5	Tp	3.4	Tp	.4	Tp	.9	Tp	12.0	Tp
488	FF 5	TAIL ARCH	JHA	86	.5	Tp	3.4	Tp	NO	NA	.5	Tp	3.4	Tp	1.4	Tp	2.8	Tp	5.0	Tp
489	EP 38	TWIG ARCH	CWA	84	3.4	Tp	.2	Tp	NO	NA	3.4	Tp	2.8	Tp	1.6	Tp	1.6	Tp	NA	NA
490	EP 24	SEA SHELL ARCH	ECA	84	3.3	Tp	1.5	Tp	NO	NA	3.3	Tp	1.5	Tp	3.0	Tp	5.0	Tp	7.0	Tp
491	SA 10	SLANT ARCH LOWER	FSA	84	3.3	Tp	1.5	Tp	NO	NA	3.3	Tp	1.5	Tp	.3	Tp	2.2	Tp	5.0	Tp
492	ND 84	RUBBLE ARCH NORTHWEST	FSA	85	1.5	Tp	3.3	Tp	NO	NA	1.5	Tp	3.3	Tp	.8	Tp	1.3	Tp	NA	NA
493	SD 15	RINGTAIL ARCH UPPER	ECA	84	3.3	TR	1.1	TR	NO	NA	3.3	TR	1.1	TR	2.3	TR	1.0	Es	7.0	Tp
494	PB 20	TUBA ARCH	SAA	84	3.3	Tp	.9	Tp	NO	NA	3.3	Tp	.9	Tp	.4	Tp	1.5	Tp	5.5	Tp
495	ND 86	DESTRUCTION ARCH	CWA	85	3.3	Tp	.8	Tp	NO	NA	6.2	Tp	2.4	Tp	.7	Tp	1.4	Tp	6.2	Tp
496	SD 53	MAGPIE ARCH SOUTH	CWA	84	3.3	Tp	.4	Tp	NO	NA	3.3	Tp	.4	Tp	.2	Tp	.5	Tp	3.3	Tp
497	UC 10	TRAIL END ARCH	ECA	84	3.3	Tp	.4	Tp	NO	NA	3.3	Tp	.4	Tp	7.0	Tp	3.5	Tp	NA	NA
498	KB 14	RECON BRIDGE	NB	86	3.3	Tp	.3	Tp	NO	NA	4.5	Tp	.7	Tp	.3	Tp	1.6	Tp	4.6	Tp
499	FF 21	SECRETIVE ARCH	ECA	86	3.3	Tp	.3	Tp	NO	NA	3.7	Tp	.4	Tp	.4	Tp	1.1	Tp	5.5	Tp
500	FF 9	HOOF ARCH	CWA	84	3.3	Tp	.2	Tp	NO	NA	3.3	Tp	1.7	Tp	3.5	Tp	.2	Tp	6.0	Tp
501	SA 49	COTTONTAIL ARCH	CWA	84	3.2	Tp	2.0	Tp	NO	NA	15.5	Tp	4.0	Tp	6.0	Tp	6.0	Tp	15.5	Tp
502	GW 22	HOOP ARCH	SAA	84	1.6	Tp	3.2	Tp	NO	NA	1.6	Tp	3.2	Tp	3.0	Tp	.6	Tp	4.0	Tp
503	FF 15	MINI SPECTACLES NORTH	FSA	84	3.2	Tp	1.5	Tp	NO	NA	3.2	Tp	1.5	Tp	3.8	Tp	1.1	Tp	NA	NA

RANK	IDENT	NAME	TYPE	YM	LOL	HM	LOD	HM	DLO	HM	OBW	HM	OBH	HM	SVT	HM	SHT	HM	SXT	HM
504	ND 75	GREY FOX ARCH	CWA	84	3.2	Tp	1.4	Tp	NO	NA	3.2	Tp	2.3	Tp	5.0	Tp	5.0	Tp	8.0	Tp
505	ND 30	HOLEY ARCH	ECA	84	3.2	Tp	.7	Tp	NO	NA	3.2	Tp	.7	Tp	.8	Tp	1.6	Tp	4.0	Tp
506	EP 48	CLIFFROSE ARCH	ECA	86	3.2	Tp	.4	Tp	NO	NA	4.0	Tp	.4	Tp	1.3	Tp	1.2	Tp	NA	NA
507	ND 13	WASH BASIN ARCH	ECA	84	3.2	Tp	.4	Tp	NO	NA	3.2	Tp	.4	Tp	1.7	Tp	5.0	Tp	5.5	Tp
508	HP 11	LEGBONE ARCH	JHA	86	.2	Tp	3.2	Tp	NO	NA	.2	Tp	3.2	Tp	.2	Tp	2.0	Tp	5.8	Tp
509	PB 15	VISOR ARCH	CWA	84	3.2	Tp	.1	Tp	NO	NA	3.2	Tp	2.2	Tp	5.5	Tp	5.0	Tp	4.0	Tp
510	EP 10	FESTOON ARCH	CWA	86	3.1	Tp	2.3	Tp	NO	NA	3.1	Tp	2.3	Tp	1.4	Tp	1.3	Tp	3.3	Tp
511	EP 46	GREASEWOOD ARCH	FSA	86	3.1	Tp	1.5	Tp	NO	NA	3.7	Tp	3.7	Tp	2.2	Tp	6.5	Tp	NA	NA
512	SW 19	DONUT ARCH	CWA	84	3.1	Tp	1.4	Tp	NO	NA	4.9	Tp	6.8	Tp	1.4	Tp	4.0	Tp	6.0	Tp
513	SD 16	DEAD JUNIPER ARCH	ECA	85	3.1	Tp	1.3	Tp	NO	NA	5.0	Tp	1.3	Tp	5.5	Tp	4.5	Tp	NA	NA
514	WS 42	SINK ARCH	FSA	86	3.1	Tp	.8	Tp	NO	NA	3.1	Tp	1.6	Tp	1.4	Tp	3.5	Tp	7.0	Tp
515	PB 17	CLAM SHELL ARCH	SAA	84	3.1	Tp	.4	Tp	NO	NA	3.1	Tp	.4	Tp	2.5	Tp	2.0	Tp	NA	NA
516	GW 10	PLANK ARCH	CWA	84	3.1	Tp	.3	Tp	NO	NA	5.5	Tp	1.0	Tp	.3	Tp	1.2	Tp	7.0	Tp
517	FF 48	WHIPPED CREAM ARCH	ECA	84	3.1	Rd	.3	Rd	NO	NA	3.1	Rd	.3	Rd	3.0	Rd	1.5	Rd	NA	NA
518	WS 37	DRY FALLS ARCH	CWA	86	3.1	Tp	.2	Tp	NO	NA	3.1	Tp	.7	Tp	.3	Tp	.8	Tp	8.0	Tp
519	SA 47	AIRFOIL ARCH UPPER	ECA	84	3.1	Tp	.2	Tp	NO	NA	3.1	Tp	.2	Tp	1.6	Tp	.2	Tp	5.0	Tp
520	PB 6	PIANO ARCH	SAA	84	3.0	Tp	2.0	Tp	NO	NA	6.0	Tp	2.0	Tp	.4	Tp	1.0	Tp	NA	NA
521	ND 44	CAT HEAD ARCH	FSA	84	2.0	Tp	3.0	Tp	NO	NA	2.0	Tp	3.0	Tp	16.0	Tp	1.4	TE	NA	NA
522	EP 28	LEAN TO ARCH	JHA	84	1.6	Tp	3.0	Tp	NO	NA	1.6	Tp	3.0	Tp	2.6	Tp	4.0	Tp	7.0	Tp
523	SW 21	SOLO ARCH	JHA	84	1.5	Tp	3.0	Tp	NO	NA	4.0	Tp	3.0	Tp	1.0	Tp	1.0	Tp	6.0	Tp
524	FF 24	QUEUE JUGHANDLE	JHA	84	1.0	Tp	3.0	Tp	NO	NA	1.0	Tp	3.0	Tp	1.5	Tp	1.6	Tp	NA	NA
525	SW 3	ONE LEGGED ARCH	JHA	84	3.0	Tp	.8	Tp	NO	NA	3.2	Tp	2.4	Tp	.6	Tp	.4	Tp	4.6	Tp
526	EP 30	WEEPING ARCH	CWA	84	3.0	Tp	.5	Tp	NO	NA	3.0	Tp	.5	Tp	1.3	Tp	2.4	Tp	7.0	Tp
527	FF 6	BISCUITROOT ARCH	CWA	86	3.0	Tp	.1	Tp	NO	NA	3.0	Tp	.5	Tp	1.5	Tp	.5	Tp	3.5	Tp

BIBLIOGRAPHIC REFERENCES

Arches National Park Historical Files, Arches National Park, Moab, Utah

Cook, R. U., "Salt Weathering in Deserts," Proceedings of the Geologists' Association, V. 92, 1981

Blair, Robert W. Jr., "Development of Natural Sandstone Arches in South-Eastern Utah," International Geomorphology 1986, Part II, ed. V. Gardiner, John Wiley & Sons, 1987

Doelling, Helmut H., Geology of Arches National Park, Utah Geological and Mineral Survey, 1985

Dorn, Ronald I., "Cation-Ratio Dating: A New Rock Varnish Age-Determination Technique," Quaternary Research, V. 20, 1983

Hunt, Alice P. and Tanner, Dallas, "Early Man Sites near Moab, Utah", American Antiquity, V. 26, # 1, July, 1960

Pretoria, J. Cooks, "Geomorphic Response to Rock Strength and Elasticity," Zeitschrift der Geomorphologie, V. 27, 1983

Rogers, J. David, The Genesis, Properties and Significance of Fracturing in Colorado Plateau Sandstones, PhD Dissertation, Department of Civil Engineering and Geological Engineering, University of California, Berkeley, 1983

United States Geological Survey, Topographic Maps:
- Arches National Park,   scale - 1:50,000, 1974
- Big Bend,   scale - 1:24,000, 1985
- Cisco SW,   scale - 1:24,000, 1977
- Gold Bar Canyon,   scale - 1:24,000, 1975
- Klondike Bluffs,   scale - 1:24,000, 1977
- Merrimac Butte,   scale - 1:24,000, 1975
- Moab,   scale - 1:24,000, 1975
- Mollie Hogans,   scale - 1:24,000, 1977
- Rill Creek,   scale - 1:24,000, 1975
- The Windows Section,   scale - 1:24,000, 1975

ADDITIONAL READING

Barnes, Fran A. Canyon Country Arches and Bridges, Canyon Country Publications, 1987

Johnson, David W. The Story Behind the Scenery, KC Publications, 1985

Lohman, S.W., <u>The Geologic Story of Arches National Park</u>, Geological Survey Bulletin 1393, 1975

Vreeland, Robert H., <u>Natures Bridges and Arches</u>, V. 2 Arches National Park, 1977.

APPENDIX
NEW ARCHES

The following list contains the names and locations of arches that have been reported and verified, but have not been completely documented since the field work for this book ended in 1986. Verification of subsequently reported arches is continuing and it is certain that the total number of arches will be well over 700 when documentation is completed. A Supplement to this book is planned which will contain detailed information on all additional arches found.

For readers interested in knowing about future publications, please contact the authors or the publisher to have your name included on the mailing list for notification of future publications.

Name	Area	Section
Atlasta Arch	SA	CtT
Attractive Arch	KB	Esc
Banded Arch	LC	SOL
Bedded Arch	SW	WCW
Buteo Bridge	SW	WCW
Centerpiece Arch-West	SW	WCW
Centerpiece Arch-East	SW	WCW
Chipmunk Arch	ND	DON
Crummy Arch	KB	SoK
Curved Arch	KB	SoK
Down Angle Arch	SW	WCW
Ell Arch	SW	WCW
Femur Arch	ND	SVN
Fibula Arch	ND	SVN
Geodesic Arch	SW	WCW
Grass Arch	SW	Del
Hideout Arch	ND	SVN
Jigsaw Arch	ND	SVN
Knee Arch	ND	DON
Missed Arch	SD	UTr
Multi-Layered Arch	FF	Upr
Omega Arch	KB	Esc
Pine Cone Arch	KB	Esc

Name	Area	Section
Plunging Arch	ND	DON
Professional Arch	KB	SoK
Ramp Arch	CA	PB
Relocated Bridge	KB	Esc
Root Cellar Arch	SW	Del
Root or Bush Arch	SW	WCW
Secret Garden Arch	FF	Upr
Shade Arch	FF	Upr
Shapely Arch	SW	WCW
Sidetrack Arch	FF	Lwr
Stick Arch	SW	WCW
Thighbone Arch	KB	Esc
Three Tier Arch-Upper	LC	SOL
Three Tier Arch-Middle	LC	SOL
Three Tier Arch-Lower	LC	SOL
Tibia Arch	ND	SVN
Touching Arch	SW	WCW
Trade Arch	KB	SoK
Tripod Arch	SW	WCW
Underground Arch	SW	WCW
Up High Arch	SW	WCW
Wolfe Cabin Arch	SW	Del

The key to the symbols used to indicate "area" and "section" can be found on page 123 which is the general key to the alphabetical list of arches.